# THE
# AMERICAN
# AUTOMOBILE

# THE
# AMERICAN
# AUTOMOBILE

**TONY BEADLE**

with **IAN PENBERTHY**

**BARNES
&NOBLE
BOOKS**
*NEW YORK*

This edition published by Barnes & Noble, Inc., by arrangement with Salamander Books Ltd.

2000 Barnes & Noble Books

M10987654321

ISBN 0-7607-1897-0

All correspondence concerning the content of this volume should be addressed to Salamander Books Ltd.

**CREDITS**
Managing Editor: Charlotte Davies
Designer: Richard Mason
Reproduction: P&W Graphics PTE Ltd and Studiotec
Printed in Italy

**DEDICATION**
This book is dedicated to my wife, Jennie, for putting up with my grumpy behavior during the final stages of putting together the text, and for not moaning (too much!) about the lack of work done around the house during the time spent researching and writing.

**ACKNOWLEDGEMENTS**
I would like to acknowledge the following for their assistance: Helen Jones Early of the Oldsmobile History Center, Mike Key, Dan Lyons, Rod Blackaller, Julian Balme and all the authors and publishers of the numerous books and magazines that provided invaluable reference material.

Special thanks to the late Nicky Wright.

# CONTENTS

# INTRODUCTION

As any automotive writer will tell you, looking back can be filled with pitfalls. Often our vision of the past is distorted, just like peering through the double curvature of the wrap-around Panoramic windshield on a 1954 Oldsmobile Starfire – the images may be twisted out of shape or highlighted in sharp focus, or even slightly colored by the tint in the glass, according to our viewpoint. In some extreme cases the alterations are so dramatic that the picture we see becomes almost unrecognizable to people who were actually there at the time. Yet we all share a common desire to capture the true spirit of the period, as embodied in the designs of the cars – from the determination of the entrepreneurs who had the dream, to the stylists that created the form, the engineers that crafted the metal, the workers that assembled the components and the customers who drove the finished result – it's just that our perception of what's on the other side of that window through time takes on a different emphasis.

There is no other nation in the world where the automobile has become so much a part of the fabric of everyday life as the USA. And throughout its life, the automobile has faithfully mirrored the dreams, needs and wants of the American people – whether it was the basic black Tin Lizzie of Henry Ford, the majestic doomed splendor of a Marmon Sixteen, the outrageous fins and lavish chrome on a '59 Cadillac, the ground-shaking performance of a Dodge Hemi Challenger or the quirky sawn-off economy of the American Motors' Gremlin – they all represent a part of a fascinating story.

But it hasn't just reflected, the automobile has also exerted a tremendous influence on the way we behave, changed the way we think, caused huge physical changes to our surroundings, and molded the landscape. For the most part, the automobile has been a machine of great benefit to mankind. But it is more than a mere collection of nuts and bolts, the car can interact with people like no other machine. Climbing behind the wheel makes you part of the machine, while retaining control of your ultimate destiny – barring poor navigation, traffic congestion, breakdowns and (heaven forbid) an accident or encounter with the highway patrol! It has given us fun, excitement, pleasure of ownership, a freedom of movement for the individual that nothing else can equal and provided work and a source of income for untold millions over the years. Oh sure, cars have been the cause of frustration, anger, misery, injury and death too, but in my opinion the good far outweighs the bad.

The variety of automobiles created during the period covered by this book is enormous, and the list of auto makers that have come and gone is also lengthy; to attempt to cover each one in detail would require more volumes than an encyclopedia. This was obvi-

ously not possible, and the dedicated historian will note omissions, some more signficant than others but, in the end with limited space available, the selection process had to be ruthless and a choice exercised.

Included are obvious, well-known classics, some popular favorites, plus others considered to be of particular historical interest or having design features of note, and there are even a few relatively obscure cars that were regarded as simply too fascinating to be left out. This is by no means a definitive history of the American automobile, and was never intended to be so. It is a celebration of the best and the worst, some brilliant successes and some dismal flops, classic marques and bizarre oddities. Maybe this book might even inspire a few enquiring minds to undertake further research and uncover previously hidden facts or information – if so, that would be an added bonus.

Tony Beadle
June 2000

**Below:** Surely there can have been few automobiles shaped more like a carapace than the 1949 Lincoln Cosmopolitan?

# 1919

World War One had ended in November 1918, the economy was experiencing a post-war mini-boom based on the euphoria of victory, and the population of Detroit was nearly four times what it was at the start of the century, thanks to the burgeoning business of building automobiles. At the heart of the Motor City's prosperity was the incredible ever-expanding empire of Henry Ford, based on the cornerstone of just one model – the Model T.

Arriving in October 1908, the Model T Ford was to revolutionize the automobile industry and help establish a freedom of movement for Americans – the car would come within reach of almost anyone. Eleven years on, the Model T was going strong and, if altered in appearance (it had a major facelift in 1917), no backwoods mechanic could fail to recognize the car or its components and know exactly how to fix whatever went wrong.

Mass production was the key to its phenomenal success, but equally important was Ford's insistence on reducing the price when possible, stimulating demand even more and creating further profits. When introduced, the Model T sold at $850, but by 1919 the 2-door Runabout was only $500. And while the first full year of production saw 17,771 put together, with the coming of the moving assembly line and its refinement of operation, in 1919 an amazing 820,455 cars bearing the Ford name were manufactured – almost double the previous year's output and nearly half the

**Above:** At just $500, the two-seat Runabout was the cheapest Model T on offer in 1919 and yet it was acceptable for use even on formal occasions. By this time Ford only offered cars in 'any color as long as it's black' but prior to 1914 Model Ts were painted in a number of hues.

**Left:** Prior to 1919, Willys-Overland was second to Ford in production, but a factory strike delayed a new model intended to combat the Model T. When it did arrive, it was priced at over $800 – way above the Ford – and could no longer compete. This Overland has just completed a seven day, non-stop publicity run in high gear.

total for the whole US auto industry. A further milestone reached in this year was the production of the three millionth Model T.

It is widely assumed that Ford could keep the price of the Model T so low because it was churned out, year after year, without any alterations. This isn't so. Changes were made all the time – models came and went, different suppliers were used and components were modified, either to cure problems or to provide a cheaper method of production.

But the original concept of a car for the masses remained and the specification was more or less constant. The engine was a four cylinder L-head of 176.7 cu.in. developing 20 horsepower, cooled by thermo-syphon action, coupled to a unique planetary transmission with two forward speeds and reverse and a multiple disc clutch, while a torque tube drive connected this to the rear axle. The wheelbase was 100 inches, wooden spoked wheels were 30 inches and suspension was by transverse semi-elliptic leaf springs.

Within that framework the Model T evolved bit by bit, and 1919 saw an electric starter and battery as standard on closed models and offered as an option on open cars. This in turn led to an instrument panel being fitted with a single gauge (an ammeter), ignition/light switch and choke knob – speedometers were installed by dealers or owners. Demountable rim wheels were also available for the first time to make tire changing easier.

The Model T became forever enshrined in American folklore for being virtually indestructible and, in spite of its quirky features, utterly reliable. Cheerfully used and savagely abused, it was a target of derision and affection in like amounts, at home on the remotest farm or in the teeming city, and it captured the heart of the nation in a manner that no other automobile in history – before or since – has come close to equaling.

**Left:** Chevrolet was started by William C. Durant with the intention of building a 'light car' at an affordable price, and had enjoyed some considerable success after a rather hesitant start, enabling Durant to regain control of General Motors in September 1915. But by 1919, Chevy's offerings had grown heavier and more expensive. Typical of the period is this Series 490 4-door sedan (Chevrolet's first closed model) which included standard equipment like a speedometer, ammeter, demountable wheel rims, tire pump and electric horn, among other things, all for a cost of $1185.

# 1920

Choosing a suitable name for a new car company must have been a vexing task for the hundreds of so-called entrepreneurs in the Twenties, as proposing to set up an automobile producing business had been a lucrative method of selling stock and raising millions of dollars to fund the business since the turn of the century. Spurred on by the successes of people like Ransom E. Olds (Oldsmobile and Reo), William C. Durant (Buick, Chevrolet and General Motors), Henry Ford and many others in making personal fortunes out of the fledgling auto industry, the crooked speculators took full advantage of the boom and the naivety of investors. The ReVere is just one of many automotive enterprises that, for one reason or another, failed to last the distance.

During this frantic time, almost every name that would look good at the head of a certificate had been used (some more than once) and the names of US automobile companies registered run the whole gamut of the alphabet, from Abbott-Akin to Zip (both of whom, coincidentally, didn't survive 1914). Yet it is surprising to find only one make of car named after the famous Revolutionary War figure Paul Revere.

When Revere made his epic ride in 1775 to warn the Massachusetts militia men that British troops were advancing on Concord, the 20 mile night time journey from Boston was regarded as an incredible adventure and rightly so. How the patriotic hero and erstwhile silversmith, engraver and dentist would have viewed a motorcar bearing his image is impossible to say, and it seems odd that when the ReVere (that's how the name was usually depicted) did appear, it was to come from the Mid-West, rather than his New England home.

The ReVere Motor Car Corporation was established in Logansport, Indiana in 1917 to begin construction of an automobile using the race-bred, four cylinder Duesenberg engine. Two of the three company's principals came from racing backgrounds – Gil Anderson had driven successfully for Stutz, while Tom Mooney had been part of the Premier team. The third, Adolph Monsen, previously owned and operated a garage in Chicago and built a few cars as part of that business, but on a strictly limited basis.

The choice of powerplant was indicative that the trio were not aiming the ReVere at the Model T market, but the stylish and sporty (and expensive) end of the spectrum. And so when the first cars were completed in 1918, they turned out to be high priced as well as high performance. The ReVere would ultimately achieve its main recognition for its speedster models – also called raceabouts, runabouts and roadsters by other manufacturers – for which there was quite a fashion in the early Twenties, but the initial offerings also included an open touring car and a Victoria.

In dividing the workload, it was Anderson who was chiefly responsible for the chassis development, with the suspension including outboard semi-elliptic rear leaf springs and (advanced for the period) provision for shock absorbers. Monsen took care of the engine, making some modifications and, in due course, producing his own version of the Rochester-Duesenberg four cylinder motor.

**Below:** Although ReVere is chiefly remembered for its high-performance roadsters, the company also produced some other excellent models, like this five passenger touring car. Based on a 131 inch wheelbase chassis and using a modified 100hp Rochester-Duesenberg four cylinder engine, these expensive cars found favor with several foreign heads of state.

**Right:** Despite being described by a sales slogan as "America's Incomparable Car" the fact that the ReVere failed to survive the Twenties was due more to the mishandling of financial matters than any shortcomings of the cars themselves.

Mooney's role is less clear, but he evidently helped out in various different capacities.

The ReVere promotional blurb was fulsome enough: "The last word in classy design built by people who know, for people who want the classiest..." and the company adopted the slogan "America's Incomparable Car". A publicity stunt saw famed racing ace, Cannon Ball Baker, drive a ReVere tourer around the USA in 1918, clocking up over 16,000 miles and the ReVere was also exhibited at several major auto shows generating a fair amount of attention for the marque.

Production had commenced in earnest at the start of 1919, and the ReVere carried a hefty price tag of around $3,850 from the factory – about ten times the cost of the cheapest Model T Ford! The company soon began to receive orders for specially-built cars for heads of state of foreign countries, one of the most prestigious being King Alfonso XIII of Spain who took delivery of a Victoria model.

Outwardly, the ReVere automobile venture seemed to be progressing nicely but, behind the scenes, things were less satisfactory. Financial control of the company was in the hands of a quartet headed by president Newton Van Zandt, and aided by vice-president A. A. Seagraves, treasurer C. H. Wilson and secretary E. R. Mattingly. ReVere stock was being sold in large quantities, no doubt

**Above:** The 1920 Packard Twin Six. This was the world's first 12 cylinder car manufactured in series quantity with over 35,000 built between 1916 and 1923. Its 60° L-head V12 of 424 cu.in engine produced 90bhp.

due to a concocted prospectus statement that a contract for the next five years of production had been agreed with an Eastern syndicate, guaranteeing a profit of $500 on every car made and amounting to a total of $45 million which attracted plenty of eager investors.

But there was no such contract, and matters quickly started to go wrong. In December 1920, ReVere was petitioned into bankruptcy by three creditors from Chicago and the court action dragged on into 1921. Then, in August of that year, Van Zandt was sued for grand larcency by a stockholder from Buffalo, New York, but the ReVere president was acquitted of the charge. Further investigations into the company's affairs precipitated its failure, and in November 1922 the factory was sold off.

However, that wasn't the end of the ReVere. By February 1923, a reorganization had taken place and the ReVere Motor Company was born, with Adolph Monsen taking up the post of vice-president and general manager. Manufacture of sedans and roadsters continued through 1924 using the Monsen derivation of the Duesenberg engine, and then in 1925 a Continental six cylinder was introduced as well.

All was not well at ReVere though for, despite the new organisational structure, the company's image and reputation never really recovered from the earlier financial scandal. Finally, in 1926, the factory closed its doors forever and the marque named after an American hero disappeared.

Prior to its departure, the last ReVere models offered balloon tires, four wheel brakes and a rudimentary form of power steering. This unusual system comprised of two steering wheels, one inside the other, which had a lower ratio to make it easier to park, but the idea died with the ReVere company.

At it's peak in 1920, the ReVere represented all that was both good and bad in the auto industry of the time. In the speedster ranks, it never quite rivaled the leading makers' models like the Mercer Raceabout and the Stutz Bearcat, although it was on a par with other less well-known marques such as Biddle,

Kissel, Marmon and Paige, but the financial wranglings of the company rather than any mechanical shortcomings were its undoing.

It was the beginning of the Jazz Age – an era of fads and freakish fashions that came and went with amazing rapidity and, despite a depressed US economy in 1920-21, a feeling of prosperity prevailed. Prohibition started on January 16, 1920, and the Chicago White Sox were accused of throwing the World Series, but politicians were fueling the consumer culture by promising "a car in every garage" and there were now around 9 million automobiles in the USA as motoring was becoming more a part of daily life rather than just a frivolous pastime for the rich.

**Above:** The Essex debuted in 1919, and in August 1920, set a new record carrying mail from San Francisco to New York in 4 days, 14 hours, and 43 minutes.

**Below:** Gaston Chevrolet won the 1920 Indy 500 at an average speed of 88.62mph in a Frontenac, built by his brother Louis after he had left the Chevrolet Motor Company following a dispute with William C. Durant in 1914. After that, none of the Swiss-born Chevrolet brothers would have any connection with the marque that bore their name.

GASTON CHEVROLET, WINNER 1920

# 1921

Proof of the rapid development of the automobile's place at the very heart of the American way of life is shown from several incidents during this year. Warren G. Harding became the first US president to travel to his inauguration in a car – a Packard Twin Six, and, at the other end of the scale, was another first – the Pig Stand, a drive-in restaurant in Dallas, Texas, where barbecued pork sandwiches were served to people to eat in their cars. Meanwhile, in an effort to regulate the ever-increasing flow of cars on the streets, the Detroit police were experimenting with synchronized traffic lights, having introduced the three-colored light two years earlier.

But the economy was still depressed at the start of the year, with 5 million people unemployed. As Ford slashed the price of the Model T to stimulate demand, grabbing over 60% of the market, the need for cheaper cars was recognized by other manufacturers. Oldsmobile had established itself as a builder of medium-priced, good quality automobiles, but reacted to the down-turn in sales by bringing out a four cylinder car – the Model 43-A. Since 1916, Oldsmobiles had all been powered by either a six or eight cylinder engine and the four was a welcome addition.

At under $1400, the 43-A was the cheapest Oldsmobile by a wide margin (their eight cylinder models cost nearly twice as much), yet they couldn't hope to approach the rock-bottom prices set by Ford. A Model T Runabout eventually sunk to $325 in 1921, but a 2-door sedan was $760 – still half the price of the new Olds. The difference in price is reflected in the annual production. While Ford churned out nearly 1.3 million cars, Oldsmobile's output was a modest 19,157, of which 13,867 were the Model 43-A.

**Above:** 1921 saw the arrival of Henry Leland's new V8 Lincoln, but although superbly engineered, the conservatively-styled luxury cars from the creator of Cadillac struggled to survive in what were difficult times and the company went into liquidation in November. Henry Ford bought Lincoln in February 1922 and thereby ensured the future of the marque.

**Left:** A Frontenac again took the chequered flag at the Indianapolis 500 Mile Race, this time with Tommy Milton behind the wheel. His winning average speed was 89.62mph.

Despite the reduction in price compared to earlier models, the four cylinder Oldsmobile remained a quality automobile, far more sophisticated and better equipped than the Ford. While the cheaper open models were more popular, the Olds 4-door sedan looked more in keeping with the times, sporting the fashionable sloping windshield, but all featured smoother body work lines, especially where the hood joined the passenger compartment.

Mechanically too, the Oldsmobile was in a higher class, with its 224 cu.in. engine putting out 43 horsepower, over double that of the Ford four. And, featuring a simple manual transmission with a single plate, dry disc clutch, torque tube drive and spiral bevel gear rear axle, the Olds was as conventional as could be. Dimensionally, the Oldsmobile was also unremarkable, sitting on a wheelbase of 115 inches with 32 x 4 tires on wooden spoke artillery wheels. It all added up to a

straightforward package that appealed to those drivers who wanted a little bit more from an automobile and were prepared to pay extra for it.

Oldsmobile might not have had the commanding presence in the market enjoyed by the overwhelming Ford juggernaut but, as a small part of the complex General Motors organisation put together by Billy Durant, it would survive and prosper. Pierre du Pont had taken over as president of GM, but it was Alfred P. Sloan who directed the essential rationalization programme needed to unravel the mess created by Durant. Part of the restructuring meant a clearer definition of the market levels in which each marque sold its products and it was decided that Oldsmobile's future was to be with bigger and better automobiles. As a consequence, the four would be discarded after 1923 and, thereafter, the Olds would use only six and eight cylinder engines.

**Below:** Although the cheaper open cars were more popular, this Oldsmobile 4-door sedan exhibits some of the fashionable trends in automobile design of the early Twenties, in particular the sloping windshield, which was also used by many other manufacturers.

# 1928

When the Hudson Motor Car Company were looking to name their cheaper range of four cylinder models planned for a 1919 launch, a map of England was used to find a name with a more up-market appeal. It seemed a strange notion as the car bearing the new badge was to be aimed at the low-buck Model T end of the market, but they finally settled on "Essex" – a county to the east of London. The Hudson people could have also saved themselves the bother of finding a map when you consider that there are towns and counties called Essex in the states of New Jersey, Vermont, Massachusetts and Delaware among others. The choice is even more surprising when you consider that at least three other auto manufacturers called Essex had been launched in the USA.

Whatever the reasons, Essex it was, and although less than a hundred cars were produced in 1918, production leapt the following year and almost 22,000 cars were delivered to the dealers. The most notable thing about Essex in the Twenties was the pricing of its closed models. In an age when open-top cars were generally more popular, and consequently cheaper, Essex made its name producing closed coachwork models for a fraction of the price charged by other manufacturers.

At $1,495, the 1922 Essex four-passenger coach model was the cheapest closed car in America, generating headlines like: "Only $300 More Than Touring Model" in publications such as Motor Age. By 1925, the Essex coach cost five dollars less than the company's open tourer, although prices did equalize later.

Derided as a "packing crate" by the opposition, the Essex coach nevertheless showed the way forward, but the illusion that it was a car produced by a company separate from Hudson gradually diminished. The exemplary F-head 180 cu.in. four was replaced by an L-head 144 cu.in. six cylinder engine during 1924, and performance suffered as a result.

For 1928, Essex enjoyed its best ever sales year, shipping almost 230,000 cars to dealers. Described in some quarters as "low hung", the Essex styling closely resembled the Hudson, but on a slightly smaller scale, with a narrower radiator and a winged mascot replacing the old-fashioned motormeter. Other new styling features included wider fenders and cowl-mounted side lights, plus a

**Right:** Walter P. Chrysler's 1928 entry into the family car market was the four cylinder Plymouth. Despite four-wheel hydraulic brakes, full pressure engine lubrication, aluminum alloy pistons and a separate hand brake, its first year sales of 50,000 were well below Ford and Chevrolet numbers. However, the timing was impeccable and the Plymouth marque would ensure Chrysler's survival in the economic depression that was to follow.

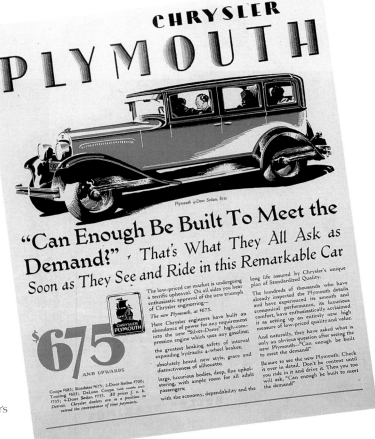

CHRYSLER

# PLYMOUTH

*Plymouth 4-Door Sedan, $725*

## "Can Enough Be Built To Meet the Demand?" · That's What They All Ask as Soon as They See and Ride in this Remarkable Car

$675 AND UPWARDS

Coupe $685; Roadster $675; 2-Door Sedan $700; Touring $695; DeLuxe Coupe (with rumble seat) $735; 4-Door Sedan $735. *All prices f. o. b. Detroit. Chrysler dealers are in a position to extend the convenience of time payments.*

The low-priced car market is undergoing a terrific upheaval. On all sides you hear enthusiastic approval of the new triumph of Chrysler engineering—

*The new Plymouth, at $675.*

Here Chrysler engineers have built an abundance of power for any requirement into the new "Silver-Dome" high-compression engine which uses any gasoline; the greatest braking safety of internal expanding hydraulic 4-wheel brakes; absolutely brand new style, grace and distinctiveness of silhouette; large, luxurious bodies, deep, fine upholstering, with ample room for all adult passengers; with the economy, dependability and the

long life assured by Chrysler's unique plan of Standardized Quality.

The hundreds of thousands who have already inspected the Plymouth details and have experienced its smooth and economical performance, its luxurious comfort, have enthusiastically acclaimed it as setting up an entirely new high measure of low-priced quality and value.

And naturally, they have asked what is only an obvious question after seeing the new Plymouth—"Can enough be built to meet the demand?"

Be sure to see the new Plymouth. Check it over in detail. Don't be content until you ride in it and drive it. Then you too will ask, "Can enough be built to meet the demand?"

shorter windshield visor on closed models. A major technical advance was the use of Bendix mechanical brakes on all four wheels.

Essex was leader of the trend which saw 88.5% of cars sold in the USA in 1928 being closed models, whereas less than a decade earlier almost 90% had been open-top – a complete reversal of public taste. While rivals like Chevrolet and Ford were still asking at least $100 more for closed models in '28, the Essex management saw that the future lay in producing enclosed cars as opposed to road-sters and phaetons.

However, the biggest news in the industry that year was the replacement for the Model T Ford. After a shaky start, the Model A went on to become another success. Meanwhile, the stock market boomed, Mickey Mouse made his debut in "Steamboat Willie" – the first cartoon with sound, and Amelia Earhart became the first woman to fly across the Atlantic. It seemed like everything was new in '28.

**Above:** It is almost impossible to believe today but, in 1927, Ford closed its production lines for six months in order to introduce the Model A in early '28. What is equally unbelievable is that both dealers and customers were willing to wait for such a long time without defecting to other makes, such was the influence wielded by Henry Ford. Although a major advance on the ancient Tin Lizzie, the Model A was completely conventional, powered by a 200 cu.in. L-head four cylinder engine, and nearly five million would be built in four years.

**Left:** The 1928 Essex Super Six Phaeton is unusual because the Hudson nameplate was leading the revolution towards closed models in the late Twenties. Using a 153 cu.in. six cylinder engine like the rest of the '28 Essex models, Phaeton carried a factory price of $750 – fifteen dollars more than the 2-door sedan – but formed part of the best calendar sales year in company history with 229,887 units produced.

front suspension comprised quarter-elliptic leaf springs and Houdaille-Hershey shock absorbers, which were also used at the rear with semi-elliptic leaf springs.

The car was based initially on a ladder frame, which was common practice at the time. However, when Cord himself drove the prototype over a patch of rough ground, the chassis flexed so much that it caused all the doors of the car to spring open. He immediately ordered Auburn's chief engineer, Herb Snow, to fix the problem, which he did by designing the industry's first X-frame chassis. This provided a much more rigid foundation for the car, and would be copied by other manufacturers as time went on.

Placing the transmission and final drive ahead of the long, straight-eight engine made for a long wheelbase, 137½ inches in fact. This was much longer than any comparable automobile of the period, but it did have an advantage when it came to designing the bodywork. The Duesenberg-type grille, long sweeping hood and flowing fenders produced a rakish appearance, which was accentuated by the low overall height of the car. Because of the front-wheel-drive layout, no central transmission tunnel was needed in the floor which not only improved foot room for passengers, but also allowed the floor to be a low, step-down design. This ensured that the car retained good headroom for passengers inside while maintaining a relatively low overall height (61 inches for closed cars and 58 inches for open models – most other cars of the period were at least 70 inches high). At the same time, a generous ground clearance of 8 1/2 inches was also possible.

Not only was the Cord L-29 a good looking car, but it was also well appointed inside. The luxurious interiors of closed cars were trimmed in good-quality broadcloth, while open cars received leather upholstery. In both cases, this was set off by silver-plated interior fittings. In addition, the front seats and steering column were adjustable, while fingertip gear shifting was provided by a small lever on the dashboard.

**Above:** Lincolns for 1929 received a taller and narrower radiator surround, while the previous leather windshield visor was replaced by a tinted glass unit. This is a two-window town sedan, reportedly owned by John Wayne.

**Below:** While the Whippet made a major contribution to Willys-Overland sales in 1929, it was another casualty of the Wall Street Crash and the Depression. Production ended in 1931.

attempt to overcome the poor sales of 1929, the price was dropped by $800 for 1931, but this did not achieve the desired results. Production was halted at the end of the year, the last 157 cars being built as 1932 models. These had a more powerful 132 horsepower, 322 cu.in. straight-eight engine. This engine had originally been intended to power a new Cord, the L-30, but with the economic situation so poor, and so few L-29s having been built (around 5,000), it was never put into production. Indeed, there would not be another Cord for four years, and in the meantime E. L. Cord would concentrate on his other business interests. Even the new car would only last for two short years, after which Cord sold his empire for a reported $4,000,000, killing off Auburn and Duesenberg in the process.

**Below:** Chevrolet's Model AC, while similar in appearance to the 1928 Model AB, had an all-new ohv six cylinder engine. The basic design of this engine remained until 1953.

Cabriolet, sedan, brougham and phaeton body styles were available, although many private coachbuilders, on both sides of the Atlantic, used the Cord as the basis for special bodywork. However, beautiful as the cars undoubtedly were, in performance terms they were somewhat sluggish. It took over 30 seconds for the L-29 to reach 60mph from a standing start, while top speed was not much more than 75mph. When compared to contemporary Cadillacs, Lincolns and Packards, the car was definitely a follower rather than a leader, but it did so in such great style.

Although, in theory, the front-wheel-drive layout should have ensured good traction on poor surfaces, in fact much of the weight of the L-29 was over the undriven rear wheels. As a result, the cars gained a poor reputation for dealing with loose surfaces. Furthermore, the constant-velocity joints were lacking in durability, and frequent replacement was necessary.

Although many of the problems that beset the car could have been solved with more development work, Cord himself was impatient to put the L-29 into production and insisted that it be introduced before 1930.

Unfortunately, teething troubles were not the only problems that would affect the sales of the L-29. Two months after the car was introduced in 1929, the stock market on Wall Street crashed, destroying the L-29's chances of becoming a commercial success. In an

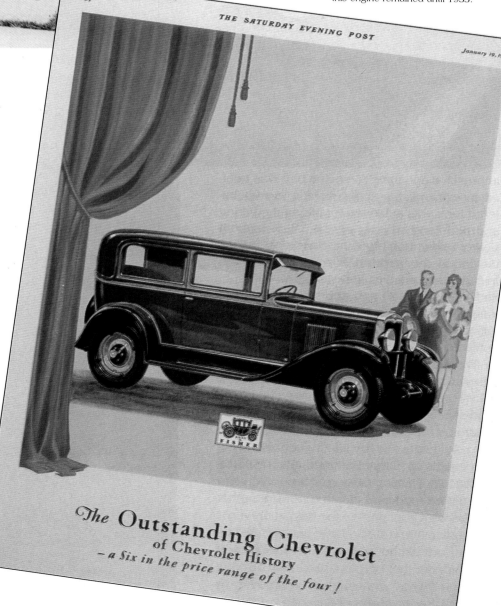

34

THE SATURDAY EVENING POST

*January 19, 1929*

FISHER

*The* **Outstanding Chevrolet**
*of Chevrolet History*
*– a Six in the price range of the four !*

# 1934

For a company whose cars were dominated by engineering considerations, almost to the exclusion of styling innovations, the arrival of the Airflow from Chrysler in January '34 must have been a surprise to many people. But even more of a surprise, perhaps, is that the Airflow indeed came directly from a desire for better automotive engineering rather than a decision to create a design statement.

Unfortunately for Chrysler, the Airflow was proof that while good engineers can be relied on to crack difficult technical problems, even the best of them sometimes fail to appreciate that styling shouldn't be completely ruled by function. The engineer's view of what looks right is usually determined by what works best, not what appeals to the potential customer. Throughout modern history there have been numerous examples of ideas that were too far ahead of popular taste and had to be abandoned as a result – the Chrysler Airflow is just one such mistake.

Inspiration for the wind tunnel research that led to the creation of the Airflow is said to have come to Chrysler engineer Carl Breer

**Below:** The Chrysler Custom Imperial Airflow 4-door Sedan. Limited production Custom Imperial models were the first to use a curved one-piece windshield in '34 and also had vacuum assisted brakes. Although featuring all the body trim of a 1934 example, the pointed grille is of the type introduced for the '35 model year by stylist Raymond Dietrich in an attempt to revitalize sales from the disastrous slump – it wasn't enough.

**Right:** The Chrysler Airflow Series CU 4-door Sedan came with an in-line eight cylinder L-head 299 cu.in. engine that developed 122bhp. Standard equipment included an automatic vacuum-operated clutch on a three-speed manual transmission. By far the best seller of the 1934 Airflow models, the CU Series was the cheapest range at $1,345, but only 7,226 of these 4-door sedans were ever built.

back in 1927 when he saw a squadron of air craft flying in formation. It set in motion a train of thought about the lack of aerodynamics involved in the design of car bodies, so he had a small scale wind tunnel constructed where he carried out tests on wooden blocks. The next stage was to have a much larger wind tunnel built at the Chrysler Highland Park research center. One of the most interesting observations arising from the experiments was that most cars produced less wind resistance when placed backwards in the tunnel. In a later interview, Carl Breer said he remembered looking out of his office window at the parking lot and thinking: "Just imagine all those cars running in the wrong direction all this time".

One of the first elements he found to reduce wind resistance was a sloping back and this led to other fundamental design changes. In order to give sufficient headroom for rear seat passengers, they had to be moved forward, which in turn caused the front seat to shift and this had a knock-on effect of pushing the engine out over the front axle – a completely new idea. But important though streamlining had become, there were many other factors that the team of Breer, Owen Skelton, Fred Zeder and Oliver Clark were working on with the new car. Improved ride qualities through better weight distribution, more interior room and greater structural strength were also targets for the engineers.

With a conventional Thirties car, the majority of the weight would be supported by the

rear axle, typically in a ratio of 60:40%. By moving the engine forward, the Airflow now had a much better front to rear balance with 55% at the front and 45% at the rear. It wasn't simply a matter of moving the engine forward, however, it had to be tilted at an angle of 5° to keep the transmission tunnel profile down. This, in turn, required a special oil pan to cope with suspension movement as one third of the block was ahead of the front axle. Longer leaf springs were used to further enhance the ride characteristics and some reports concluded that the Airflow came close to fulfilling the "Floating Power" phrase used in Chrysler advertising. Also, seat width was increased by a whopping ten inches to give unrivaled roominess for six people to travel in comfort.

Structurally too, the Airflow differed considerably from the norm, using an all-steel cage fixed to the chassis rails, rather than the traditional method of wooden reinforcement members for the steel body panels favored by most other manufacturers. The lightweight cage, resembling a modern NASCAR racing stock car safety frame, closely followed the roof and body lines providing a rigid mounting for the panels and was a step along the road towards full unitary construction and the elimination of a separate body and chassis. One other feature of note was the first use of a one-piece curved windshield on the special Custom Imperial limited production models.

But no matter what technical advancements were achieved with the Airflow, it was the body styling that would sell the car to the public. Today we can look at the "waterfall" grille and rounded front end and appreciate what they were doing, but back then it was seen as an ugly beast. That wasn't the case at the New York Automobile Show where the car made its debut, and enough of the more sophisticated metropolitan audience were sufficiently impressed to place orders which added up to several thousand in total. And several high-profile personalities in the fashion and design world expressed enthusiasm for the ultra-modern shape. It was a fairly promising start, but by no means all of the big city observers liked the design, and some warning signs might have been noticed.

The immediate problem faced by Chrysler was fulfiling these initial orders. Getting the radical design into production proved more difficult than had been envisaged and there was a three or four month delay (depending on the model) before deliveries began. This hold-up proved to be critical. In the interim, rival manufacturers were able to circulate negative rumors about the strange-looking Airflow and without any cars in use to counter this propaganda, Chrysler suffered from a loss of consumer confidence in the new automobile. It also has to be admitted that when the first cars were actually delivered there was some shortfall in the build quality, which didn't help at all.

It wasn't just Chrysler that was affected; DeSoto used the Airflow design exclusively for its '35 model range and sales tumbled as a result. The Chrysler marque fared slightly better because of the line of more conventional models with the Airstream name that were produced alongside the Airflow and so

**Above:** The Brewster nameplate was revived in 1934 by the Springfield Manufacturing Corporation of Springfield, Massachusetts, to produce custom-bodied cars, usually based on a Ford V8 chassis. They featured a sensational heart-shaped grille, split bumpers and flaring fenders. Built to the highest standards, and priced at $3,500, ostentatious Brewster models like this convertible sedan were inappropriate for the time and the company was wound up in 1936 after production of between 100 and 300 cars.

**Left:** Typical of the conventional style of Chrysler's Dodge and Plymouth divisions in 1934 is this Dodge Senior Six sedan produced for export. It consists of a Plymouth body, chassis and running gear with minor trim alterations to make it look like a Dodge.

helped limit losses. In a year when auto industry sales rose by 40% the combined total for Chrysler and DeSoto dropped by almost 10% to about 50,000 units. Of those, only 15,000 were Airflow models – it was a dismal verdict on a technically superior vehicle.

Thankfully for the corporation as a whole, Plymouth and Dodge hadn't used the Airflow shape and their sales remained buoyant. The situation wasn't as disastrous as it might have been for Chrysler, partly due to sales of the standard Airstream models, but also to the fact that the Airflow had been designed to keep tooling and manufacturing costs down.

The Chrysler panic buttons were hit and stylist Raymond Dietrich was hired to rescue the situation. He introduced a grille with a peak to replace the original waterfall design for '35 but sales still declined. Chrysler kept faith with the Airflow until 1937, giving it annual facelifts to try and improve public acceptance but the resistance to the unusual shape just couldn't be overcome and it was dropped.

Setbacks of a more permanent kind were suffered by the criminal fraternity during 1935 as bank robbers Bonnie Parker and Clyde Barrow were killed and became enshrined in folk lore. And Public Enemy Number One – John Dillinger – was killed by the FBI, as were hoodlums Pretty Boy Floyd and Baby Face Nelson. It proves that just like crime, it doesn't always pay to be first in the automotive field with a revolutionary idea, no matter how sound the engineering behind it!

**Right:** The Packard Eleventh Series for 1934 (the sequence started in 1924 with the First Series) included many magnificent models such as this convertible coupe. Packard sales improved to 8,000 and dealers would often bring cars to prospective customers' homes for test drives as part of the service.

# 1935

Sometimes the past can come back and hit you in the face, reminding you that it's all been done before. To use an automotive analogy, it's like looking in the rear view mirror and seeing that engraved message warning that "objects may be closer than they seem". Since Chrysler introduced the Plymouth Voyager and Dodge Caravan in 1984, minivans, MPVs or people movers have become some of the biggest selling models of the Nineties and nearly every manufacturer has an example. But look at the Stout Scarab of 1935, read the specification and marvel at how farsighted was its creator William B. Stout.

While the Scarab was influenced by his pioneering work on all-metal aircraft, Stout's background also included automotive jobs. His first taste of car design was in 1913 when he was an editor on Motor Age, but his proposed cyclecar never made it into production due to lack of finance. Stout had better luck with the Imp cyclecar when he was general sales manager for McIntyre, but that was a commercial failure and he moved to Scripps-Booth at the end of 1914 where he was chief engineer. That position was also brief, and in 1916 he joined the aircraft division of Packard.

All his life, Stout was a prolific inventor (he filed more patents than anyone else except Thomas Edison) and he introduced the internally-braced, cantilevered all-metal wing and corrugated aluminum outer skin to American aviation. Stout also had a gift for self-promotion, as shown by a letter he sent to Detroit industrialists, to raise money for a project, which said: "We want to build a metal plane. If you join us it will cost money. One thousand dollars. No more, no less. And for your thousand dollars you will get one definite promise. You will never get your money back."

But it was joining forces with Henry and Edsel Ford that really got things going. The Fords built Stout a new facility in Dearborn, Michigan, and the Stout Metal Airplane Co was established as a division of The Ford Motor Company. The result was the 2-AT, the first all-metal aircraft built in the USA, which had exceptional load carrying capabilities. In 1925, Henry Ford decided to buy out William Stout's share of the company, and he became the head of an independent airline while still developing aircraft. Stout Air Services operated Ford 4-AT Tri-Motor airliners, and was the first airline to offer in-flight meals (sand-

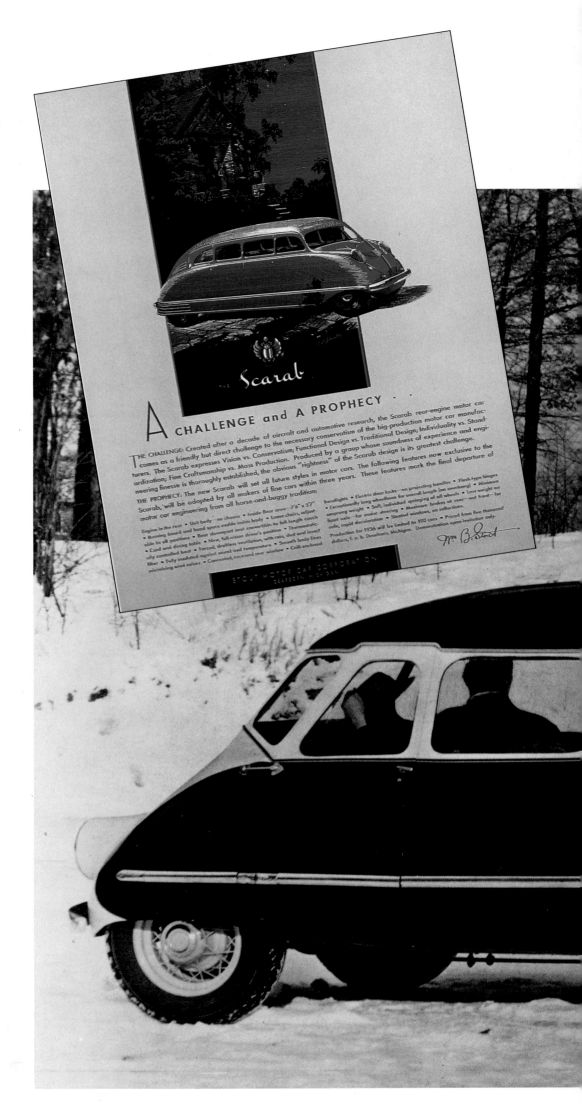

A CHALLENGE and A PROPHECY

**Left:** Stout Scarab advertising consisted of "A challenge and a prophecy..." but the prediction that the unusual car would be a major influence on automobile design was about half a century out.

**Below:** The minimum body overhang due to the wheels being positioned at the extremities and the aerodynamic shape were part of the futuristic Scarab's unique features, but poor rearward vision was a handicap.

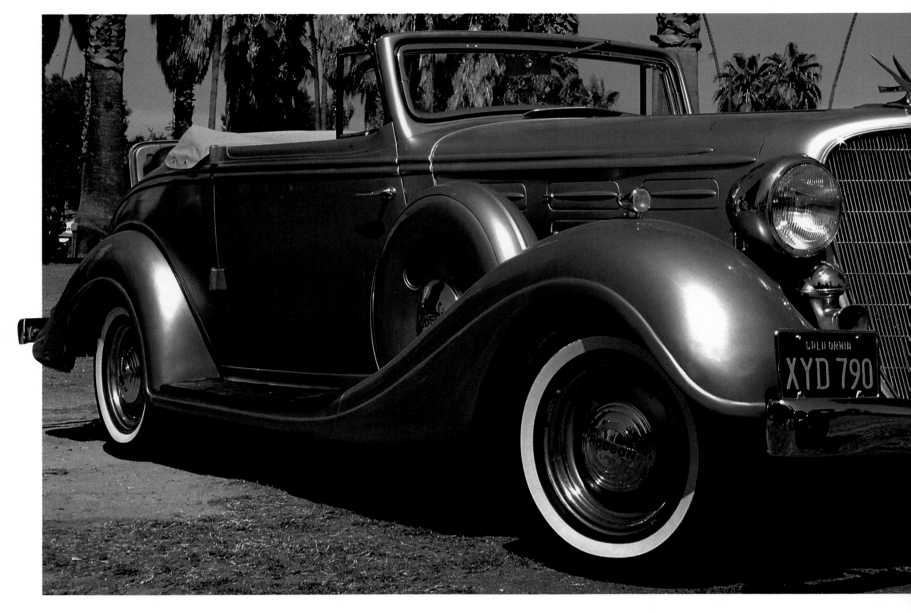

wiches and coffee) and employ uniformed Flight Escorts. Stout's aircrew also wore the company uniforms of blue trimmed with gold braid, a suggestion by Henry Ford that it would "lend dignity to their profession".

Stout sold his airline to the newly-formed United Airlines and turned his mind to other things. In 1932, he started Stout Engineering Laboratories in Detroit where he built the first Scarab prototype. It wasn't until 1935, however, that he deemed the Scarab was ready for production when he introduced a second, steel-bodied version (the original had a duraluminum alloy body). Everything about the Scarab was unusual – unit construction and streamlined in shape, it had a rear-mounted 85hp Ford V8 coupled to a transaxle/differential unit modified from a three-speed transmission, plus coil spring suspension all round.

The Scarab interior was equally unorthodox: in a huge 7ft 6ins by 5ft 7ins floor area, only the driver's seat was fixed, the others were loose to enable them to be moved to any position. A folding table was provided for eating or playing cards and there was a rear

davenport seat which converted into a full-length couch. One magazine described the Scarab's cabin thus: "The interior of the car is extremely comfortable and roomy, with a table and movable chairs. It gives passengers the feeling of traveling in a hotel room".

**Above:** Hudson's '35 sedan models had all-steel roofs but were otherwise the same as '34 models. The main new item was a 93hp, 212 cu.in. six cylinder engine alongside the 254 cu.in. 113 hp straight eight used before.

Whether people would want to travel in such surroundings is another matter, but Stout took the Scarab on trips to promote it and drew large crowds whenever he stopped. A report on a visit to Bartlesville, Oklahoma, describes Stout as "one of the nation's foremost mechanical engineers, responsible for many modern perfections in both aeronautical and automotive design...the Scarab seems destined to mark a new milepost in motor design".

Stout's advertising outlined the advanced features – draftless ventilation with rain, dust and insect filter; thermostatically-controlled heat; electric door locks; insulation against sound and temperature; smooth lines minimizing wind noise – things we now take for granted. Stout made this prediction: "The new Scarab will set all future styles in motor cars. The following features now exclusive to the Scarab, will be adopted by all makers of fine cars within three years. These features mark the final departure of motor car engineering from all horse-and-buggy tradition".

Stout's advertisements for the Scarab issued a bit of a challenge: "Created after a decade of aircraft and automotive research, the Scarab rear-engine motor car comes as a friendly but direct challenge to the necessary conservatism of the big-production motor car manufacturers. The Scarab expresses Vision vs Conservatism; Functional Design vs Traditional Design; Individuality vs Standardization; Fine Craftsmanship vs Mass Production. Produced by a group whose soundness of experience and engineering finesse is

thoroughly established, the obvious 'rightness' of the Scarab design is its greatest challenge".

Stout's confidence was misplaced. He priced the Scarab "from five thousand dollars" which placed it in Cadillac territory. And to enhance exclusivity, production was limited to 100 cars in 1936, with demonstration by invitation only! Despite its merits – and there were quite a few – the Scarab's concept and styling proved too advanced for the period. In the end, less than ten were built (sources differ between five and nine) and a couple of those found their way to Hollywood where such an outrageous-looking vehicle would have fitted right in with the movie star set.

These days, the streets and highways are crowded with MPVs and minivans, and while it might have pleased Stout to see his prophecy come true, it would undoubtedly have given him more pleasure had his Scarab been the success he hoped for. As it was, like so many visionaries, Stout's ideas were ahead of their time and his dreams ended in failure.

Failure of a more traumatic nature was facing farmers after years of drought and the southern plains turned into the notorious Dust Bowl as dust clouds darkened the skies. Forced to become migrants, many headed west in their jalopies in search of work. Those who could afford new cars found General Motors switching to all-steel Turret-Top roofs without the customary fabric insert. Other metal tops in the news were on beer cans which appeared for the first time; was it a coincidence that Alcoholics Anonymous was also founded?

**Right:** Ford's slogan for 1935 was 'Greater Beauty, Greater Comfort, and Greater Safety' and the DeLuxe Phaeton is a good example of the longer, wider and faster automobiles being produced by the company. The year's most popular Ford was the 2-door Tudor sedan which sold over 322,000; the more expensive Phaeton sold only 6,073, but the lack of roll-up windows probably didn't help. Note the front doors are now front-hinged and this was the last year for outside horns and wire wheels.

**Left:** Oldsmobile added the all-metal 'Turret-Top' roof as part of a complete restyle for 1935 although the car's mechanics stayed much as before. This MGM publicity photo shows movie star Freddie Bartholomew polishing his new Olds 4-door Touring Sedan, a gift from studio head Louis B. Mayer following his success in the leading role in David Copperfield.

# 1936

In October 1936, the first 300-mile international road race was held at New York's Roosevelt Raceway at Westbury on Long Island. The track had been built on the site of the airfield from which Charles Lindbergh had taken off on his daring solo transatlantic flight in 1927, and the racers were vying for the George Vanderbilt Cup. It was ultimately won by Italian Tazio Nuvolari in a Scuderia Ferrari Alfa Romeo. The highest-placed American finisher, however, was Mauri Rose, who took eighth place in an Offenhauser-powered Miller car.

Rose's placing was not much for American sports fans to cheer about but, earlier in the year, they had good reason to be happy. Black athlete, Jesse Owens, triumphed at the Olympic Games in Berlin, much to the chagrin of Adolf Hitler and his Nazi followers. Their racist doctrine could not contemplate the success of anyone other than a blond, blue-eyed arian and Hitler stormed out rather than present Owens with his gold medal.

It would not be long before the Nazi hordes would be storming through Europe, but such a prospect would be far from the minds of Americans that year. US car buyers, particularly in the luxury market, would be

considering the new streamlined Lincoln Zephyr. This radical design employed a novel method of construction and was technically advanced in many ways.

The Zephyr began life outside the Ford Motor Co, being conceived by John Tjaarda, a stylist at Briggs Manufacturing Co. Briggs built bodies for Ford, and the new design was intended as a project to sell to Ford. An early prototype was constructed in 1934, but it was far too radical for production. Although it was powered by a Ford flathead V8, this was mounted in the rear with a swing-axle final drive sprung by a transverse leaf spring. The cost of making this set-up work, plus the likely buyer resistance to such an unusual arrangement, even if it were backed by the Ford name, made the idea a non-starter.

**Above:** Seen from above, the streamlined shape of the Lincoln Zephyr, with its tapering nose, is quite obvious. Head lights set into the front fenders and full fender skirts at the rear added to its sleek look.

However, the overall streamlined shape of the car appealed to Edsel Ford, who felt that it had possibilities as a front-engined car. Edsel had been responsible for transforming the fortunes of Lincoln during the Twenties and early Thirties. When he took charge of the

**Above:** The new 267.3 cu.in. flathead V12 engine was similar in design to Ford's V8, but had its cylinders set at a narrower angle. Despite lubrication problems, it performed well giving the Zephyr a top speed of 90mph.

**Above:** Two body styles were offered in 1936: a 2-door sedan and a 4-door sedan. The teardrop shape was in evidence throughout the car, including the rear lights and fenders.

**Right:** Buyers had a choice of taupe broadcloth or tan bedford cord upholstery but, if they paid extra, they could have the interior trimmed in leather, as shown here. This 4-door has a glazed divider between front and rear seats.

# THE AMERICAN AUTOMOBILE

division in 1922, Lincoln had only recently been saved from receivership by his father, Henry Ford, and was building expensive, old-fashioned cars. Under Edsel, the company soon began producing some of the most beautiful automobiles ever created.

Henry Ford believed that a car should be engineered first, with the bodywork designed to suit. But Edsel had other ideas. He placed good styling first and foremost, so much so that he authorized the creation of Ford's first styling department under the direction of Eugene T. Gregory. The latter was now given the task of refining Tjaarda's design to allow for the installation of an engine and radiator at the front of the car.

In the original, rear-engined design, the nose of the car had been very narrow and pointed; Gregory managed to widen this sufficiently to accommodate the engine, radiator and radiator grille, while retaining the sense of a narrow, pointed nose. The result was a beautiful, streamlined body, based on a 122 inch wheelbase, that was quite unique for its day. Much use was made of the teardrop shape, not just in the overall style of the body, but also in individual features, such as tail lights, fender skirts and grille emblem.

The uniqueness of the car's styling was matched by its method of construction. Even in its rear-engined prototype guise at Briggs, the car had featured unibody construction, the body panels being welded together with various strengthening members to produce a strong structure that had no need of a separate chassis. The fabric roof insert, found on all other closed Ford cars at the time, was also disposed of and the Zephyr had a solid steel roof panel in its place.

The narrow tapering nose of the Zephyr needed a small, narrow engine. At the time, all Lincolns were powered by V12 engines, and it was felt that the new car would have to be similarly equipped to be considered a Lincoln. However, the existing powerplant was too large for the sleek design, so Lincoln's chief engineer, Frank Johnson, designed a new engine to suit the car. While this was based on Ford's successful flathead V8, it naturally had four extra cylinders. To achieve the narrow profile, the cylinder banks were angled at 75° (they were set at 90° in the V8). The one-piece, cast-iron block was fitted with aluminum cylinder heads and alloy steel pistons. With a bore and stroke of $2^{3/4}$ and $3^{3/4}$ inches respectively, the new V12 displaced 267.3 cu.in. and produced 110 horsepower at 3900rpm.

Backing the engine was a three-speed manual transmission with floorshift. This was connected to a torque-tube drive, which was standard Ford practice.

While the engine and bodywork were completely new, some aspects of the car were definitely behind the times. Not only was the Zephyr equipped with mechanical brakes on all four wheels, but its suspension system was also outdated: transverse leaf springs were fitted at front and rear with solid axles. While the mechanical brakes would be replaced by Bendix hydraulic units in 1939, the transverse springs would soldier on for

**Right:** Paramount starlet, Gloria Shea, poses for a publicity shot on the front fender of a '36 Chevrolet Master Deluxe sport coupe. The Master series was updated this year with a larger, more rounded grille, while the Standard models took on a similar style. The revisions obviously worked, as Chevrolet gained the number one spot in automobile sales that season.

some time to come. Even the new engine received a lot of criticism, particularly concerning the lubrication system. To ensure that the engine ran reliably, owners were advised to change the oil every 1000 miles. Some engines never made it to the 30,000 mile mark before expiring.

Although sales were slow when the first Zephyrs appeared in November 1935, they soon picked up, and total production for the year came to 15,000 cars, a big improvement on Lincoln's performance for the previous year, which totaled 1,400 cars. No doubt, its revolutionary styling produced some initial resistance, but the Zephyr was well priced, at a fraction of the cost of earlier coach-built models offered by the company.

When the Zephyr went into production, Briggs built most of the car, while Lincoln carried out final assembly work, such as fitting the engine, transmission and suspension along with the hood and fenders, then painting and trimming the cars. However, this arrangement was terminated shortly after the car was introduced. When the Zephyr needed updating for 1937, this was handled by Ford's styling department, who made subtle changes to the design that not only significantly improved the car's appearance, but also kept costs to a minimum by utilizing most of the original tooling.

The Lincoln Zephyr would continue to be updated and restyled until 1949. Throughout, it remained a sleek, streamlined design in keeping with the original.

**Above:** In 1936, Errett Lobban Cord made a last attempt to move in to the specialty market, with the 810. The new Cord had striking "coffin nose" styling by Gordon Buehrig and the range comprised two sedans, a phaeton and a convertible, all on a 125 inch wheelbase and powered by a 125 horsepower Lycoming V8. The car became the 812 in 1937, with an optional supercharger, but production was halted that year following Cord's departure from the auto industry.

**Right:** Racers round the first turn during the Vanderbilt Cup 300 mile international road race at Roosevelt Raceway.

# 1937

Disasters in the air were major news in 1937. After a successful transatlantic crossing, the massive German airship Hindenburg exploded while coming into land on May 6 with great loss of life. Out over the Pacific, pioneer aviatrix Amelia Earhart disappeared and no trace of her, her companion or her airplane was ever found. While ostensibly she was on a record-breaking flight, it was rumored that she was working for the government and spying on the Japanese, who shot her down. Whether or not this is true, no one will ever know, but it is far more likely that the weather, machine problems or simply fatigue caused her to crash and be swallowed up in the vastness of the ocean.

In the world of international auto racing, Americans faced a disappointing result in the Vanderbilt Cup at Roosevelt Raceway. The first three machines across the finish line were all from Europe. In the lead was Bernd Rosemeyer, whose Auto Union averaged 82.5mph to win; in second and third places respectively were Dick Seaman (Mercedes) and the American, Rex Mays (Alfa Romeo).

In Detroit, the United Auto Workers union had settled a running dispute with GM. However, there were riots following labor disputes at Ford and US Steel.

But there were triumphs too in 1937, among them being the opening of the Golden Gate Bridge across San Francisco Bay. With its soaring towers, this stately suspension bridge was a masterpiece of engineering that remains as impressive today as it was 60 years ago.

While many buyers of automobiles that year would have marveled at the Golden Gate Bridge, a significant number of them were also impressed by the new LaSalle. With a longer wheelbase and a V8 engine, the car was snapped up and production rose to a record level. Total Cadillac production that year was 46,000 cars, and LaSalle accounted for 32,000 of them.

Interestingly, the styling of the '37 LaSalle could be traced back to 1934, when it had

**Below:** In 1934, the restyled LaSalle had been chosen as official pace car for the Indy 500 race. That honor was bestowed on the marque again for 1937, when a convertible coupe led the procession around the famous track. Although originally styled in 1934, and with only minor changes since, the LaSalle had a graceful, streamlined appearance that in no way looked dated.

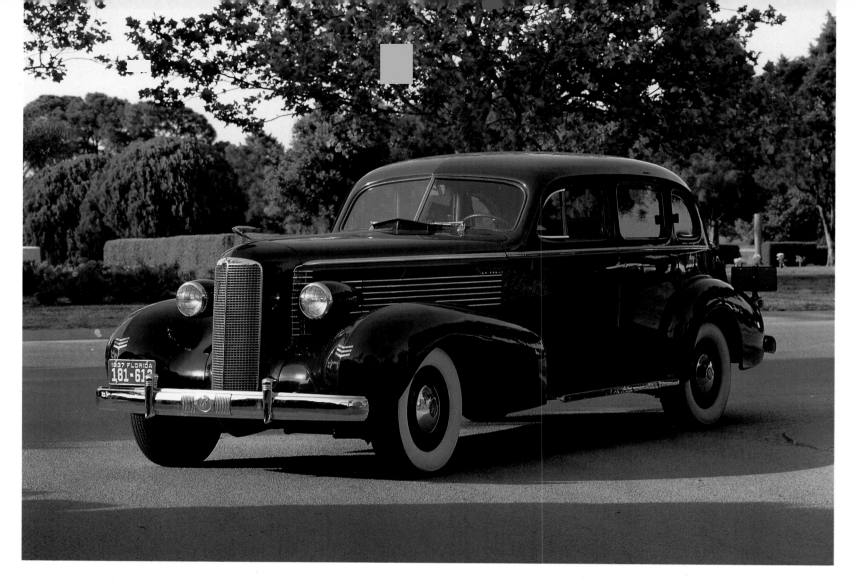

definitely been ahead of its time. The car received a completely new look in 1934, following a poor showing in the early part of the decade. While the car had originally been conceived to fill the gap between the bottom-of-the-range Cadillacs and the top-of-the-range Buicks, by the beginning of the Thirties, there was not much to choose between it and the less expensive Cadillacs. Although the difference in price was about $500 (a substantial sum in those days), the Cadillacs actually seemed to provide better value for money, and their production outstripped LaSalle.

Rather than drop the LaSalle line altogether, GM executives decided to give it a more positive identity so that it was no longer perceived as simply a cheap Cadillac and, therefore, would appeal to a wider audience, other than the traditional buyers of luxury cars. LaSalle could trade on the prestige of being associated with Cadillac and the upmarket body builders Fleetwood, but there would be no doubt that it was not a Cadillac. Moreover, this was emphasized by the $1000 price difference between the LaSalle and the bottom-of-the-line Caddy.

The new streamlined body style had many features that would not be found on other automobiles until later in the decade. Among these were airfoil-shaped fenders that were full and low at the front, blending into the radiator shell and concealing the frame rails. The teardrop-shaped headlights were

supported on the radiator shell and the grille was tall, narrow and oval. The hood sides featured a line of oval ports rather than the normal louvers. The windshield was raked to match the sloping grille and the doors were all of the suicide type, hinged at the rear.

Body styles comprised 4-door sedan, club sedan and convertible sedan, and 2-door coupe and convertible coupe. These were all mounted on a new X-frame chassis with a wheelbase of 119 inches. GM's new "Knee-Action" coil-sprung independent front suspension was adopted, while semi-elliptic leaf springs supported the rear Hotchkiss drive, which replaced Cadillac's more traditional torque-tube arrangement. Double-action shock absorbers were fitted all round, while a rear stabilizer bar was also incorporated to improve ride and handling. Unlike Cadillacs that year, the LaSalles benefited from Bendix hydraulic brakes.

During the early Thirties, LaSalles had been given Cadillac's 353 cu.in. V8, but the new model had Oldsmobile's 240.3 cu.in. flathead straight-eight with aluminum pistons and five main bearings. It produced 95 horsepower (10 less than the V8) at 3700rpm and was backed by a three-speed manual transmission, also of Oldsmobile design. At the time, however, Cadillac were keen to conceal the source of the engine and other driveline parts, stating that they were built at the Cadillac factory, and they were prepared to

**Above:** In addition to the 4-door touring sedan shown, the model range also included a 2-door sedan, a convertible sedan, a convertible coupe and a sport coupe. These stylish cars offered good value for money, particularly with their Cadillac V8 engines, and sold well in 1937.

# 1938

Unlike the previous year, 1938 proved a good one for aviation when millionaire Howard Hughes made history by flying his twin-engined Beech airplane around the world in a record time of 3 days, 19 hours and 17 minutes. He wasn't the only one remembered for achieving a remarkable feat that year. Orson Welles caused mass panic across the US, with his broadcast of "The War of the Worlds" radio play, and thousands of Americans truly believed their country was under attack from alien spaceships. They need not have worried because, as anyone picking up Action Comics' first edition would have found, Superman also made his debut.

Among the technological achievements that year was the invention of the Xerox photocopier by Chester Carlton, and the development of nylon products by Du Pont. Teflon and fiber glass also made their appearance.

Although some auto makers were noted for technological innovation, Packard was not one of them. Nevertheless, their cars offered refined luxury, a timeless appeal, and good performance. During the Thirties, the bodies of their cars had become more streamlined in keeping with general styling trends but, even in 1938, they were still using an upright grille design that had been introduced in the early part of the decade. However, that did not matter, as it suited the elegant image of the cars. Packard were at the top end of the market, producing low-volume, carefully-built cars for the wealthier, more discerning buyer.

Given their potential market, the Packard range of 1938 was surprisingly comprehensive, offering a wide choice of models and body styles. These included a six cylinder series, two eight cylinder series and a twelve cylinder series. Although in styling the cars appeared similar to the 1937 models, there were substantial changes. The previous flat, one-piece windshield was replaced with a two-piece V-shaped windshield on all series and, in addition, all body styles had pontoon fenders, which partially enveloped the sidemount spares where these were fitted.

At the bottom of the Packard range was the Packard Six which, for 1938, received a 7 inch increase of wheelbase taking it to 122 inches. The chassis was fitted with a completely new, all-steel body, rather than the composite wood-and-steel of previous years. Although eventually all car bodies would be

**Left:** Packards form the basis for many custom body packages. This Greber is a typical example. Unlike production '38 Packards, its radiator shell and surrounding "catwalk" has been chromed. The pelican emblem on top of the shell was a $10 dollar option in 1938.

**Above:** Along with the twelve cylinder models, the Super Eights were the top-of-the-line Packards in 1938. They offered elegance and performance in a variety of body styles ranging from coupe to limousine.

# 1939

As America celebrated the arrival of a new year on the eve of 1939, in Europe the ominous clouds of war were gathering. Later in the year, the storm would break: German Chancellor Adolf Hitler would send his troops into Czechoslovakia, then Poland, prompting Great Britain and France to declare war on Germany. This was the beginning of a terrible conflict that eventually would span continents and last for six long years.

Although the United States took a neutral stance at this stage of the war and would not take a belligerent role until after the Japanese strike on Pearl Harbor in 1941, under President Roosevelt, she increasingly provided military aid of all kinds to the Allies, in particular the British. Without America's assistance in this way, the events of the early years of the war might have taken another direction altogether.

Helping to cement the special relationship between the US and Great Britain, King George VI and Queen Elizabeth toured the United States in 1939. Although they would cross the Atlantic by ship, other travelers could take advantage of a more rapid means of travel, for that year saw the inauguration of Pan American's regular transatlantic air service, which made use of Boeing Clipper flying boats.

To escape the dreary news from Europe – and at home, where the economy remained stagnant – Americans could take in a movie and see Clark Gable in "Gone With The Wind", or Judy Garland in the "Wizard of Oz". Or they could visit the World's Fair, which had opened in New York.

"Economy" was a word that also played a major part in some of Ford's advertising that year, although in a different context. In an attempt to compete with the top-of-the-range Oldsmobiles and Dodges, and lower-range Buicks and Chryslers, Ford had launched a completely new model range for 1939 under the Mercury name. The new cars – a convertible, a coupe, a 2-door sedan and a 4-door town sedan – fitted neatly between the standard Ford offerings and the much more luxurious and larger Lincoln Zephyrs. Their overall styling was similar to both the Lincoln Zephyr and the de luxe Fords, but at 116 inches, the wheelbase was 9 inches shorter than the former and 4 inches longer than the latter. Apart from the slightly larger size, the immediate identifying feature between the Mercury and Ford was that the Mercury had horizontal grille bars, while the de luxe Fords had vertical bars. The Mercury coupe also had a distinctive roofline and side glass both of which were quite different from those of the Ford.

Mechanically, the Mercury was similar in construction to the Ford, but from the outset it was fitted with Lockheed hydraulic brakes, whereas both the Ford and Lincoln Zephyr had only switched to hydraulics that year. It was powered by a 95 horsepower version of Ford's famous flathead V8, and it soon gained a reputation as being a hot performer for a big car. Despite this, Ford emphasized the fuel economy of the Mercury, which they claimed could be as much as 20 miles to the gallon and which few cars of any size could match at the time.

Like most of Ford's products, the Mercury sold very well from the outset, establishing the Mercury name, which would continue in the company's line-up from then on. A slight increase in the size of the wheelbase, to 118 inches, would follow in 1940 and the cars would continue to sell well until all civilian automobile production was stopped at the beginning of 1942 to devote capacity to the war effort. Up to that time, the Mercury had always been regarded as an upmarket Ford. However, after the war was over, the parent company would form the Lincoln-Mercury division, and all future Mercurys would be offered as the less expensive versions of the company's luxury cars, rather than the more luxurious forms of their bread-and-butter automobile range.

**Above left:** At a glance, the Mercury town sedan looked similar to the 4-door Ford, with the same roofline, hood and fender shape. However, the horizontal grille bars are unmistakable.

**Far left:** Studebaker's Champion series arrived in 1939. Powered by an in-line flathead six, this Deluxe sedan came with broadcloth upholstery, quarter windows and dual windshield wipers.

**Left:** Willys-Overland spent much of the Thirties in receivership, but by

# 1941

By 1941, most of Europe was under the German jackboot; only Great Britain stood defiant, but bloodied, refusing to be subdued. Through the lend-lease scheme, America was providing military equipment and supplies to the embattled British, despite officially being non-belligerent. As an explanation, President Roosevelt argued that if there had been a fire in his neighbor's house he would have lent that neighbor a hose to put it out. In addition to actual equipment, the US also provided naval escorts for convoys carrying it across the Atlantic, helping to protect it from U-boat attack. Moreover, the US Navy and Coast Guard mounted their own anti-submarine patrols to protect Allied vessels when entering and leaving American ports.

Although Britain was holding out against German aggression, British Prime Minister, Winston Churchill, knew that there was no chance of turning the tide of the war against the German forces. He needed the USA to declare war on Germany, but America had not been attacked, nor were there any treaties that bound her to come to the aid of any victims of German aggression. That situation would change at the end of the year.

At the start of 1941, despite the ominous rumblings from across the Atlantic, it was business as usual for Detroit. At Chrysler, it was a face-lift year, the new models being similar in appearance to the 1940 offerings, although the bodies were wider and the cars had a lower stance. A six-bar grille replaced the previous year's nine-bar unit, and the cars could be ordered with or without running boards. Ever since the lack of success achieved by the radically-styled Airflow model which appeared in 1934, the overall

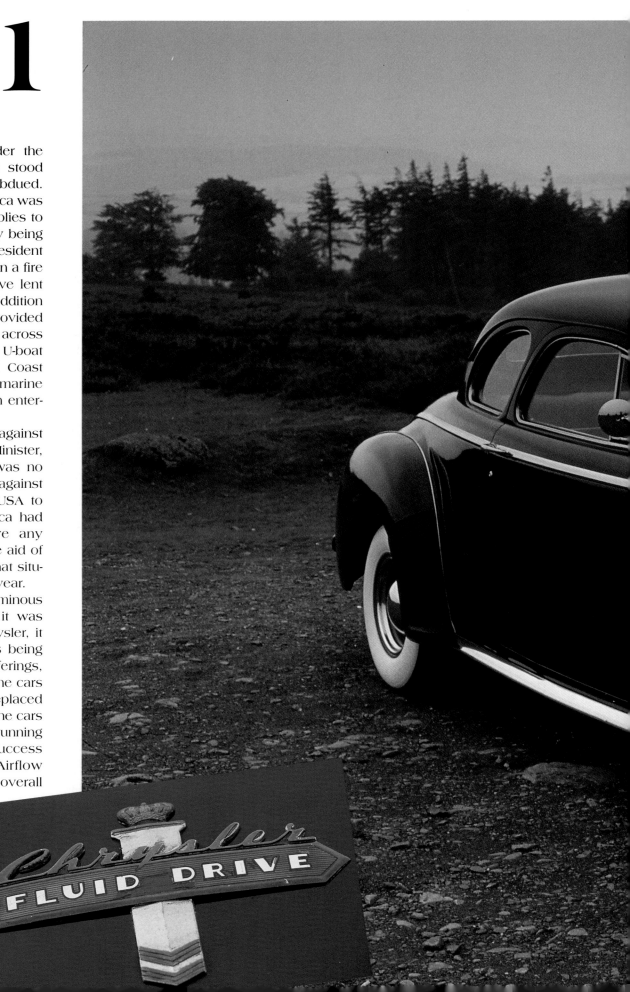

**Right:** Although not spectacular, Chrysler's styling for 1941 projected the company's dependable image and steady progress through proven

# 1946

Emerging from the war, most manufacturers could only offer revamped 1942 models to the eagerly-awaiting public. It didn't matter. As long as it had four wheels and an engine, you could find a buyer willing to exchange their savings for it. This pent-up demand gave false hopes to quite a few entrepreneurs who attempted to enter what appeared to be an extremely lucrative business – most of these newcomers ended up losing their shirts.

But if the cars seemed familiar, much else had changed since Pearl Harbor. Global conflict led to huge advances in technology and America was propelled into the atomic era, with jets, rockets and computers. These space age influences would form themes in every automobile produced in the USA (and beyond) but, for now, a more conservative approach was necessary to get cars delivered to customers as quickly as possible.

There could be few more traditional people in the industry than Chrysler president K. T. Keller (the initials stood for Kaufman Thuma, but nobody ever dared use those names) who had taken over the reigns from Walter P. Chrysler in 1935. Keller's concept of car design was firmly rooted in the past, as can be judged by part of a talk he gave in 1947: "Automobiles are looked at and admired. The buyer is proud of his car's symphony of line; its coloring and trim express his taste; he welcomes the applause of his friends and neighbors. But he bought the car to ride in, and for his wife, and children, and friends to ride in... Though at times one might wonder, even headroom is important. Many of you Californians may have outgrown of the habit, but there are parts of the country, containing millions of people, where both the men and the ladies are in the habit of getting behind the wheel, or in the back seat, wearing hats."

Engineering took precedence over styling at Chrysler, and maintaining sufficient clearance for headgear obviously restricted the designer's options, resulting in a rather more upright look than most other cars. One commentator described the early 1940s Chrysler body thus: "It won't knock your socks off, but it won't knock your hat off, either".

And it is from this rather staid background that the magnificent Town & Country model was born. As the woodwork suggests, its origins lay with a station wagon, but not the usual rectangular timber box built on the back

of a sedan body. It was David A. Wallace, general manager at Chrysler, who decided to add a station wagon to the catalog – a model new to them. However, Wallace specified a wagon with the curved lines of a sedan and this somewhat perplexed the bodybuilders who normally manufactured the "woodies".

Faced with reluctance, Wallace decided to bring the project in house and gave the problem to his own team of engineers. The solution was arrived at after much hard work and,

**Below:** The Chrysler Town & Country 2-door hardtop coupe was a prototype that never made it into production as the sales team decreed that only 4-door sedans and convertibles would sell. Only seven hardtop coupes were built in 1946. This pillarless design pre-dates the first hardtops from GM by three years and was the pioneer of a body type which figured in every manufacturer's line-up for decades .

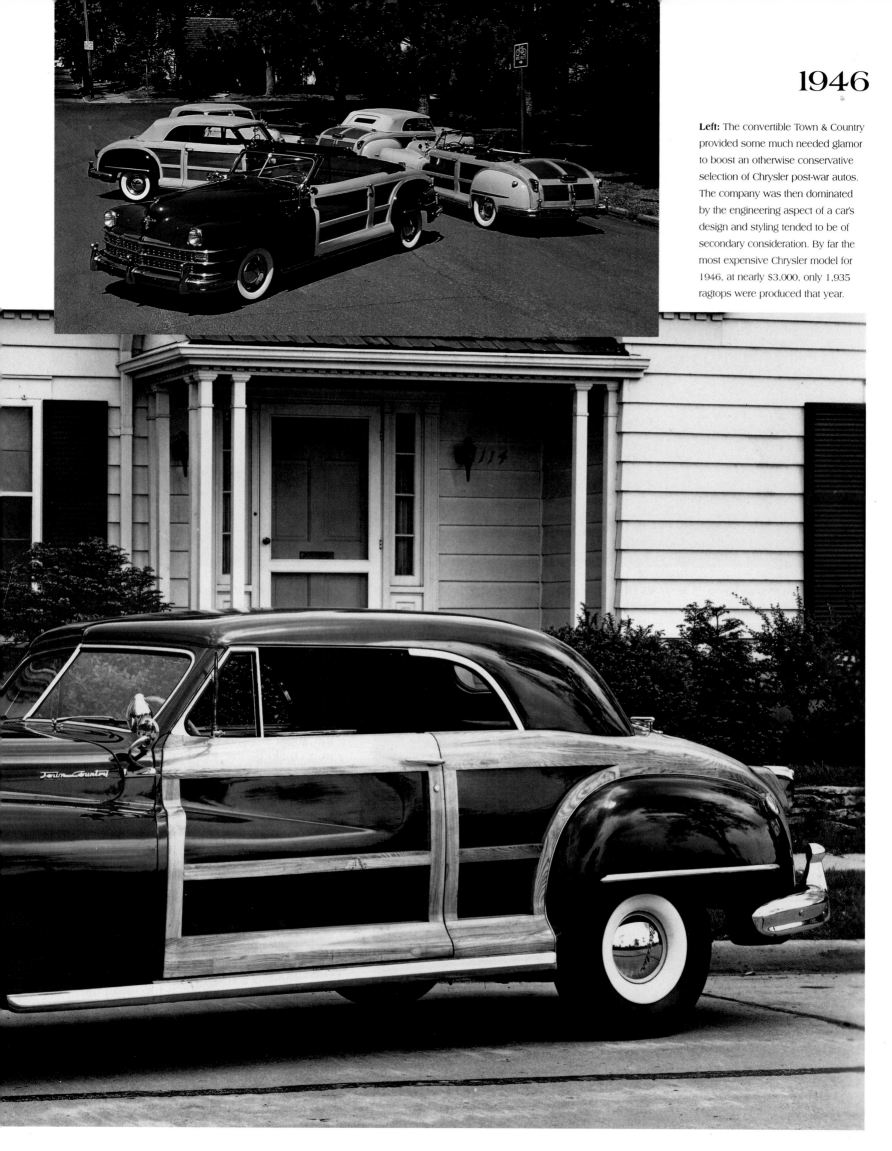

# 1946

**Left:** The convertible Town & Country provided some much needed glamor to boost an otherwise conservative selection of Chrysler post-war autos. The company was then dominated by the engineering aspect of a car's design and styling tended to be of secondary consideration. By far the most expensive Chrysler model for 1946, at nearly $3,000, only 1,935 ragtops were produced that year.

# 1947

The US auto industry lost two giants in 1947, William C. "Billy" Durant died on March 18 and Henry Ford on April 7. Both were founders of huge corporations, but only Ford and his family were to benefit. Durant wound up nearly broke and, in an attempt to spare the 4 million ex-servicemen returning to civilian life the same fate, the G.I. Bill was introduced.

"First by far with a postwar car" was Studebaker's proud boast when their 1947 models were introduced in April 1946. And there's no disputing the fact that the design, generally credited to Raymond Loewy, represented a major leap forward in automobile styling with the front fenders flush with the body. In fact, Studebaker were beaten into announcing their radical new models by the fledgling Kaiser-Frazer company who also brought out a slab-sided car (designed by Howard "Dutch" Darrin) in January. However, the Kaiser-Frazer

**Right:** Studebaker advertising carried the message "First by far with a postwar car!" and it would take the other major Detroit manufacturers a couple of years to catch up with the new designs from South Bend, Indiana.

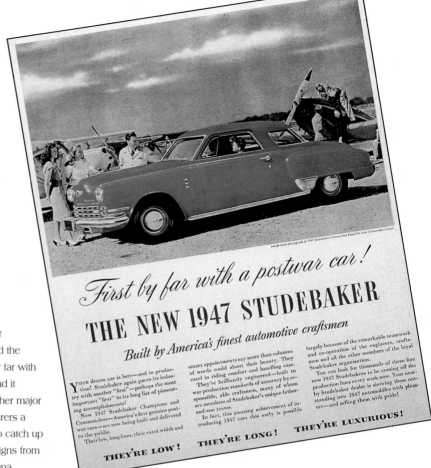

*First by far with a postwar car!*

## THE NEW 1947 STUDEBAKER

*Built by America's finest automotive craftsmen*

**THEY'RE LOW!**　　**THEY'RE LONG!**　　**THEY'RE LUXURIOUS!**

**Below:** The Commander Regal DeLuxe five-passenger Starlight Coupe was one of the top line Studebakers for '47. Most distinctive was the slab-sided front fenders integral with its main body.

offering was plainer and lacked the creative innovation of the products from South Bend, Indiana. And, if Studebaker was miffed at being upstaged in this way, at least their new cars went into production in May and were available to the public in June, well before the first Kaiser-Frazer cars hit the road in October.

Studebaker achieved a two to three year styling lead over the "Big Three" – primarily because of their use of an outside design studio rather than having company stylists and draftsmen tied up with military work during the war. However, the story behind the new design is far from straightforward. Raymond Loewy Studios were the consultants, and establishing the advanced lines began in 1942 with the design team headed by Virgil Exner and Robert Bourke and assisted by clay modeler Frank Ahlroth. Loewy would make regular visits to the factory from New York to check on progress, but it seems his flamboyant personality upset some of the factory management – in particular Roy Cole, engineering vice president.

Virgil Exner also resented Loewy for taking the lion's share of the credit for design work he felt was his. So when he was approached by Cole early in 1944 to start a rival design project at home, in direct competition to his work for Loewy, Exner barely hesitated. To ensure that the Loewy design would fail to be accepted by Studebaker management, Cole deliberately gave Bob Bourke false dimensions for the car, resulting in a full-size mock-up being prepared which was both shorter and narrower than required.

Consequently, when the Loewy proposal was rejected for looking out of proportion, Cole was able to unveil Exner's effort for com-

**Above:** The rear styling of Studebakers gave rise to comments about it being difficult to tell which way the car was going, and you can see why. The difference between the rear window configurations: the wrap-around on the Starlight coupe (center) and ordinary coupe and sedan can easily be seen.

parison and it easily won the approval of the Studebaker hierarchy. Despite a desperate attempt by Loewy's team to re-size their design in just seven days, Cole had already put the production tooling in hand for the Exner model. As can be imagined, Raymond Loewy was outraged and immediately fired Exner, who was at once taken on by Cole to continue his design work for the company.

Therefore, it is not easy to attribute the design precisely. Although Exner is acknowledged as stipulating the flashier, more upright front end, it was very much a team effort. By the end of the war, there were 39 Loewy people working at the factory on styling and design, including noted designers: Gordon Buehrig, John Reinhart, Bob Koto, John Cuccio, Ted Brennan, Vince Gardner and Jack Aldrich – all of whom made a contribution.

Exner and Cole may have undermined Raymond Loewy's personal influence at Studebaker, but the overall design had been developed by his group under his guidance for several years, and many of his team continued to work on the cars. For example, Vince Gardner was responsible for detailing the '47 front grille, and John Reinhart designed the dashboard.

The 1947 Studebaker's most obvious styling feature – the wrap-around rear window and steeply sloping trunk – is found in its most extreme form on the Starlight coupe, but is equally prominent on the sedan models. This gave rise to jokes about how difficult it was to tell which way the car was going but, for Studebaker, it was heading in the right direction and the company moved to eighth place in the sales charts for '47, overtaking Oldsmobile for the seventh spot in '48.

Studebaker were not the first to use a one-piece, curved windshield, but the extensive glass certainly provided outstanding all-round visibility. "Wide Vision" was an apt name for the windshield and, combined with the split rear windows, it gave an unrivaled feel of light and space to the interiors. In fact, the insides of the '47 models were more spacious than their predecessors – up to 11 inches more hip room for example – although the overall height had dropped by four inches in line with the trend for longer and lower cars.

The dashboard looked ultra-modern with three round dials grouped together and framed by the steering wheel; most other manufacturers would continue to position the clock on the passenger side for some years in order to achieve a symmetrical layout. Another innovation was the use of back light illumination for the instruments to cut out glare; a method pioneered on aircraft during the war. Otherwise, the upholstery and trim

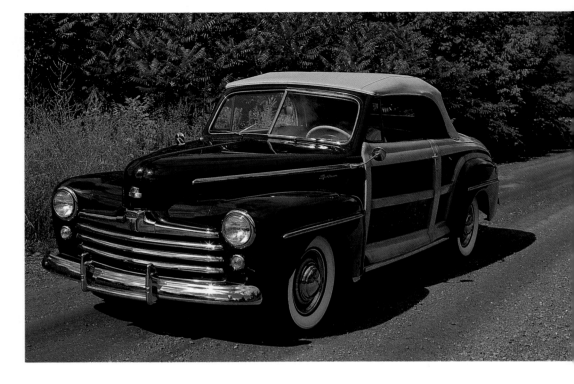

**Above:** The Sportsman convertible woodie was an attractive variation of the Ford ragtop but, at around $500 dearer than the all-steel convertible, only 2,274 were sold in '47. The body design was much the same as the '42 models with a face-lifted grille. The Sportsman was dropped after '48.

**Right:** The Pontiac Streamliner Sedan Coupe was typical of the carry-over models produced in immediate post war years by most manufacturers. The sweeping fastback style (called "Sport Dynamic" by Pontiac) was on the way out, as it restricted rear vision, passenger headroom and trunk space. Although reliable and competitively priced, Pontiac models were generally regarded as rather old-fashioned and were aimed at middle-aged buyers as opposed to the young.

was unremarkable and Loewy expressed his concern at the contrast between the new exterior styling and the old-fashioned interior. Studebaker would not budge, claiming that a lot of their customers were old retired people and wouldn't accept brightly-colored interiors.

While the Commander series of models at the top end of the Studebaker catalog rode on a 119 inch wheelbase (the Land Cruiser 4-door sedan was stretched a further four inches to give generous leg room to rear seat passengers), it was the smaller Champion series (112 inch wheelbase) that proved to be the most popular. Indeed, Raymond Loewy claimed he was the first man in the industry to use the term "compact car" when describing the Studebaker Champion.

Where the body shell and chassis engineering bristled with new ideas, the engine definitely did not. Although new powerplants had been researched and even a V12 considered, at the end of the day, a practical, cost-effective updated version of the flathead six cylinder from prewar models was settled upon. Champion models used a 169.6 cu.in. 80 horsepower version, while the larger Commanders had a 226.2 cu.in., 94hp engine. Transmission was a three-speed manual across the board, with a column gear shift, and an optional automatic overdrive. An interesting device was the Automatic Hill Holder (introduced on the 1936 Studebaker President)

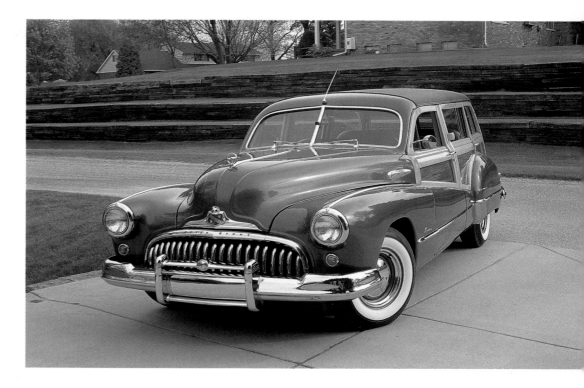

which operated the brakes when the clutch pedal was depressed and prevented the car from rolling backwards.

The new 1947 Studebakers received complimentary media reaction. Motor Manual stating: "This is indeed tomorrow's car today!" It might not have quite been tomorrow's car, but it was sufficiently advanced that the design remained virtually unchanged until 1950, when Loewy (getting his own back on Exner) won the redesign contest with his famous "bullet-nose" creation. It wasn't until the 1953 model that the final traces of the '47 design were eliminated and, even then, it didn't look that dated, proving just how futuristic the original concept had been.

**Above:** Another model coming to the end of its life was the wooden-bodied station wagon. Buick was the last company to produce a true wooden wagon in '53, but this '47 shows how wood cladding had replaced a structural feature on the sides, although the rear door remained an all-timber construction.

# 1948

Americans had plenty to celebrate in 1948. The country was getting back on its feet after the war and life was returning to normal. To top it all, US athletes picked up no less than 38 gold medals at the Olympics held in London, England. It was also election year and there was a new President in The White House – Harry S. Truman. Later in the year, Truman was to sign the Marshall Plan, guaranteeing $6 billion for overseas aid. Some of that aid would be needed in Berlin, Germany, which was being blockaded by Soviet forces in one of the first moves of what would become the Cold War. Berlin was deep in the Soviet-occupied area of Germany, but the city itself had been split into zones administered by the Americans, British, French and Soviets. To keep their zones of the city alive, the Allies organized a massive, round-the-clock airlift, which kept the inhabitants supplied with all the essentials for daily life.

Back in the States, residents of San Bernadino, California, saw history in the making, as the first McDonald's hamburger stand opened. From this small beginning would grow first a nationwide chain of restaurants, then a world-wide chain that eventually would even penetrate the Soviet Union.

Fast food was not the only area of advance in 1948. The development of the transistor at the Bell Laboratories would soon lead to a burgeoning electronics industry, while the latest development in photography was the Polaroid camera.

In Detroit, the auto manufacturers were also making strides forward. In the years immediately after WW2, they had simply dusted off their pre-war designs, made a few cosmetic changes, then built them as fast as they could to satisfy the demands of a car-hungry public. Buyers did not mind that the designs were four or more years old; after years of not being able to buy a new car, anything with wheels would do. Besides, they simply had no choice; it was the only way for companies to pick up the reins of business after years of wartime production.

By 1948, however, new models were beginning to appear, often resulting from development work carried out in secret during the war, and utilizing techniques of manufacture founded in the war work. Experience gained in the manufacture of non-automotive products, particularly aircraft and aircraft components, opened the eyes of designers and engineers to new possibilities in automobile design and construction.

Hudson was one manufacturer that offered a new car for 1948 which was a real winner and, in some respects, unique compared to the rest of Detroit's offerings that year. It was known as the Step-down Hudson.

The new Hudson was based on a unibody design which, although not a new idea for an American car (Nash and Lincoln had already produced unibody designs), it was an innovative move at that time. As utilized in the Step-down design, the unibody arrangement gave greater passenger comfort and safety, together with a sleek, attractive appearance. However, there were pros and cons to this construction. Without the heavy chassis, a much lighter structure could be built saving both materials and cost. On the negative side, it was both difficult and expensive to make alterations to the design. This meant that the substantial changes in appearance, which had become an annual ritual in Detroit, were

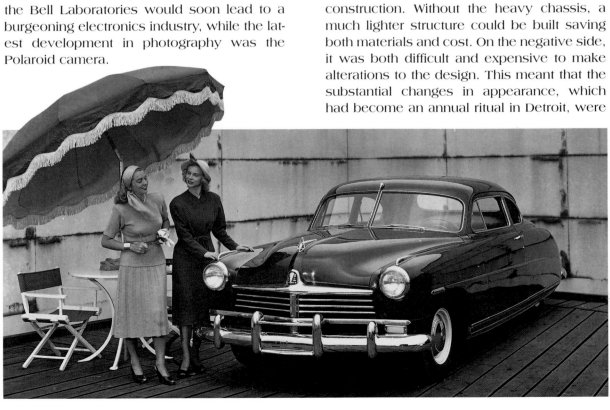

Left: One of the most striking aspects of the Step-down Hudson was its height. The lowered floor provided a low seating position and, hence, a low roofline, emphasizing the sleekness of the design. This was accentuated by the close-fitting, wrap-around bumpers.

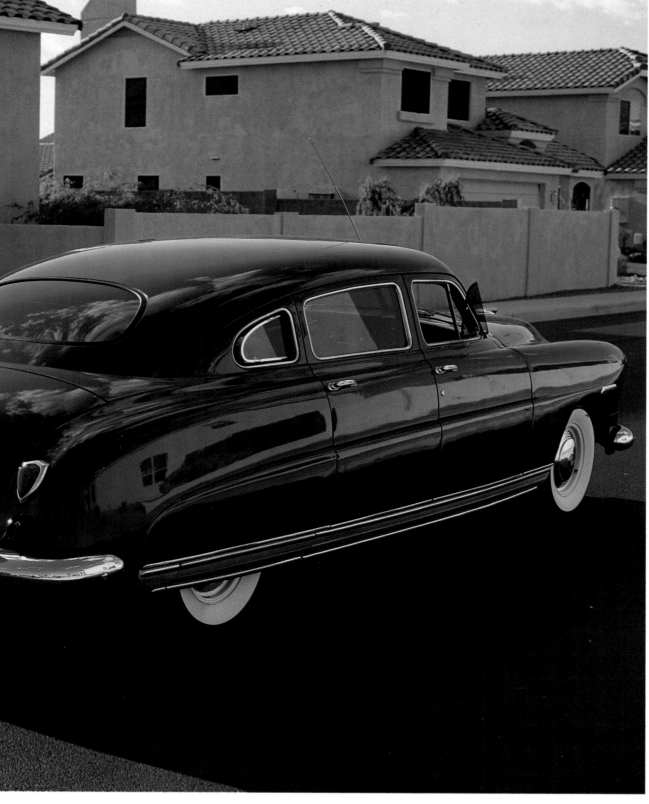

**Left:** This 4-door sedan clearly illustrates the low roofline of the Step-down Hudson. Despite the shallow height of the side glass, a substantial windshield and back light were incorporated into the design, although they had to be laid down somewhat to fit. This is particularly obvious with the back light.

**Left:** The unibody design incorporated box-section stiffeners to strengthen the structure and support the engine, transmission and suspension. A unique feature was the arrangement of the perimeter rails, which passed outside the rear wheels. Convertibles were made by sawing off the roof of club coupes and adding extra stiffeners under the floor, to the sides and around the opening of the passenger compartment.

out of the question. This would prove to be a major problem with the Step-down Hudson but, in 1948, the rapturous reception afforded the car outweighed doubts about the future.

Based on a 124 inch wheelbase, the body was designed to incorporate box-section stiffeners, which effectively formed a strong cage around the passenger compartment and provided support for the engine, transmission and suspension. These formed perimeter rails that ran under the doors and outside the rear wheels keeping intrusion into the passenger compartment to a minimum.

The "Step-down" name referred to the design of the passenger compartment itself. Aware that a low center of gravity would improve the car's handling and ride quality, Hudson designers arranged for the floor to be level with the bottom of the main perimeter rails, rather than sitting on top, which was normal practice with a separate chassis. To get into the car, it was necessary to step over the side rails and down onto the floor.

With a lower floor, it was possible to lower the position of the seats within the body and, consequently, the roofline while retaining good headroom inside. At 60 inches high, the new Hudson was four to six inches lower than most of its competitors, yet it provided as much, if not more, headroom. At the same time, ground clearance was not compromised. A two-piece driveshaft allowed the central floor hump to be quite low, improving comfort for passengers sitting in the middle of the seats.

Hudson engineers also improved the ride for passengers by cradling them between the axles, rather than having them sit over the axle at the rear, so the rear seat was positioned ahead of the axle. This allowed for a wider seat without requiring a wider body. Further elbow room was provided by arranging for the side glass to drop into the doors at an outward angle, allowing recesses to be formed in the door trim panels.

Although the roofline was lowered, the beltline was of conventional height, making the side glass quite shallow in depth – the bottom edge of the glass was level with passengers' shoulders. However, the windshield and back light were comparable in area to taller cars, although these were canted somewhat.

Power for the Step-down Hudson came from a choice of six or eight cylinder in-line engines. The former was a new powerplant – the Super Six, which had a capacity of 270 cu.in and developed 121 horsepower, while the latter was Hudson's tested Super Eight, a 254 cu.in. engine of 128 horsepower. Among the transmission options offered was overdrive, Drive-master and Vacumotive Drive, which had been available on previous mod-

els. Drivemaster was a form of automatic transmission, while the Vacumotive Drive gave automatic operation of the clutch alone.

The suspension was conventional coil-sprung independent at the front with parallel leaf springs at the rear. However, a heavy front stabilizer bar and rear panhard rod were incorporated to assist handling and ride.

A wide range of models was offered in the Super and Commodore series, comprising of 4-door sedans, 2-door broughams, club and standard coupes and convertible broughams.

When the Step-down was shown to Hudson dealers late in 1947, they could not believe their eyes. Worried about how long they could continue selling outdated pre-war designs in the face of steadily rising competition, they found the long, low and sleek automobile everything they could have wished for, and more. It was well received by road testers, too, who praised its styling, "roadability" and its comfort. For the next three years, the new Hudson would boost the small independent company's profits tremendously as the public stepped up to step down.

**Top and above:** The Tucker Torpedo was the brainchild of Preston Tucker, who had made a fortune during WW2 from the design of a gun turret mounting used in bomber aircraft. Fascinated by automobiles, after the war he set out to develop a car that would offer advanced engineering, styling, performance and levels of passenger safety. Powered by a 355 cu.in. rear-mounted, air-cooled, aluminum flat-six, the Torpedo could reach 60mph in 10 seconds and had a top speed of 120mph. For safety, its interior featured a padded dashboard and seatbelts, while a central third head light turned with the steering so that the driver could see around corners at night. Sadly, Tucker's enterprise failed with accusations of fraud and dirty tricks played by Detroit's "Big Three" automobile makers. Only 50 examples of the futuristic Torpedo were completed.

**Above:** Cadillac's new model for 1948 was to set a styling trend that would become a prominent part of all Cadillac designs throughout the Fifties and be copied by most other manufacturers. The '48 Caddy was the first of many to feature tail fins. The car's designer, Franklin Q. Hershey, had developed the idea after seeing the Lockheed P38 Lightning airplane prior to WW2.

**Left:** The Frazer first appeared in 1947 and featured a high level of interior appointments in addition to its advanced, slab-sided styling with integral fenders. Built by Kaiser-Frazer, it outsold the products of the other independent auto makers until 1949, when co-founder Joe Frazer left the company. Although the company continued under the Kaiser name, never again would it enjoy the profits of that brief post-war period.

# 1949

The Berlin airlift came to an end and, still in the sky, James Gallagher made the first non-stop flight around the world in a Boeing B-50A Lucky Lady II, while another Boeing, the Stratocruiser, introduced new standards of airline passenger luxury. On the ground, more than 6 million cars poured out of factories and aviation influences abounded in the designs.

There was a momentous transformation in Ford's fortunes as their output nearly tripled and they zoomed into the number one spot, overtaking arch rivals Chevrolet. On the face of it, this tremendous success can be attributed to the brand new automobiles they had to offer, but there's more to it than that.

For a start, the 1949 model year spanned almost eighteen months, as the restyled cars were launched in June 1948 and remained on sale right up until November 1949. This early announcement also shortened the '48 model year considerably and reduced sales of the pre-war designs on offer in that year, which were much the same as the '46 and '47 Fords.

Even taking all this into account, it has to be said that the '49 Ford was worthy of all the media attention and phenomenal sales that followed. The Ford is significant because it was the first low-price car with a slab-sided body devoid of any of the traditional fender lines. Other makes such as Hudson (another landmark in automobile styling), Nash and Kaiser-Frazer also produced similar concepts but they were not as successful nor as cheap as the Ford. Chevrolet and Plymouth, meanwhile, still had pronounced rear fenders and an obvious dip between head lights and hood.

In fact, the slab-sided Fords were regarded as so flat that they soon earned the nickname "shoeboxes", though today it's hard to equate the curved lines with a shoebox. Engineering was revolutionary too (for a Ford!); this was the beginning of exciting times for the blue oval brigade. Following the death of founder Henry Ford in 1947, his grandson Henry Ford II introduced swinging changes and sought to rid the company of old-fashioned practices.

One of young Henry's most stalwart supporters was executive vice president Ernest Breech, and it is chiefly due to his efforts that the company won through. Breech also had a significant effect on the styling of the '49 Ford models, as we shall see later on. But the first things to disappear were the transverse leaf springs and beam axle suspension that old

**Above:** Ford advertising vigorously suggested "There's a New Ford in your future" and highlighted its "Mid Ship" ride and "Sofa-Wide" seats which attracted over a million customers.

**Left:** Despite a higher price tag, the 1949 Ford Custom Club Coupe proved itself to be a more popular choice than the standard version. Evidently most people weren't bothered about the possible saving of $96, and 150,254 Custom coupes were produced against only 4,170 of the cheaper ones. The extra money gave you such essentials as chrome window trims instead of rubber, a horn ring on the steering wheel, twin sun visors, dual arm rests and a chrome strip along the body sides.

89

# THE AMERICAN AUTOMOBILE

**Right:** The new Rocket overhead valve 303 cu.in. V8 engine was a hot performer and, consequently, an Oldsmobile 88 convertible made a good choice as the pace car for the 1949 Indianapolis 500. Here an Olds 98 convertible (not the official pace car) is posed alongside one of the legendary Novi-engined race cars, the Mobil Special Kurtis roadster.

**Below:** Nash brought out radical Airflyte-styled cars in 1949, soon to be dubbed "bathtubs". The unitary construction (without separate body and chassis) was a first for a mass production US manufacturer. Nash claimed the shape produced 20% less drag, but under those curves lurked an old-fashioned in-line six. "There's Much of Tomorrow In All Nash Does Today" ran the slogans. Nash was replaced by Rambler in 1958.

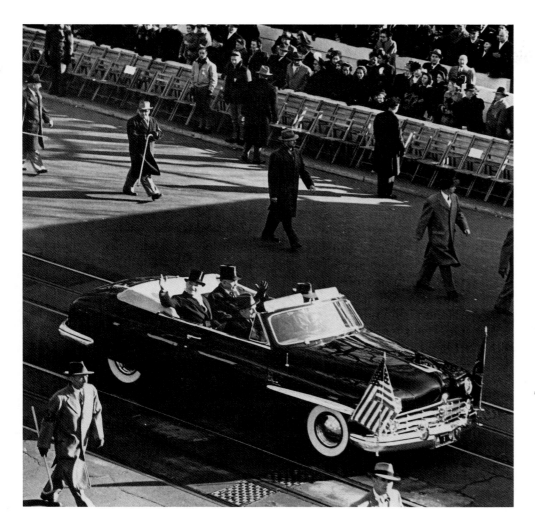

**Above:** For his inauguration on January 20th, President Harry S. Truman rode to the ceremony in style in a Lincoln Cosmopolitan convertible. Totally restyled for '49 with a modern streamlined appearance, prestige, luxury and distinction were all attributes that Lincoln promised its owners saying "you may drive it everywhere with pride". Recessed headlights and wide chrome grille helped differentiate the bigger Cosmopolitan from similar-shaped Mercury models (some Mercury body panels were shared with the smaller Lincoln EL series), but all Lincolns also had a new 336 cu.in. V8 for improved performance.

Henry insisted upon, to be replaced with coil spring independent front and longitudinal leaf rear suspension. Gone too, was the two-speed rear axle and in its place optional overdrive.

The engine was moved five inches forward to create a lower profile, yet provide greater internal space within a slightly shorter and narrower body. This allowed more leg room for the people in the front seat, and with the rear seat now positioned ahead of the rear axle (instead of between the wheels), an extra six inches of width for the passengers in the back. Advertising emphasized this additional comfort by describing the seats as "Sofa-Wide" and promoting the "Mid Ship Ride" and Hydra-Coil front springs. The new Ford design also created 57% more trunk space, now denoted as a "Deep Deck Luggage Locker". And if that wasn't enough, then surely the Magic Air temperature control system, Magic Action brakes or Picture Window visibility would do the trick?

It's estimated that around 28 million people visited the dealers' showrooms in the first three days after the new models were announced. What drew them were attractive cars that had progressed from initial design to production in just 19 months (in those days, average lead times were about three years). Haste wasn't without its problems, of course, and the build quality on the first '49s wasn't as good as it might have been. Body rattles

plagued early vehicles and a number of alterations were made to alleviate problems. This situation persisted throughout the '49 model run and wasn't fully resolved until the 1950 models came along. But it didn't stop the '49 Ford becoming a huge hit and the company outsold Chevrolet by a large margin, with 1.1 million cars coming off the assembly lines.

Indeed, the success of the 1949 models is often credited for saving Ford from oblivion – it really was that desperate. Whether an organization of such magnitude would have disappeared completely is open to conjecture but this automobile has warranted a special place in Ford's long and varied history.

The genesis of such a ground-breaking model was not without complications and there have been many claims as to how the design came about. The first stage in the saga began when Ford's head designer, Eugene T. "Bob" Gregorie showed his ideas to Ernest Breech in 1946. Breech liked the proposal, but felt it was too big to be marketed as a Ford, and in September '46 he pronounced that Gregorie's prototype would instead be used for the more upmarket Mercury range.

This naturally left a big hole in the planning process, and Gregorie immediately started work preparing an alternative design for the Ford. At the same time Breech contracted his friend George Walker (who operated a design consultancy that had done a lot of work for Nash) to come up with some ideas. On the staff were Elwood Engel, Joseph Oros, Richard Caleal, Holden Koto and Bob Bourke. When it came time to make the presentation, Gregorie submitted one clay model and the Walker studio put up three for consideration.

Although there seems to have been very little to choose between them, Breech picked one of Walker's designs. Gregorie left Ford a short time later although they remained on friendly terms. Walker's team proceeded to develop the design and developed the spinner in the center of the grille. Precisely who thought up this idea is debatable. Until recently it was accepted that the front end of the '49 Ford was the work of Caleal, Bourke and Koto – the latter two either working directly for Walker, or moonlighting from the Loewy studio (and the '50 Studebaker with its similar spinner was definitely a Bourke creation for Loewy). However, Oros has stated emphatically that the spinner was his creation.

Whatever the truth, it is apparent that there were many influences during what must have been a hectic period. George Walker took most of the credit at the time and used it to good effect to promote his agency, but it was Ernest Breech and Henry Ford II who had the final say on what went into production.

# 1950

The dark clouds of war gathered again as US troops were sent to South Korea to help fight off the invasion from the north, and President Truman declared a state of emergency. Another rather sinister spectacle, closer to home, was the communist witch hunt conducted by Senator Joe McCarthy, but Boston University president Daniel Marsh was more concerned with television turning 150 million Americans into "a nation of morons".

Sometimes, the hardest task for a designer is altering a car to make it look different from last year's model. Occasionally this results in a classic, but mostly it looks exactly what it really is – a face-lifted version of the earlier car.

Annual changes put pressure on stylists to produce alterations significant enough for the customers to know this was a new car, yet without making fundamental modifications to the structure. Cost restrictions meant that the body sheet metal and major engineering components were used for at least three years, so often a designer was restricted to reworking the front end, the body moldings and fancying-up the rear. The chance to re-design the car every year wouldn't come until later.

Faced with "improving" their elegant 1949 creations, staff at the GM Art & Color Studio, who had responsibility for Buick, decided a bold statement was required – and they don't come much bolder than the buck-toothed grille! While overall responsibility was Harley Earl's, pin-pointing which designer should take the credit (if credit's the right word) for the row of exaggerated bumper guards is not easy. Various people have laid claim, but as most of them are now dead, it's probably impossible to give a definitive answer.

We do know that Ned Nickles, Harlow "Red" Curtice, Edward T. Ragsdale and Henry Lauve were involved. Nickles and Lauve worked under Earl, Curtice had been Buick general manager until 1948 when he was promoted and Ragsdale was manufacturing manager. Nickles is regarded as the leading Buick stylist at that time and is acknowledged for contributing such features as the VentiPorts and sweepspear side decorations. Lauve claimed the dummy porthole VentiPorts and the "Toothy Wonder" grille were his idea.

There seems no dispute as to who was involved with introducing the hardtop body style – Nickles, Ragsdale and Curtice – although, yet again, details of precisely how

**Above:** There was no mistaking a Buick in 1950! No other car could match those chrome teeth filling a gaping grille. Behind the Roadmaster's bucktooth smile was a trusted 320 cu.in. straight eight engine and Buick's own Dynaflow automatic transmission. Note the four elongated VentiPorts.

**Left:** Chrome "sweepspear" decoration on the body sides was another Buick trademark. The Roadmaster convertible was the most expensive model (apart from a limited production station wagon) at almost $3,000 and sold in correspondingly low numbers. Other Buicks were more sought-after, though, and model year production rose to around 670,000 cars.

**Above:** The 1950 Chevrolet DeLuxe Fleetline 4-door sedan is virtually identical to the first proper post-war designs introduced a year earlier. The beginnings of Fifties styling flamboyance are evident, together with the increasing use of chrome, even on lower-price cars, but the sleek fastback shape was soon to go out of fashion as restricted rear vision was a problem. The brand new two-speed Powerglide automatic was a Chevy breakthrough at the cheaper end of the market, but the ancient Stovebolt six was still the only engine available.

**Above right:** The Studebaker Starlight Coupe was about as original as a design could get. The large chrome spinner in the center of the grille has obvious aircraft connotations and the wrap-around rear window was another unusual feature. Although regarded today purely as a classic example of innovative styling, the controversial shape created huge public interest and the company enjoyed its best year ever.

it came about are far from conclusive. The concept dates from 1945 and, depending on who you believe, either Nickles or Ragsdale came up with the suggestion of a body style that looked like a convertible but had a steel roof. The most quoted source of inspiration is Ragsdale's wife, Sarah, who liked convertible models for their looks but didn't enjoy driving them with the top down because her hair got blown around. Nickles believed that Ragsdale saw a model of his and took up the idea.

The role played by Curtice was pivotal. Although no longer officially involved in the day-to-day running of Buick, he remained very much in charge, dominating easy-going general manager Ivan L. Wiles who had taken over his position. The idea of a huge division like Buick being treated as a personal fiefdom

might seem incredible today, but Red Curtice held a unique position, having taken the marque from the depths of depression, through the traumas of war and into the boom years of the Fifties. So it was Curtice, either working directly or by pressurizing people behind the scenes, who directed how Buick progressed.

And progress Buick certainly did. While it is easy to fault the amount of chrome used or the bizarre aspects of the design, in its day the voluptuous Buick was a highly-regarded automobile, only one step down from a Cadillac, and to be behind the wheel of Buick was a sign of a successful career. Forecasting the growth of the automobile market, in 1945 Curtice had persuaded General Motors' chief executive Alfred P. Sloan to fund an expansion programme to increase Buick's manufacturing capacity to over half a million vehicles a year. It was a couple of years before that total was reached, but 1950 saw it exceeded by a wide margin and Buick leapt to number three in the sales charts, behind Chevrolet and Ford – a remarkable achievement.

The curvaceous nature of the Buick was accentuated by a body line that sloped down from the top of the headlight and dipped in front of the rear wheel before climbing back up and giving a distinct definition to the rear fender. This was at a period when most other body styles tried to eliminate the rear fender shape and harks back to Harley Earl's 1939 Y-Job Buick concept car which foretold many of the styling ingredients that were to become identified with Buick in the 1950s.

One of the smallest of these styling artifacts was the gunsight or bombsight hood ornament. Back in 1946, Nickles produced a design that would be suitable for mass production, based on the Y-Job ornament, and the feature remained until 1958. Undoubtedly more of a Buick trademark were the VentiPorts on the sides of the front fenders. Nickles is almost always credited for these (copied from a fighter plane exhaust stubs) when he cut holes in the hood of his '48 Roadmaster convertible and fixed lights behind them wired to the distributor so they would flash like exhausts.

Ragsdale was horrified at seeing Nickles' customizing and complained to Curtice that the young designer had ruined a perfectly good car. Curtice looked for himself and, far

from censuring Nickles, incorporated the portholes in the 1949 Buick models. Initially these VentiPorts were said to release fumes from the engine compartment and were fully functional. For various reasons – not least reports of inebriated passers-by using the orifices to urinate on the engine – the holes were blanked off and they became purely decorative. For 1950 models, the VentiPorts were elongated to look like slots; the more expensive models had four per side, while others had three.

The excess chrome on postwar Buicks was explained by Nickles as coming about due to a shortage during the war. Once free of restrictions, designers used chrome for glamor and perhaps overdosed on the shiny stuff. Nickles was quoted as saying: "...we were entertaining people with chrome on cars..." and it surely did that. Not all designers took such a sanguine attitude in later years, Henry Lauve calling it 'Club Sandwich Chrome' and you can see what he means. Lauve also said that the huge teeth only came about because "...we wanted to be different..." Again, there can be little argument that they succeeded!

However, looking at the era in which the 1950 Buicks were conceived, they were totally appropriate for their time. Big, bold, brash, certainly – yet they established keynote features that would instantly tell you that the car was a Buick from a block or more away, not something that can be done that easily in the Nineties. Stylish? Yes, the 1950 Buick had style aplenty and it showed.

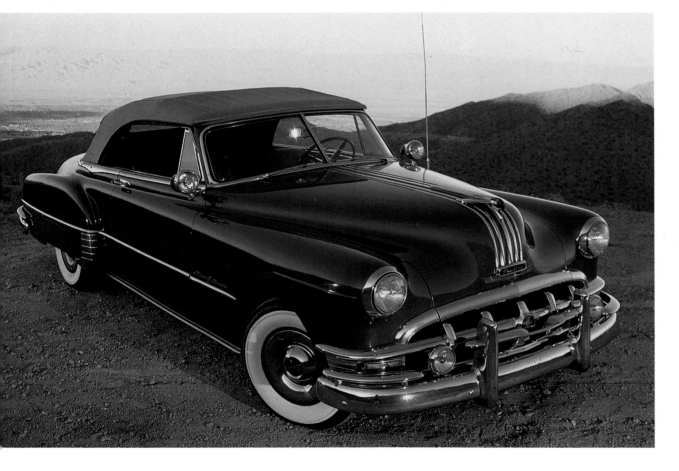

**Left:** The Pontiac Chieftain convertible was another General Motors product that only had limited revisions from the previous year, although the massive grille seems fairly restrained when compared to that of the Buick. The characteristic Silver Streak styling of chrome strips running back over the hood had been around since the Thirties and the Indian Head ornament (which lit up at night) remained as a fixture until 1957. This car has the 268 cu.in. straight eight L-head engine, but in-line six cylinder powerplants were also available.

# 1951

The war in Korea was dragging on, although the US Army was on the offensive and had recaptured Seoul, and it came as something of a shock when president Harry S. Truman sacked General Douglas MacArthur for defying the civil authority in April. Further shocks were felt when an atomic bomb was tested in Nevada, just 45 miles from Las Vegas, and the first hydrogen bomb was detonated on an atoll in the Marshall Islands, in the Pacific Ocean. But probably the biggest explosion in America was the increasing television audience which had risen to 9% of all homes and continued to escalate at an ever faster rate.

Truce finally came to Korea in November, and things became easier for some drivers who chose to buy a Chrysler with the auto industry's first viable power steering system, called "Hydraguide". At the lower end of the market, three-speed automatic transmissions could now be had on Ford and Mercury cars – the Ford-O-Matic and Merc-O-Matic units, built in conjunction with Warner Gear – but it was something of an exaggeration for Mercury to advertise its '51 models using the slogan "Nothing like it on the road!"

The Mercury nameplate suffered from something of an identity crisis – it was usually looked upon as a fancy Ford rather than a junior Lincoln. The 1951 models (the last of a three year phase starting with the '49 designs) were more Lincoln in appearance, although beneath the bodywork there were mostly Ford mechanical parts.

In an attempt to give Mercury automobiles a more upmarket image, the Lincoln-Mercury division was formed in October 1945. This also gave Lincoln an independent dealership network whereas its cars had previously been sold in selected Ford showrooms.

As we know from the story behind the creation of the 1949 Ford models, it was Ernest Breech who decided that Bob Gregorie's initial design should be used for the Mercury range. But the development of the shape that was to become inextricably linked with the Fifties wasn't quite as straight-forward as simply changing the name on the hood.

In fact, the evolution of the 1951 Mercury involved three generations of the mighty Ford dynasty and, in some ways, encapsulated the end of the old autocratic regime that had grown up under the ailing Henry Ford and the new beginnings heralded with the arrival of

**Left:** According to the advertisement copy writers, there was nothing like a '51 Mercury on the road, but its striking similarity to the models of the previous two years was unmissable.

**Below:** There were few major changes to the Mercury '51. The 4-door sedan was the top seller and one third of the buyers opted for Merc-O-Matic automatic transmission.

# THE AMERICAN AUTOMOBILE

**Right:** Totally redesigned by John Reinhart, the 24th Series Packards for '51 were acclaimed as "the most beautiful car of the year" by the Society of Motion Picture Art Directors. The line up consisted of three main levels of models – the lower priced 200 (back) had a "toothless" grille with a 288 cu.in. engine and 122 inch wheelbase; the mid-range 300 (center) had a 5 inch longer wheelbase and bigger engine; the top of the line 400 Patrician (front) only came as a 4-door sedan.

**Below:** The Packard 250 convertible was a mid-year introduction, together with a companion 2-door Hardtop coupe. It was based on the shorter wheelbase of the 200 series, but used the larger 327 cu.in. in-line eight cylinder L-head engine. Four dummy louvers on the rear fenders and fancy interiors featured in these models.

his grandson, Henry Ford II. Gregorie first started work on the design when Edsel Ford was in charge of styling and, although the two shared many ideas, they were by no means in total agreement. Edsel Ford tended to favor a lighter touch, especially on details like bumpers and grille, whereas Gregorie was more inclined to use broader brush strokes.

The death of Edsel Ford on May 26 1943 was a turning point. Grief-stricken at the loss, Octogenarian Henry took even less interest in the cars bearing his name, and left important decisions to others – mainly Harry Bennett and Charlie Sorensen – as the battle waged for control of the Ford empire. Vice-president, "Cast Iron Charlie" Sorensen saw the Gregorie proposals and encouraged the stylist to make the cars even bigger and more rounded, equating size and luxury to the voluptuous curves of "those big Italian gals".

But Sorensen was part of the old guard and on his way out, eventually to be deposed early in 1944. However, the internal power struggle wouldn't be fully resolved until some time after Henry Ford II became company president in September 1945. Young Henry hired new management to replace Bennett and his cronies and, in one of his most crucial appointments, was to take on a group of ten young ex-USAAF officers headed by Charles "Tex" Thornton, who quickly became known as "The Whizz Kids" throughout Ford. Ernest Breech was then persuaded to join the company and things really started to happen.

One effect was a rationalization of the Ford, Mercury and Lincoln models. It was decided that Mercurys would use a 118 inch wheelbase chassis (required for the larger body shell shared with Lincoln) of similar dimensions to pre-war designs although completely new in concept, while Fords would sit on a four inch shorter platform. Meantime, Lincoln used two slightly longer configurations – 121 and 125 inches – as befitted their status as a luxury marque.

Although Bob Gregorie had left Ford in 1946, his design for the 1949 Mercury went into production with very little modification. Subsequent face-lifts in '50 and '51 improved the overall look, adding extended rear fenders and vertical tail lights. The bodywork may have altered little, but a brand new feature on the 1951 was of more significance to the buyer – the Merc-O-Matic automatic transmission.

Coupled to an outmoded Flathead V8, the automatic put the Mercury's performance into the "leisurely" bracket or, as Mechanix

Illustrated tester Tom McCahill put it: "...the winged Mercury parked his track shoes outside the door and joined the ladies over a comforting pot of tea". Mercury adverts highlighted economy, promising to "Squeeze the last mile out of a gallon", and stressed that it wasn't expensive either, saying they gave customers "more car per dollar". The hot rodders' favorite had been turned into something different, something more comforting to Mr and Mrs Joe Average – for it was they who were buying new automobiles. The difference appealed and, with sales over 310,000, raised Mercury to number six in the charts.

But if the '51 Mercury was a success with the older generation when new, it would gain a far more long-lasting image as a Fifties icon from a most unlikely source – the death of a film star. Had he lived, it is impossible to predict what would have become of James Dean, but one thing is certain – he would never have driven a Mercury except in a movie. The fact that his second starring role in "A Rebel Without A Cause" (released in 1955 shortly after his fatal car crash) featured him as a super cool teenager fighting the establishment and driving a mildly customized Mercury was to endow the car with a presence that endures today.

The association with James Dean fixed the "bathtub" Mercury as an automobile with attitude – performance didn't matter, it was all about looking cool as you cruised to the drive-in. Over the years, Hollywood periodically reinforced this image, notably in the 1970s blockbuster "American Graffiti" in which the customized Mercury was used by a delinquent gang of youngsters.

From comfortable family transport for the suburban dweller to an everlasting symbol of teenage rebellion, surely no other car has made such a remarkable transition as the Mercury?

**Below:** Lee Wallard won the 1951 Indianapolis 500 in his Belanger Motors Special at an average speed of 126.244mph. This marked the 28th consecutive victory on Firestone tires at the Brickyard, and was proclaimed in adverts with the slogan "Safety-proved on the Speedway for your protection on the highway", stressing that 500 miles on the track equalled five years of average driving.

# 1952

Many US industrialists profited hugely from government contracts during the Second World War, and one of the most famous was Henry John Kaiser who had interests in ship-building and construction. Like other tycoons who made vast fortunes over the years, Kaiser thought he could take on the established Detroit auto makers and beat them at their own game. And, just like all "outside" attempts to launch a new postwar car, Kaiser's venture ended in failure.

Henry Kaiser's dream was a small, cheap car that would provide basic transportation for everyone. In the early 1940s, he had predicted producing a new car for $400 – a suggestion which proved to be totally unrealistic, yet one Kaiser often repeated in his quest for publicity. It was in an attempt to revive the flagging fortunes of his auto company, that he decided to launch the new small car in September 1950 and borrowed 44 million dollars to finance the tooling required.

Stylist Howard "Dutch" Darrin produced a prototype based on his 1951 full-size Kaiser design but, instead, Henry decided to go with another concept put together by American Metal Products of Detroit. Based on a 100 inch wheelbase chassis, the compact Henry J (as it came to be called) 2-door sedan was notable for its sloping fastback and small tail fins. The fins were part of Darrin's attempt to improve the looks of the car, and he made several other changes, including his trade-

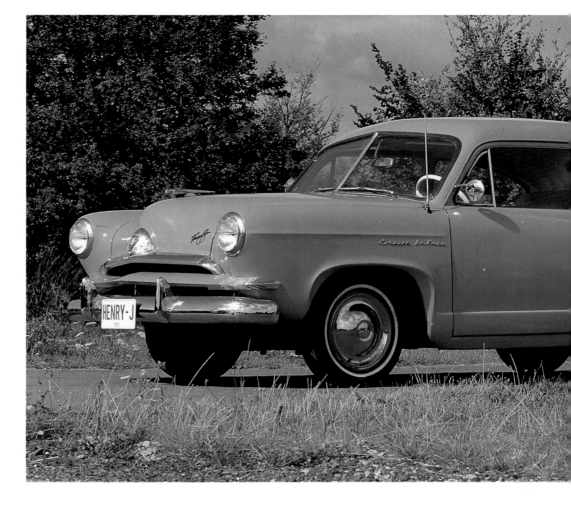

**Above:** The small Henry J 2-door sedan was launched as an economy car that anyone could afford. Priced at $1664, the top of the line Corsair DeLuxe version came with glove box and opening trunk lid – items that came as standard on even the most basic cars. The 161 cu.in. six cylinder engine gave a 0-60mph time of 14 seconds. The central bar of the grille should be chrome, not painted.

**Right:** Outwardly, the 1951 and 1952 Chrysler models were identical, but under the hood of Saratoga and New Yorker models was the first legendary Hemi V8 – a 331 cu.in. overhead valve engine that produced 180bhp in standard form. The Windsor Highlander convertible only had a 119hp 264 cu.in. L-head in-line six cylinder engine and so was far more sedate.

**Right:** In an attempt to boost flagging sales in '52, Kaiser managed to persuade department store chain Sears Roebuck to market the car using their Allstate brand name. Little more than a Henry J with a different grille and interior, despite aggressive promotion, less than 1,600 Allstates were sold in 1952, and the scheme was dropped in '53 after fewer than 800 orders had been taken.

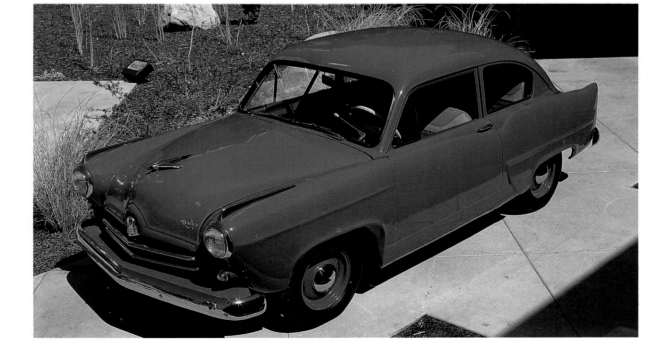

mark feature – a slight dip in the bodywork just behind the door. Power for the Henry J came from either a 68hp flathead Willys 134 cu.in. four cylinder engine or a 161 cu.in. six that gave 80 horsepower.

Initially it seemed as though Kaiser had come up with a winner as almost 82,000 Henry Js were sold in 1951. That seems to have saturated the market though, as sales more than halved in '52, then halved again in '53. In 1954, the car's last year, only 1,123 were sold and that was the end. Henry Kaiser's mistake was to believe that there was a huge market for a cheap car with no trimmings. He was quoted as saying, "We feel that we have accomplished our goal at a price which will be within the budgets of millions who have never been able to afford a new car." But Kaiser had failed to understand that most Americans in the early Fifties preferred to own a car that looked glitzy rather than one classed as "a poor man's automobile".

While Kaiser's aim was to produce a cheap, no-frills automobile, that didn't prevent copywriters from filling the company sales litera-ture with fulsome descriptions. Calling the mundane flathead engines "Supersonic" was par for the period, but stating that the feeble four cylinder "Lunges like a lion (without the roar!)", was definitely over the top! Other animal connotations were used, such as "Tough as an Ox, nimble as a Kitten" but, in an attempt to make the Henry J appeal to as wide an audience as possible, there were also statements like "You'll be the object of envy at the doors of the smartest shops".

The Henry J saw some international competition use too. Three cars were entered in the 1952 Monte Carlo Rally, and one actually finished in 20th place – an incredible achievement. But even had a Henry J won the event outright, it would not have been enough to stop Kaiser's dream becoming a nightmare.

Sales plummeted and debts mounted. Kaiser amalgamated with Willys-Overland in 1954, and the following year Kaiser-Willys ceased manufacture of passenger cars. Henry J. Kaiser's venture into the automobile world was estimated to have lost 100 million dollars in a decade.

# 1953

Ford and Buick shared 1953 as their Golden Anniversary Year and Charles E. Wilson, president of GM, made his famous (and often misquoted) statement: "...for many years I thought that what was good for our country was good for General Motors, and vice-versa". What eventually turned out good for Chevrolet was the arrival of a brand new sports car.

Whenever the reasons behind the birth of the Corvette are chronicled, it is usually suggested that it was GIs returning from Europe with an enthusiasm for British or Italian sports cars that led to the creation of America's favorite two-seater. While not wishing to diminish this idea, it is worth pointing out that, in 1952, little more than 11,000 new sports cars were registered across the entire USA – approximately 0.025% of the nation's new car market.

Given this perspective, it is easy to understand why the big Detroit automobile makers were not exactly fighting each other to enter such a small, specialized sector of the marketplace. That it should be Chevrolet – traditionally a purveyor of affordable, yet mundane, family sedans – to introduce such a

bold departure from the norm, is almost entirely due to the efforts of two men – Harley Earl and Ed Cole.

As the stylist supremo at General Motors, Harley Earl used his considerable influence to mount almost a personal crusade to prove that his company could build a car as good as the Jaguars and Ferraris he so admired. Chief engineer Cole, on the other hand, saw a sports car would boost the Chevrolet name and give it a more youthful image. In addition to the two major players, the names of Robert McLean and Maurice Olley should be added. Newly arrived from Cal Tech, when laying out the chassis design, young McLean decided to reverse the normal procedure and started at the back axle, then worked forward to obtain the 50:50 weight distribution specified. Most of the suspension and steering details came from Olley (an ex-Rolls Royce engineer) and their efforts helped give the Corvette its road-hugging profile, thanks to the lower slung engine and drivetrain.

Following the debut of the prototype EX-122 Corvette in the GM Motorama – a glamorous cavalcade of exotic cars that toured the USA throughout the Fifties – Chevrolet dealers found themselves inundated with enquiries about the sporty two-seater. It seemed Earl and Cole had produced a winning concept and the car was put into production without many alterations. This wasn't so easy. Using glass-fiber for a concept car was fine, but

**Right:** The Corvette grille with thirteen teeth was designed to have the Chevrolet family look although the regular 1953 Chevy models only had three teeth up front. A lack of a full front bumper caused some commentators to worry about possible damage to the fiber glass body when parking and stainless steel mesh head lamp stoneguards were removed in some states because they did not conform to local motor vehicle regulations.

**Below:** The convertible top for the first Corvette was very much an afterthought that looked ungainly in appearance. Awkward to erect, with drop-in side windows that had to be stored in the trunk when not in use, it impaired the driver's all round vision considerably and completely spoilt the sleek lines of the car. Harley Earl's preoccupation with jet and rocket styling themes can be seen in the tail lights but otherwise Chevrolet's first sports car has quite a European look.

adapting the design and building techniques for the assembly line was another matter.

Compromises were inevitable; the Chevy engineers and designers were further hampered because they were forced, in the most part, to use existing mechanical components to save time and keep the cost of the project down to a minimum. This meant that the Corvette came with a six cylinder Stovebolt engine and a Powerglide two-speed automatic transmission. Of course, Cole's team tweaked the old Chevy six to produce 150 horsepower and push the speedo needle round to almost 110mph, but it just wasn't in the same league as Jaguar's twin overhead camshaft powerplant.

Thomas Keating, Chevrolet's general manager, described the new two-seater thus: "In the Corvette we have built a sports car in the American tradition. It is not a racing car in the accepted sense that a European sports car is a race car. It is intended rather to satisfy the American public's conception of beauty, comfort and convenience, plus performance."

On June 30 1953, the first ever Corvette (one of only 300 built in that year) was driven off the end of a short, six-car-length assembly line tucked away in a corner of the Chevrolet

**Above:** The dramatic new Studebaker Commander Starliner hardtop was the most elegant of Raymond Loewy's designs and won a Fashion Academy Award, but production difficulties held back sales.

**Below:** The DeSoto Firedome V8, with hemispherical combustion chambers on a 276 cu.in. engine, produced an impressive 160bhp.

plant in Flint, Michigan. Joining together the 46 separate glass-fiber panels that made up the body, getting them to cure and mounting it on the chassis was a labor-intensive task and, at times, the process was a slow and uncertain affair.

Because of the apparently huge demand and the shortage of cars, it was decided to allocate the available Corvettes to celebrities and prominent figures in the first instance. However, when the cars fell short of expectations, this method of selective distribution backfired and generated some rather unwelcome negative publicity. Only 183 Corvettes were sold in '53, and production had to be held in check the following year as manufacture was transferred to St Louis. It didn't help that, priced at $3490, the Corvette was over a thousand dollars more than an MG and out of reach of the majority of young drivers it was supposedly aimed at.

Despite Thomas Keating's pronouncement, comparisons between European sport cars and the Corvette were inevitable. And, not unexpectedly, the Chevy two-seater didn't stand up well against such competitors. It wasn't just the less-than-exciting six cylinder engine, or Powerglide automatic, but also the dashboard and whitewall tires that didn't belong on a sports car. And even those people prepared to accept the lack of performance were far from satisfied with the level of standard equipment – no external door handles, clumsy clip-in side curtains instead of wind-up windows, a primitive convertible top that let in rain and dust – and distressing rattles from the glass-fiber bodywork.

Most other automobile manufacturers would have swiftly abandoned such a troublesome project as this. The fact that a huge company like Chevrolet kept the sports car alive and that the Corvette itself survives to the present day comes back, once again, to the influence wielded by Harley Earl and Ed

Cole. Maybe some of it was simply a matter of pride and Earl protecting his reputation, unwilling to accept that his creation was, by most standards, a failure. Or perhaps Cole realized that when the new V8 engine arrived, Chevy would take on a whole new performance image – he certainly never lost his enthusiasm for the car.

In many ways the 1953 Corvette is an anachronism. At the time it was a car that Chevrolet should never have made. A giant company busy churning out 1.3 million family cars a year had no logical reason to undertake the construction of a tiny quantity of hand-built vehicles, using a curious combina-tion of special materials and stock compo-nents. But among many other facets of his character, Harley Earl was a dedicated car enthusiast and designing a sports car that would be internationally acclaimed obviously represented to him a challenge that he just couldn't resist.

His first attempt, while regarded as a Fifties classic today, fell woefully short of the type of car he wanted to emulate. But at least it was built and, in time, it would develop into a true sports car and one that Harley Earl, Ed Cole and all those Corvette designers and engineers that followed them could truly be proud of.

**Above:** A very special Buick was the Roadmaster Skylark Anniversary Convertible for 1953. Unique styling features included fenders with full round wheel openings, no VentiPorts in the hood, and sweepspear trim plus special body emblems. A lower roof line and 40-spoke Kelsey-Hayes wire wheels added to the opulent look, while the leather interior came as standard with a package of luxury accessories. At $5,000 the Skylark was the most expensive Buick and cost more than some Cadillacs; it's no wonder only 1,690 were produced.

# 1954

A ten year, $50 billion expansion program of the US highway system was announced by Vice-President Richard Nixon, and General Motors produced its 50 millionth car (a Chevrolet) on November 23rd at Flint, Michigan, which was paraded through the city streets in front of huge crowds.

Until the 1952 model year, the cars produced by Lincoln were aimed squarely at Cadillac customers and consequently designed for luxury motoring. Performance and road holding were of secondary consideration. This supposedly all changed when Earl S. MacPherson – vice president and chief engineer of Ford's Lincoln-Mercury Division – announced that, henceforth, the main target would be the Oldsmobile Ninety-Eight.

There was some sense in MacPherson's proposal as Lincoln had fared pretty badly against the outstanding 1949-51 Cadillacs, and the design team were given a strict brief to work to. However, excellent as the resulting car was, it wasn't quite the Oldsmobile equivalent that had been foreseen. Size-wise it came close – while the Lincoln had a one inch shorter wheelbase than the Olds 98, its overall length was an inch more. However, the Lincoln tipped the scales at nearly 400 pounds heavier – a weight definitely more in the Cadillac class. Under the Lincoln's hood, the new Y-block 317.5 cu.in. overhead valve V8's 160 horsepower rating was on a par with the smaller capacity Olds engine, but 30bhp down on the larger Cadillac powerplant.

Unfortunately, the '52 Lincolns were the subject of a massive 25% price hike over the previous year and, because of this, most Oldsmobile models would seem quite a bit cheaper by comparison. Therefore, in many respects, the Lincoln team were only partially successful in achieving their aims.

But bald dimensions and stark statistics can't possibly give you a feeling of what great cars the 1952-54 Lincolns really were. Gone was the bulbous carapace of an overblown Mercury body, and in its place was revealed a true "jet age" creation. And, not only did they look good, thanks to some splendid engineering the Lincoln was able to boast excellent performance, superior road holding and impressive reliability. When discussing their mechanical aspects, one recent commentator described them as "engineers' cars" – an apt appraisal.

Even so, over the years, many good automobiles have failed to sell in sufficient numbers. Fortunately for Lincoln, when it came to sales promotion they had two major advantages – the Carrera PanAmericana and Tom McCahill. That an automobile intended for upmarket American buyers could compete in, and win, the gruelling 1,900 mile Mexican

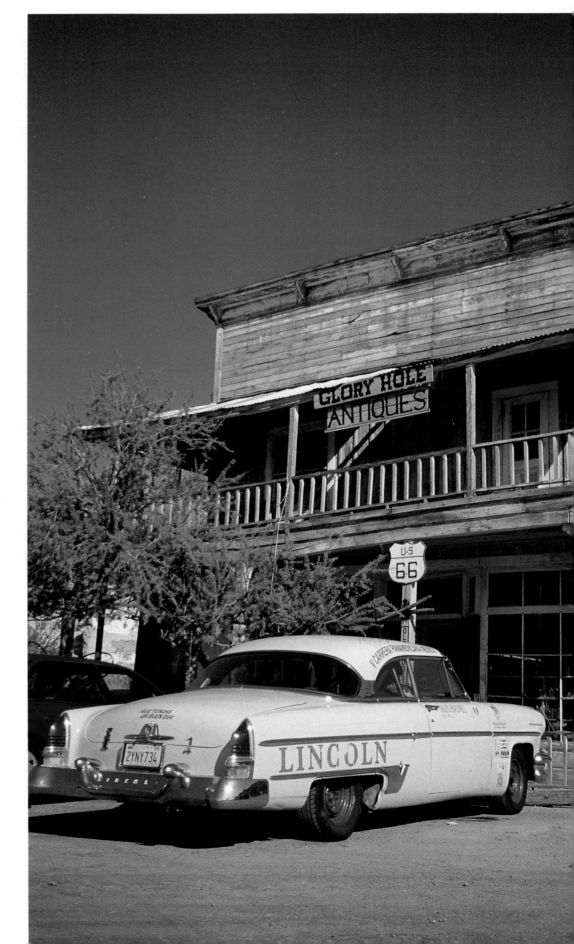

**Below:** The Lincoln Capri has been prepared as a replica of cars used in the Mexican Carrera PanAmericana road race back in the early '50s. The MacPherson suspension, strong chassis and highly efficient 317 cu.in. engine earned these Lincolns a reputation as performance machines.

cross-country road race was a truly remarkable feat, and thanks in no small part to the skilled preparation carried out by Bill Stroppe and wizard mechanic Clay Smith. Mind you, they had a good platform to work with, plus an ample factory supply of special "export" engine and suspension components – not forgetting some daredevil drivers!

In the 1952 event, Lincoln not only won the Stock Car Class, they also took 2nd, 3rd and 4th places. Winning driver Chuck Stevenson likened the experience to "riding a steel bridge across Mexico" when assessing the durability of the Lincoln chassis. A repeat performance followed in '53, with Lincoln again capturing the top four spots. 1954 also

**Below:** The clean front end design of the Lincoln was achieved by using the bumper as the central bar of the grille opening. Capri sales rose by 10% in 1954 to 29,500 and Hydra-Matic transmission (bought from arch rivals General Motors) was standard across the Lincoln range.

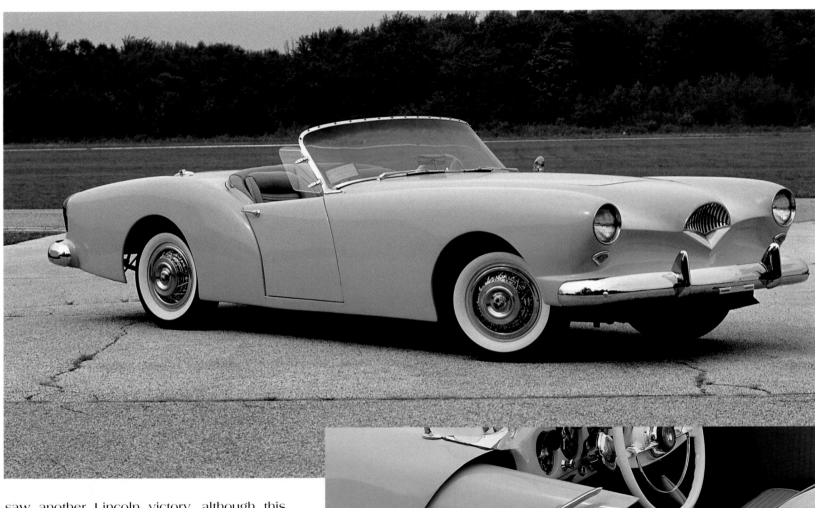

saw another Lincoln victory, although this time things weren't quite so straightforward. In fact, four of the factory-backed cars dropped out very early on and it was a private entrant who captured first place, although a surviving team car did take second place. Three wins in three years produced excellent publicity and Lincoln made good use of the successes.

Tom McCahill wasn't a race driver, but a well-respected writer who was responsible for road test reports in the immensely popular Mechanix Illustrated magazine and, consequently, a man of considerable influence. McCahill was a devoted fan of the 1952-54 Lincolns, even to the extent that he bought a '53 model for his own personal use! His review of the 1952 Lincoln could hardly have been more enthusiastic: "This is one of the finest handling big American cars I have ever driven...in the luxury and comfort departments I found it unbeatable...this car held the turns like a leech. It was a true pleasure to steer. This is undoubtedly one of the finest American cars ever built." It wasn't all praise, mind you, McCahill berating Ford for fitting too small an engine in the big car.

Two years later, McCahill was still enjoying the ride: "Last year I wrote that the 1953 Lincoln was America's finest and safest automobile. This still goes in 1954. These are magnificent road cars that will out-ride and

out-corner any other American car I have ever driven." He was happier about the engine too as that had been uprated to 205 horsepower. But the prime reason for McCahill's unstinting approval of the Lincoln's handling capability came from the new ball joint front suspension. This system did away with the traditional king pin arrangement, making the cars more stable at high speed (the Lincoln race cars could reach 130mph) and had been used before on some European cars.

The design of the Lincoln ball joint suspension (the forerunner of the suspension type currently used as standard equipment on cars around the world) was the result of a

**Above:** The futuristic fiber glass bodied Kaiser-Darrin two-seater sports car was designed by Howard "Dutch" Darrin using a Henry J chassis and 161 cu.in. Willys in-line six cylinder engine. Three–speed transmission with overdrive gave nearly 100mph top speed and 0-60mph could be done in 13 seconds. The car had unique sliding doors, and a folding top with an intermediate half-up position. Less than 500 were produced before the closure of the Kaiser company.

joint development program between Ford and the Thompson Products Co – with chief engineer Earl MacPherson obviously involved in the project. And it was MacPherson's name that was adopted to describe the new suspension – basically a refinement of earlier methods, not a completely different design – and the MacPherson Strut has become an automotive synonym, much like the domestic Hoover or Thermos names.

Superior engineering is all very well, but what the potential customer first sees when he enters the show room is the body of the automobile, not its chassis or suspension. But here too, the Lincoln was very highly thought of. The 1952 line represented the first cars that Lincoln-Mercury's chief stylist, William F. Schmidt, had directed from start to finish, and although George Walker was still retained by Ford as a styling consultant, he only seems to have had a limited input into the design work. The other in-house designers working with Schmidt were Don DeLaRossa (exteriors), L. David Ash (instru-

ment panels and details) and Don Beyreis (interiors and trim).

Following the Ford corporate styling theme, the Lincoln featured a more angular top half, emphasized on sedans and hardtops by a slightly flatter roof line and a greater area of glass. The prominent high set head lamps protruded over the bumper (in direct contrast to the recessed head lamps of the preceding models), adding to the aggressive look. The bumper itself was also positioned higher and did dual duty as the central bar of the grille opening. This integrated bumper-grille gave a very clean front end and was used by many other manufacturers in subsequent years.

A comprehensive brochure issued by Lincoln, detailing their success in the 1953 Carrera PanAmericana, carried the phrase "A Motor Car Revolution" on the cover. This was an exaggeration, and a tongue-in-cheek reference to the Mexican setting of the race, but in many ways the 1952-54 Lincolns were certainly evolutionary – so maybe we can forgive the word-play.

**Below:** Starfire was the new name for the Oldsmobile 98 convertible in '54 and it originally came from the Lockheed F-94 jet fighter, but was used on an Oldsmobile dream car displayed in '53. Apart from the obligatory annual body changes, the most noticeable styling feature is the Panoramic double curvature wraparound windshield that appeared on all '54 Olds models. The Starfire engine was a 185 horsepower version of the 324 cu.in. Rocket V8 and 6,800 were sold, with a factory price of $3,248.

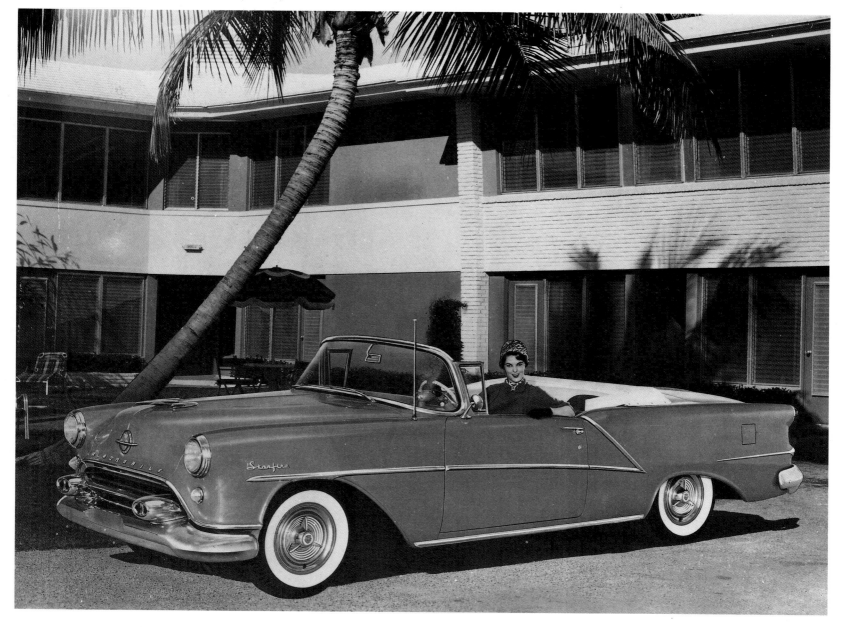

# 1955

Back in '55, cars were generally regarded as being for family use and categorized by body style – sedan, coupe, convertible or station wagon. If you wanted a sports car, you could look to Chevrolet's Corvette or to the Ford Thunderbird, or maybe even consider one of those itty-bitty European jobs. Combining the two as a sports-type passenger car wasn't really an option.

However, then came the Chrysler C-300. Styled by Virgil Exner, engineered by Robert M. Roger and powered by the legendary Chrysler FirePower Hemi V8, it was a revelation. Fast enough in standard form to set speed records over 127mph, and win NASCAR races when modified, the 2-door hardtop coupe could also seat six people in comfort. Part of the completely new-look Chrysler line in 1955, dubbed the "100 Million Dollar Look", it heralded a massive upturn in the marque's success as sales leapt an astounding 50% over the previous year.

At the very heart of the C-300 was the Hemi engine – so called because of its hemi-spherically-shaped combustion chambers – a configuration long regarded by engine experts as being the most efficient for producing maximum power. The problem with this design was that the valves were canted over at an angle to fit in to the hemi chamber and it required two rocker shafts and a complex arrangement of pushrods and varying lengths of rocker arms to make it work. This increased the cost of manufacturing the cylinder heads and the Hemi was replaced in 1959 by a more conventional wedge-head design.

Introduced in 1951, the Hemi displaced 331 cu.in. and pumped out an impressive 300 horsepower at 5,200rpm – providing the inspiration for the 300 Series name. As fitted to the '55 C-300, breathing through twin four-barrel carburetors with a full-race camshaft and an 8.5:1 compression ratio, the Hemi quickly earned Chrysler the "US Speed Champ" title. Naturally, the cars were great for racing and Tim Flock qualified a Chrysler on the pole at Daytona in 1955 and went on to win the race. He repeated the feat a year later and there's no doubt that the 300 Series would have been a major force in motor racing for some years if the manufacturers hadn't withdrawn it from competition in 1957.

The body design of the 1955 Chryslers evolved from a long line of concept cars built by Ghia in Italy under instruction from famed stylist Virgil Exner. The result was a complete break from Chrysler's previous "engineering-led" policy pursued by company president K. T. Keller, who had by now retired. His successor, Lester L. "Tex" Colbert, got rid of the old six cylinder engines and gave the styling department a freedom that was to produce some of the most striking automobiles of the Fifties under the "Forward Look" banner.

The C-300 was produced to compete with the limited-production Chevrolet Corvette and the Ford Thunderbird sports cars; not so

**Below:** Part of stylist Virgil Exner's new "One Hundred Million Dollar Look" for Chrysler, the C-300 was the high performance model of the 1955 range. It proved to be a race-winner and record setter, and was the first of the famed Letter Series of Chryslers, even though it didn't carry an "A" suffix. Only 1,725 of these 2-door hardtop coupes were built in '55.

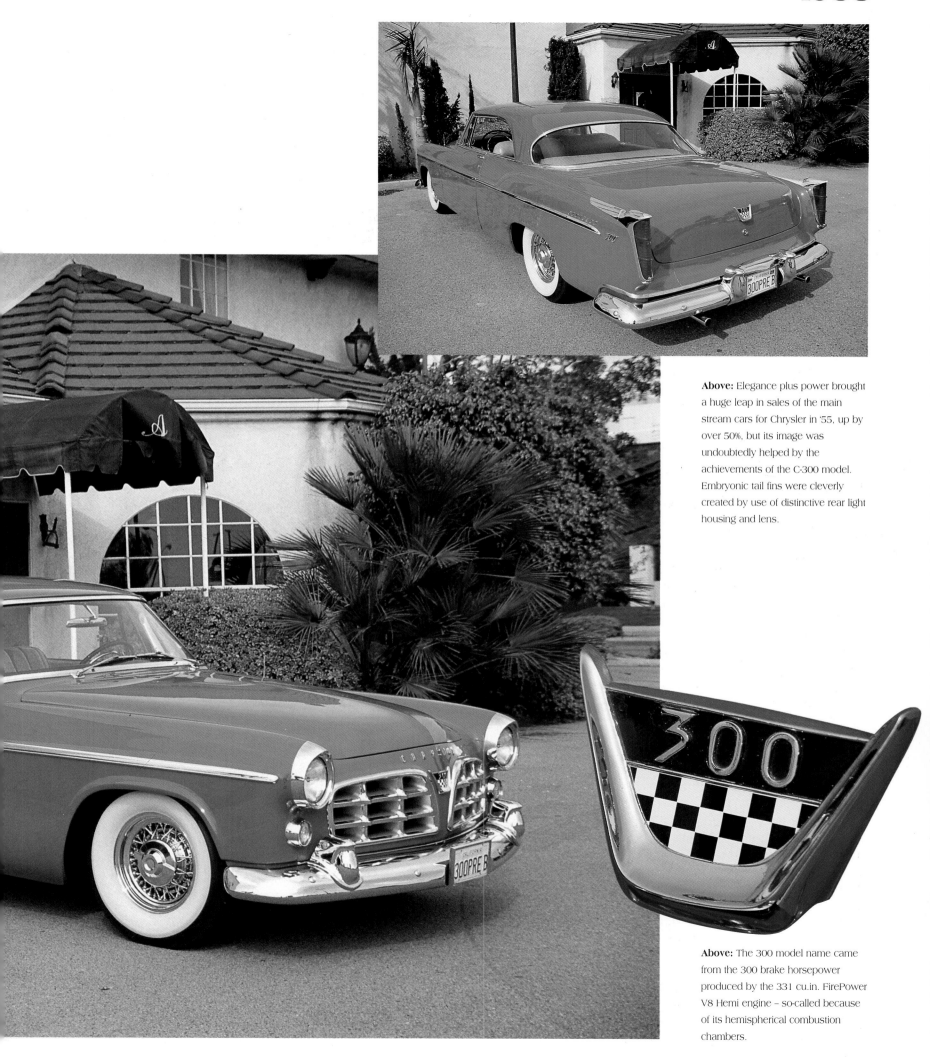

**Above:** Elegance plus power brought a huge leap in sales of the main stream cars for Chrysler in '55, up by over 50%, but its image was undoubtedly helped by the achievements of the C-300 model. Embryonic tail fins were cleverly created by use of distinctive rear light housing and lens.

**Above:** The 300 model name came from the 300 brake horsepower produced by the 331 cu.in. FirePower V8 Hemi engine – so-called because of its hemispherical combustion chambers.

# THE AMERICAN AUTOMOBILE

much for sales purposes, but more to improve Chrysler's performance image. Unable to create a special 2-seater model (although Ghia show cars of this configuration had been designed by Exner), Chrysler used what they had got. The starting point was a New Yorker 2-door hardtop body, with rear quarters from the Windsor and the grille from the Imperial to add prestige, although the New Yorker front bumper was retained.

The C-300 was a complete contrast to most other offerings of the time, when garish two-tone paint jobs and an excess of chrome was deemed the way to go. It had very little ornamentation, not even outside mirrors, and was only available in three colors – red, white and black. Even without its outstanding performance, this elegance would have set the C-300 apart from the rest. In 1955, this model represented status, luxury and performance in an exclusive package that was priced beyond the reach of the general public.

Rather surprisingly for such an expensive automobile (it was just about double the price of a Chevrolet or Ford), the C-300 didn't have air conditioning – even as a factory option. Another omission from the performance point of view was that the disc brakes used on the Imperial weren't included in the specification, although the drums all round with power assistance were thought to be more than adequate. Uprated springs and heavy duty shock absorbers helped put the cornering capability in a superior class when compared to the Chryler models, and a beefed-up PowerFlite automatic transmission with a higher stall speed torque converter produced rapid acceleration – 0-60mph in under 10 seconds.

Options such as power steering, power windows, radio, heater, tinted glass, and four-way power adjustable front bench seat could all be used to enhance the tan leather and vinyl trimmed interior. Regarded as highly desirable today, was the possibility of having

**Right:** Chevrolet had a banner year in '55, thanks to a totally redesigned car and a brilliant new V8 engine. This Bel Air convertible was chosen as the Pace Car for the Indy 500, and put Chevrolet at the top of the sales charts with over 1.7 million sales – a record for any auto manufacturer at the time.

**Below:** The Packard Caribbean convertible had attractive new body lines, but they covered an old floor pan. With powerful 275bhp, 352 cu.in. V8 and Twin Ultramatic transmission plus a unique torsion bar suspension, the '55 Packard was something special. But production difficulties were to prove a major setback and only 500 were built.

Kelsey-Hayes wire wheels fitted at a whopping $600 a set.

It goes without saying that this exclusivity would result in very few C-300 models being produced, only 1,725 in fact, and it is estimated that there are approximately two hundred survivors. But the influence of the C-300 went far beyond mere sales figures. It was to be the founding member of a legendary automotive dynasty – the so-called Letter Series Chryslers. Following the favorable reactions from the media to the '55 offering, the following year a face-lifted 1956 version was designated the 300B. This became an annual feature of the Chrysler model line-up, with a change of suffix letter, until the final 300L in 1965 – although the 300 Series itself lasted as a distinct model group until 1971.

As was the trend, all American automobiles were getting longer, lower and wide and size was an important aspect of the C-300 (and all the other 1955 Chrysler models). However, the extra inches on length and width had some unforeseen side effects. While a three inch longer car might not make much difference parked on the driveway, nose-to-tail on the assembly line it soon added up and manufacturers found themselves having to extend their production lines by up to 30 feet to accommodate the new designs. Police and city officials also voiced doubts over how these bigger cars were going to fit into existing parking places.

In purely economic terms, 1955 was a boom year in the auto industry with nearly 8 million cars being churned out by Detroit. Disneyland opened in California, the rock 'n' roll era arrived with Bill Haley and his Comets topping the charts with "Rock Around The Clock" and the minimum wage was raised to $1 per hour. On the flip side, Martin Luther King was leading a bus boycott in Alabama protesting against segregation, and James Dean died in an auto accident.

There were many great cars made that year, but the merits of the Chrysler FirePower Hemi engine cannot be denied and, equally, it is impossible to ignore the sheer class of Virgil Exner's design. If ever there was a prize for the perfect combination of performance and appearance, then the '55 Chrysler C-300 must surely rank as one of the top contenders of all time.

**Below:** The 1955 Cadillac sales brochure simply oozes class and style, as befits such a luxury automobile and status symbol. The tempting cover strap line of "Just imagine it's yours!" is matched by the equally evocative phrases inside, including: "Perhaps it's time to stop dreaming about a Cadillac and start enjoying one!" – back in 1955, plenty of people did just that, and who can blame them?

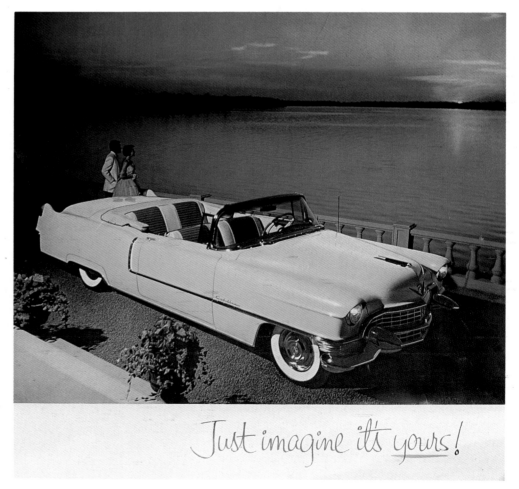

*Just imagine it's yours!*

# 1956

We like Ike. That was the message resounding through the nation as Dwight Eisenhower was returned for a second term as President in a landslide victory over Adlai Stevenson. Yet to be crowned "The King", Elvis Presley was hitting the charts and grabbing headlines thanks to songs like "Heartbreak Hotel", "Don't Be Cruel" and "Blue Suede Shoes". Another title holder, world heavyweight boxing champion Rocky Marciano, announced his retirement from the ring.

The phrase "cause and effect" is something that comes to mind when looking at Ford's Thunderbird. That it was made in response to arch rival Chevrolet bringing out the Corvette isn't in doubt, but that it would also have the consequence of ensuring the survival of the GM model was certainly something that was far from Ford's intention. It is also ironic that, having rescued the Corvette from oblivion and provided evidence of a viable market for a US-built sports car, the Thunderbird would quickly be taken out of that sector and turned into a luxury four-seater.

The reason for the decision was numbers, and it proved to be a correct direction for the second generation Thunderbird to take in 1958, but that's taking us away from the original concept. There is a story that the idea for the T-Bird first came about following the visit by Ford general manager Lewis D. Crusoe and styling consultant George Walker to the 1951 Paris Auto Show in France. Seeing all the European sports cars on display, Crusoe is supposed to have asked Walker why Ford didn't have anything similar, and the consultant (probably to keep his paymaster happy) replied that they were already working on just such a design. Immediately following this conversation, Walker was then said to have phoned his office back in the USA and told them to get something put together in time for his return.

It seems unlikely that these events ever actually happened. George Walker was a deft manipulator of the facts and often claimed credit for car design work that he personally was only involved with on an administration level. It has also to be remembered that there were an awful lot of young designers in the industry and their enthusiasm for the sports car would have generated many illustrations and drawings on the "what if we built one of those?" basis. Therefore, it can be assumed

that Ford (in common with most other manufacturers) had, over the years, been carrying out various design studies on sports cars but not progressed them any further because of the perceived limited sales potential.

When Chevrolet brought out the Corvette in 1953, Ford had to respond quickly, and unveiled a full-size wood and clay mock-up of the Thunderbird at the Detroit Auto Show in February 1954. At a press conference held in the Ford Styling Rotunda at Dearborn, Ford's sales manager L. W. Smead announced: "The Thunderbird is a new kind of sports car. We are convinced it will set a new trend in the automobile industry. It provides all of the comforts, conveniences and all-weather protection available in any of today's modern

**Right:** A removable fiber glass top was a special feature of all the first generation Thunderbirds, but although the small round portholes (new on '56 models) are often regarded as an integral part of the car's design, these were actually a no cost option. Hardtops could be ordered without them – although seemingly few ever were. Performance was improved with 225hp, 312 cu.in. V8 giving a zero to 60mph time of 9 seconds, and top speed of around 120mph, but Ford classified the Thunderbird as a "personal car" and handling wasn't in the true sports car league.

# 1956

**Below:** Several changes were made to 1956 Thunderbirds following feedback from owners of '55 models. The externally-mounted spare wheel is the most obvious feature – intended to give more luggage space in the trunk – but weight distribution was affected. Other alterations to improve driver comfort included wind wings on the windshield to prevent buffeting when enjoying topless motoring, and vent doors in the front fenders to feed fresh air into the passenger compartment. The rear bumper also had exhausts exiting through slots in the corners.

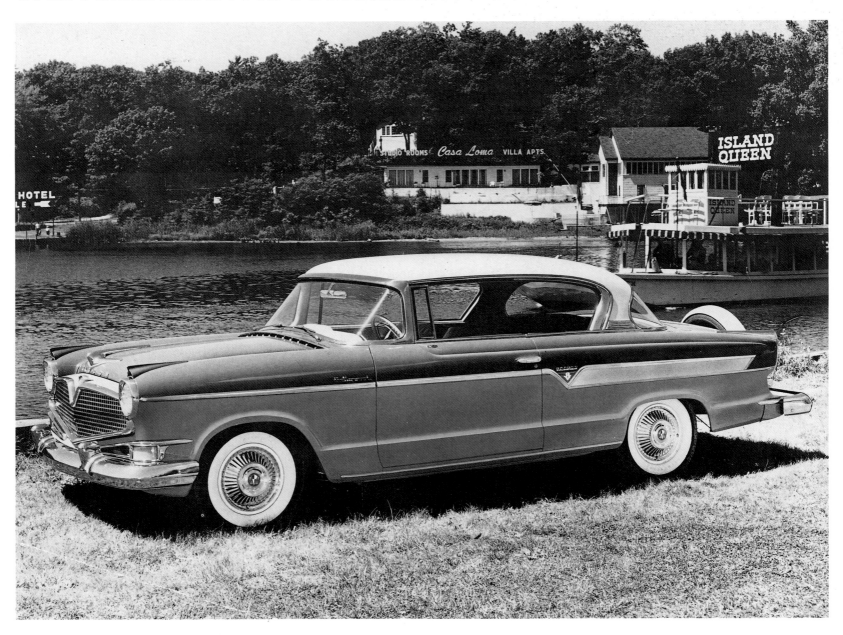

**Above:** Following the merger with Nash in 1954 to form American Motors Corporation, Hudson models became little more than Nash bodies with different grilles, interiors and rear ends. This 1956 Hudson Hornet Custom Hollywood hardtop coupe illustrates just how disastrous the marriage turned out to be as, in an attempt to provide a separate identity, so called "V-line" styling was used with bizarre results. Not surprisingly, sales dropped and only 10,671 Hudson models (excluding rebadged Ramblers) were produced in '56 and the Hudson name was dropped the following year.

automobiles. It represents a successful combination of graceful, low-silhouette styling, spirited performance and outstanding roadability with dependable all-steel body construction."

The references to the Corvette's features are obvious enough. In addition, the T-Bird came with a V8 engine and the choice of manual or automatic transmission, an attractive glass fiber removable hardtop, wind-up windows (power optional) and, using standard Ford components, it could be serviced at a regular dealership.

Production of the Thunderbird wasn't due to begin until September 1954, by which time Ford were placing much more emphasis on the level of driver and passenger comfort than speed or handling when discussing the model, possibly giving a slight hint of where the company thought its future might lay. W. R. Burnett, chief of passenger car engineering said: "Although the Thunderbird has the performance and attributes of most sports cars, management also felt that it should have a few more comforts to make it more appealing

to a wider segment of the public." Burnett also used the term "personal car" to describe the T-Bird, this being Ford's way of elevating it above the other run-of-the-mill sports cars.

Compared to the Corvette, Thunderbird sales were incredible – almost 16,000 a year in 1955 and '56, compared to a paltry 700 1955 Corvettes and only 3,400 of the revamped '56. It was clear that Ford had a better grasp of what the American buyer of the Fifties wanted from a sports car.

In this respect, a great deal of the credit for the Thunderbird's acceptance must go to Ford's chief of styling Frank Q. Hershey and his design studio team, headed by Rhys Miller. Also involved in the creation of the T-Bird were Damon Woods, David Ash and Bill Boyer. Between them, they produced a car that echoed the best features of European sports car design yet could be easily identified as American in origin with immediate connection to the rest of the Ford model line-up. Key elements were the proportions of a long hood and short rear deck, combined

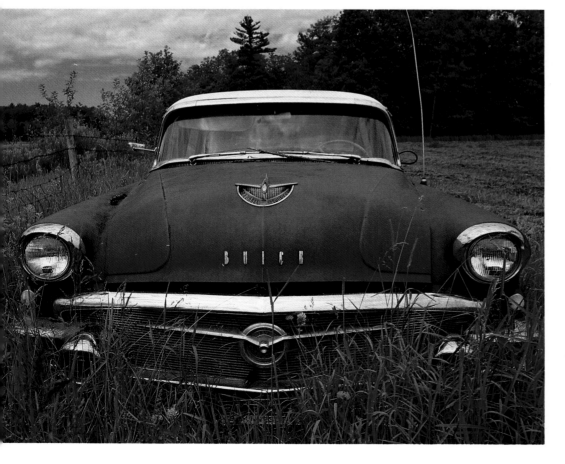

**Above:** From the start, the Lincoln Continental Mark II was hailed as a truly classic automobile. It was an attempt by Ford to create an image car that would outshine the best Cadillacs. Unfortunately, Ford lost money on every Mark II it produced.

**Below:** Buicks had a mild face-lift for '56, and came with more powerful engines. About 635,000 rolled off the assembly lines in 1956; how many of them ended up like this we wonder?

with the low profile found in all classic Fifties front-engined sports cars, plus embellishments that could only have come from Detroit.

But Hershey and his designers weren't infallible and for the '56 Thunderbird, there were a few minor alterations that had to be carried out for purely practical reasons. The most easily-spotted of the changes was the Continental Kit mounting of the spare wheel to make more trunk space available for luggage, but this wasn't universally approved of – some critics said it detracted from the car's appearance and added wind resistance. On

the other hand, this set-up was also said to help give a better balanced weight distribution. Small vent door flaps were introduced behind the front wheel arches to feed the interior with cool air after complaints from overheating drivers and passengers! In a similar vein, "wind wings" were added to the sides of the windshield to help reduce buffeting when the top was down.

If you chose to drive with the hardtop in position, in '56 this would more than likely come with the famous portholes on either side. These little round windows were apparently copied from car designs of the 1930s, and some writers have said that Bill Boyer was the man behind this idea. Non-porthole hardtops were still available but the porthole version offered as a no cost option proved to be far more popular and has become indelibly associated with the '56 T-Bird.

Long forgotten is the fact that Ford were also using safety as a selling point in those days. Okay, maybe a Life Guard package consisting of a collapsible steering column and anti-burst door locks isn't in the same league as dual air bags, but we are talking 1956 here! The offer of seat belts was another item that didn't prove too enticing to potential buyers, who were more likely to ask, "Why are you fitting seat belts – isn't the car safe?" How times have changed!

American Indian folklore was said to describe the Thunderbird as a good luck omen, being a mythical bird supposed to cause thunder, lightning and rain. A 1954 Ford press release went on to state that, among many things, the Thunderbird symbolized 'power, swiftness and prosperity'. If that is true, then Ford could hardly have picked a more appropriate name.

# 1957

Headlines were dominated by racial integration conflicts, the radio was reverberating to the sound of rock 'n' roll and Russia launched Sputnik 1 to take a commanding lead in the space race. Hollywood mourned the deaths of silver screen idol Humphrey Bogart and comedian Oliver Hardy. But in the realm of automotive history, 1957 will forever be the year of the Chevrolet Bel Air.

In terms of styling, the 1957 Chevrolet is almost a unique example, for it has enjoyed undiminished affection since its introduction. It has been the subject of numerous songs, featured in films whenever a Fifties classic is required and was once dubbed "the most popular used car in history". Today, four decades on, there are enough suppliers of restoration and reproduction parts that it is practically possible to build a complete new car. Surely no other car from the 1950s can boast such an enthusiastic following.

A look at the outline specification doesn't explain the reasons behind this phenomenon – a face-lift of a three year old bodyshell and a smaller V8 engine than both the Ford and Plymouth rivals – but that simplistic descrip-

**Below:** The swept-back tail fins and ribbed silver anodised aluminum fender trim accentuate the sweeping lines of the '57 Chevy Bel Air. The gold V on the trunk lid indicates that the car has a V8 engine, the potent Turbo-Fire 283 cu.in. unit. As with the front, the rear bumper is a more integrated part of the body design and incorporates the tail lights in bold clusters. The fender skirts were optional extras.

tion doesn't do the '57 Chevy justice. It is, quite simply, a styling and performance classic. Not that this was apparent to the designers and engineers working on the car, far from it. In fact, studio head Clare MacKichan has been quoted as saying that there didn't seem to be much continuity of thought from one year to the next, and even some of the ideas that weren't used on the 1956 models somehow got resurrected and put on the '57!

The massive new front bumper had even earlier origins, with sketches dating back to 1949 and in 1953, designer Carl Renner produced an illustration that looked almost identical to the final '57 bumper. Apart from the bumper and front end, perhaps the most striking aspect of the 1957 Chevrolet is just how much longer and lower it seems in comparison to the previous two years, despite sharing the same basic bodyshell. This was due

to Earl's quest to reduce height and increase length in the belief that it produced a better looking automobile. To keep the cowl profile low, a revolutionary ventilation system was devised which drew fresh air from inlets in the front fenders above the headlights, rather than at the base of the windshield.

The hood had dual lance-shaped "windsplitz" instead of the typical central jet aircraft-style ornament, used by other cars, for a low, smooth look. Elsewhere, the body revamp for '57 was so clever that, not only did it look different to the 1956 models, it was considered a great improvement. Undoubtedly one of the Fifties' most memorable and recognizable styling details is the ribbed aluminum panel used as part of the rear fender decorative trim on the Bel Air – it is an image, almost a trademark or a logo that couldn't be mistaken for anything else.

**Above:** Among the most striking features on the 1957 Bel Air was the massive front bumper, which became an integral part of the body shape rather than an add-on. The convertible shows the low profile to great effect; the hood height was reduced by introducing fresh air vents above the headlights and eliminating the need for intake at the base of the windshield. In place of the traditional central hood emblem, twin spears also helped achieve the lower look.

The other big news for the '57 Chevy was the engine and fuel injection. With a .125 inch diameter bigger bore, the small block V8 now displaced 283 cu.in. and was becoming a high performance legend. In standard two-barrel carburetor form, the compact power-plant was rated at a healthy 185 horsepower and, when equipped with fuel injection, the Chevy could produce one horsepower per cubic inch – an accomplishment at the time, although Chrysler had done the same with the FirePower Hemi engine somewhat earlier. It meant a very rapid car in a straight line – even a base V8 model with a Powerglide two-speed automatic could top 100mph and accelerate to 60mph in 11 seconds.

Priced at over $500 (very expensive in '57 when a basic Chevrolet was little more than $2,000) the optional Ramjet mechanical fuel injection unit initially looked like a technical innovation – it claimed to improve fuel econo-my as well as horsepower. Designed by GM and made by Rochester Carburetor Inc, after they had tested and modified it, in everyday use the Ramjet started to show problems. In particular, the fuel nozzles would get clogged and heat absorption from the engine caused rough idling. So the fuel injection option was dropped from the Chevrolet family car cata-log after 1958, although an improved version remained as a Corvette item until 1965.

Another unsuccessful Chevy development in '57 was the Turboglide automatic transmis-sion. Modeled on the Buick Dynaflow, it was more expensive to make than the existing Powerglide unit and, while smoother-shifting when performing properly, it proved less reli-able and hard to repair when faults occurred. The Turboglide lasted better than the Ramjet, surviving until the end of the '61 model year, but both ventures were only relatively minor blemishes on the

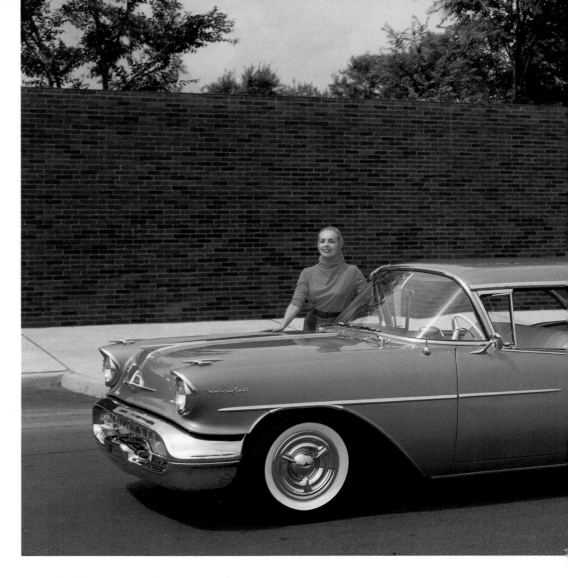

record of an automotive masterpiece.

It seems strange then to learn that, in 1957, Chevrolet failed to dominate the new car mar-ket in the same way as before. In fact, taking model year sales into account, Ford took first place. Competition was fiercer than ever and despite price reductions, '57 was not the great year the auto industry had anticipated. Indeed, come the fourth quarter of the year, the beginnings of the economic slump that was to devastate US car sales in 1958 started to have an effect and demand fell sharply.

Another blow to Chevrolet came when the Automobile Manufacturers Association passed a resolution in June forbidding their members

**Above:** Similarities between the Oldsmobile Holiday sedan and the Chevy are obvious, but the Olds looks more refined. One curious feature is the three-piece backlight which seems in contrast to the huge double curvature windshield and hardtop style.

**Below:** A spectacular debutante in '57 was the Ford Fairlane 500 Skyliner retractable hardtop. At the touch of a button, the steel roof would fold into the trunk turning coupe into convertible. Its complexity and high cost limited production to just three years.

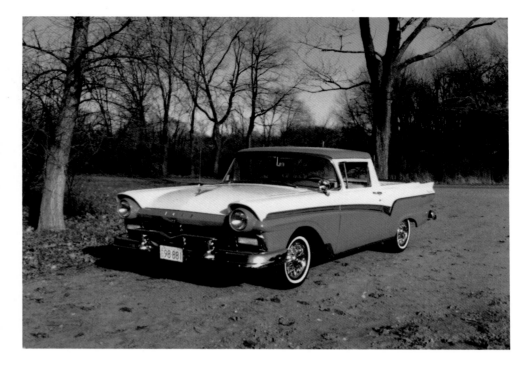

"Appreciably faster on all counts" and, in a test carried out by the same magazine later in the year, the Chevy came out ahead of both Ford and Plymouth. Fast cars gave rise to doubts about people's ability to cope, however. James Whipple of Car Life suggested that drivers would need "quicker reactions and better judgement than ever before", but concluded: "Beneath the excitement created by the sensational (for light, low-priced cars) horsepower, the '57 Chevy is an excellent automobile with a tested, stable design and a very satisfactory level of quality and workmanship".

With all this talk of power, it is easy to forget that Chevrolet then offered three models – starting with the One-Fifty, Two-Ten, and top of the range Bel Air – and the cheaper models came with much less horsepower. And while today's collector car money would go on the more expensive Bel Air coupes and convertibles, in 1957 it was the 4-door sedans that sold better than anything else.

**Above:** Another first for Ford in '57 was the Ranchero, a sedan-pickup which basically came from a standard Ranch Wagon station wagon with the rear half converted into an open bed. This set a trend for further car-based trucks in the American market that were to prove popular for many years to come.

to participate in motor racing. However, while the men in the Chevy front office were following the AMA ruling and stating "they were no longer in racing", there was plenty of help out of the back door for those drivers who could put a Chevrolet into the winner's circle.

Using a racing driver to test a model was a device used by magazines in the Fifties, and Speed Age got stock car ace Johnnie Tolan to test a '57 Bel Air 4-door sedan on the track and in the Los Angeles traffic. He reported: "I was really impressed with the new Chevy – liked its looks as well as its performance..." Journalist Walt Woron writing for Motor Trend also liked the Chevy's performance, calling it

**Right:** Plymouths were totally redone for '57, and many people regard them to be among the best designs ever produced by Virgil Exner. The low, clean lines, huge expanses of glass and the tallest tail fins on offer put them ahead of the competition in many respects. The Fury 2-door hardtop coupe had unique gold anodised aluminum Sport Tone body trim panels, upswept front bumper ends, a 290 horsepower V8 and other extra embellishments to denote its top-of-the-range status.

# 1958

The banner headline in the Detroit Free Press read "Reds claim their missile can reach the whole world" as America was smarting after the Sputniks demonstrated the Soviet lead in the space race, but the main picture on the newspaper's front page was of an Edsel. However, the economy was in recession and car sales in '58 dropped by about 20% compared with the three previous boom years.

In automotive terms, the Edsel name has become associated with spectacular failure – almost since it was launched in September 1957. Yet the surprise is, the Edsel disaster happened not by chance, but following years of solid market research and meticulous planning by the Ford Motor Company.

At the start of the 1950s, it seemed to Ford that it didn't offer enough models to cover the entire market and was losing out in certain sectors, particularly the middle price bracket. Back then, if an owner was happy with a car they would buy a replacement from the same manufacturer. And if they had become more prosperous (or just wanted to give the neighbors the impression that they had – keeping up with the Joneses was quite an obsession that the dealers happily exploited), they traded up to a more expensive, and therefore more prestigious, make from the same corporation.

According to a company executive: "Ford

was actually growing future prospects for the competition". In order to fill the hole, a Special Products Division was set up to develop a new mid-range to augment the offerings of Mercury. The code name given to this project was the "E-Car". This led to press speculation that the new car would be called the Edsel. Ford strenuously denied this, saying the E was for "Experimental" and not Edsel! But, no matter how large the company, making a 100% new car is unlikely to make economic sense so the E-Car was planned as a hybrid of existing Ford and Mercury major components with its own front and rear end sheet metal, its own engine, interior and dash panels.

The one thing the E-Car wouldn't share would be the Ford or Lincoln-Mercury dealerships, it would have its very own sales network. A vast recruiting campaign was organized and dealers were signed up from competitors across the country.

The pressure was now on to give the car a name. Over six thousand suggestions were considered from all sorts of sources – including poet Marianne Moore who came up with humdingers like "Mongoose Civique" and "Utopian Turtletop"! Four names that got a more favorable reaction were: Ranger, Pacer, Corsair and Citation. Although these were eventually chosen as the model names, Ford

chairman Ernest Breech didn't like them or any of the alternatives and, early in 1956, he made the decision to call the car the Edsel – named after Henry Ford's son who had died in 1942. Initially the Ford family were against the suggestion, but Breech persuaded them.

This choice of name was the first mistake. Outside Detroit's inner circle, the word Edsel had no significance. While certainly no worse than Buick, that General Motors marque had, by then, been in existence for over fifty years and was well established in people's minds.

Then came the second mistake. The Edsel had probably the biggest new car build-up in history. The publicity was so widespread that the public were expecting a miracle machine to appear, not just another new car.

The third problem with the Edsel was timing, and this would prove to be crucial. The plan was to launch the 1958 Edsels in June 1957, thereby pre-empting the competition – traditionally cars were launched between September and November. But Edsel production didn't start until July and the launch was put back until September to ensure that dealers would have cars on display for the big day.

This three-month delay was a huge setback. After strong early 1957 model sales, the market suddenly slowed up in midsummer and dealers had to offer discounts to clear stocks and make way for the new '58 models. The US economy went into recession and the demand for middle- to upper-priced cars evaporated in favor of smaller, cheaper

**Above:** Probably the most hyped car in history, the Edsel was a gigantic disaster for Ford. The unusual "horse collar" grille was blamed for the lack of sales, but the car was introduced just when market for larger, more expensive cars went into decline.

**Left:** The convertible Edsel looks sleek in side view, and certainly no worse than any contemporary models. The Pacer version was in the next range up from the basic Ranger specification, having more chrome trim, extra equipment and slightly plusher upholstery.

**Right:** An extensive advertising campaign was mounted and in '59, one slogan used was: "The car that makes history by making sense" – the Edsel certainly made history, but for all the wrong reasons.

This is the **EDSEL**

"The emphasis is on engineering, but the accent is on elegance"

The Edsel is as stylish in its performance as it is in its looks

**1958 EDSEL**
New member of the Ford family of fine cars

EDSEL DIVISION · FORD MOTOR COMPANY

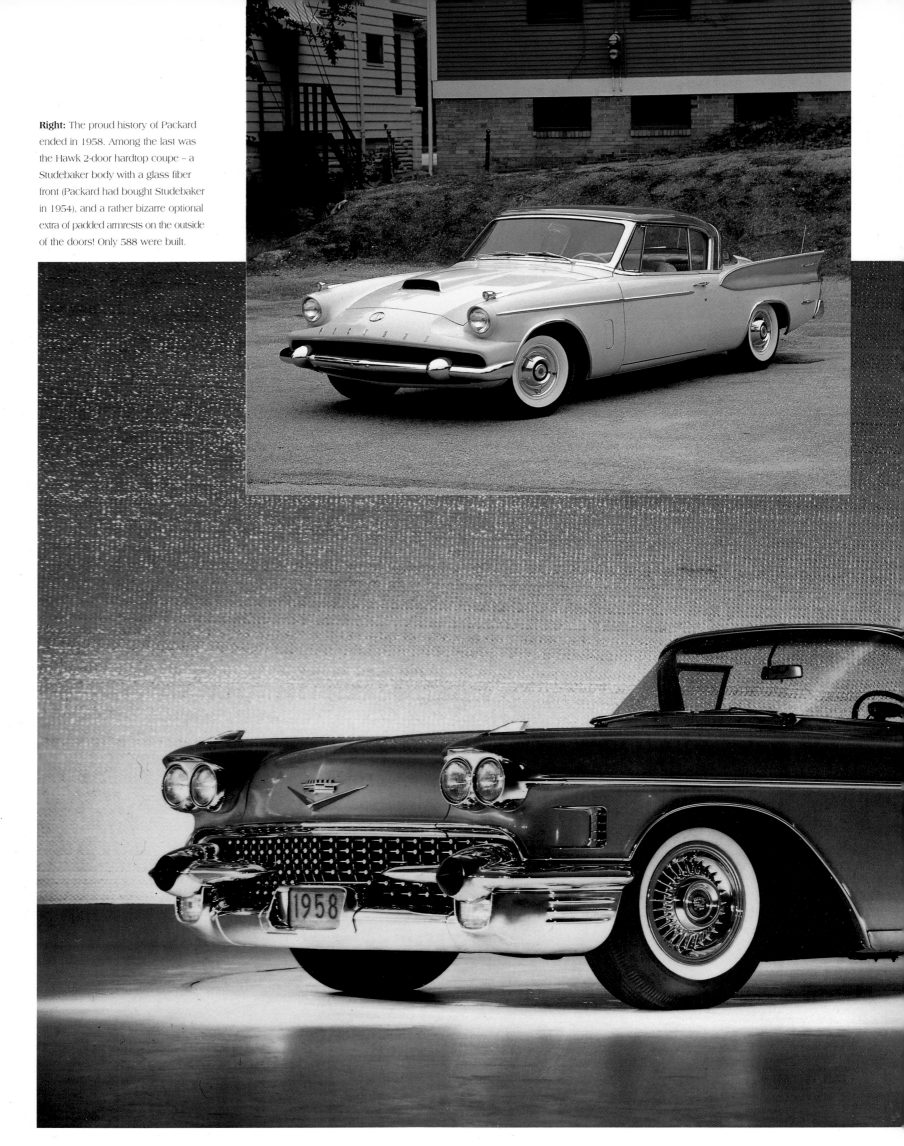

**Right:** The proud history of Packard ended in 1958. Among the last was the Hawk 2-door hardtop coupe – a Studebaker body with a glass fiber front (Packard had bought Studebaker in 1954), and a rather bizarre optional extra of padded armrests on the outside of the doors! Only 588 were built.

models. So, at the very time the Edsel burst on the scene, the market went into a severe decline. In other words, the goal posts had been moved! Despite these three problems, the Edsel could still have succeeded. And Ford's need for the car was still valid. But the final blow was the controversial styling.

The most famous feature is the "horse collar" grille. Although many European marques had a vertical grille for many years – Jaguar, Alfa Romeo, Mercedes – somehow the Edsel didn't have the same effect.

When an automobile is successful, people clamor to associate themselves with it. In the case of the Edsel, practically everyone who worked at the Ford Design Center denies any

# 1959

The history of the twentieth century is, more often than not, divided up into decades and each ten year period given its own separate identity. It is curious that this convenient method of grouping so often, and in so many ways, reflects the changes that take place in society. In purely automotive terms, nothing can surely equal the 1959 Cadillac tail fin as a symbol of the end of an era.

The Fifties was the age of the tail fin and, after having reached such heights, there was nowhere to go but down. 1959 was also the year that Harley Earl retired from his position as head of styling at General Motors and the towering Cadillac fins are looked upon as his final extravagance before bowing out. It has to be said that Earl would have found it hard to adapt to a changing environment of simplicity and economy rather than outrageous, ever bigger automobiles. It was a problem that other designers, working at rival auto makers, would also struggle to come to terms with.

At the time, there were few, if any, signs of misgivings. Designer Bill Mitchell (who took over from Earl) described the tail fins thus: "From a design standpoint the fins gave definition to the rear of the car for the first time. They made the back end as interesting as the front, and established a long-standing Cadillac styling hallmark." Whether the addition of a rear "grille" which closely resembled that of the front was such a good idea is open to debate, but the feature didn't last very long.

Lower than ever before, though no longer or wider, the '59 Cadillac not only attracted comments about its styling it also drew some favorable reports about how it drove. Jim Whipple, writing in Car Life, said: "The car rode as level as any I've ever driven..." But it wasn't totally perfect, as shown by a report in Motor Life which stated: "Flaws are noted only at high speeds, when some swaying motion sets in, and in fast corners when the tires protest loudly as the heavyweight goes through a bend". Of course, the Cadillac was built for luxury motoring and comfort, and not intended for slalom racing, so it can be safely assumed that few were ever pushed to the same limits by their owners.

Mind you, thanks to a new 325 horsepower (345hp in Eldorado models), 390 cu.in. V8 engine under that hood, the Cadillac was no slouch when it was time to get going, 0-60mph in under 11 seconds or thereabouts. And if

you were in a real hurry, a top speed of close on 120mph was possible. Pretty impressive for a car weighing over 5,000 pounds and close to 19 feet in length. Sales moved ahead too, topping 142,000 and keeping Cadillac in the top ten (just) of US auto manufacturers.

The array of Cadillac models included convertibles, two-door hardtop coupes, and two different four-door hardtop sedans plus the Fleetwood limousines. Prices started at about $5000 and went up to $7400 for an Eldorado,

**Below:** The convertible '59 Cadillac looked like a de luxe rocket ship. The grille featured double-decker construction with mirror-image quad head lights incorporated into a massive bumper. The series 62 was the lowest priced, but standard equipment included power steering, power brakes, automatic transmission, windshield washers and two-speed wipers. 11,130 were produced.

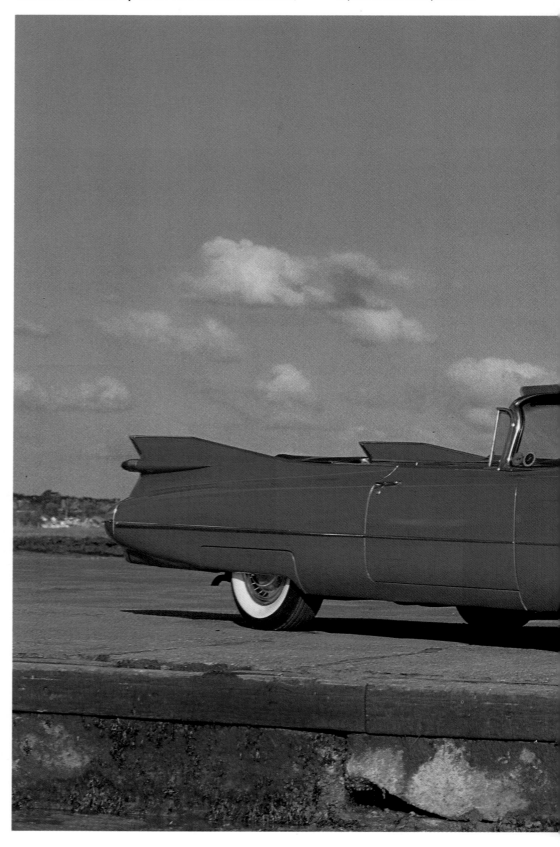

**Right:** The rear of the '59 Cadillac is unique thanks to soaring razor-edged fins with four bullet-shaped tail lights, and there has surely never been a more distinctive styling feature on any automobile in history. But the Harley Earl trademark had reached its limit and would shortly disappear with the coming of a new decade and a growing demand for less ostentatious and more economical cars.

with the Fleetwoods more than $9,500. But easily the most expensive was the Eldorado Brougham 4-door, the only Cadillac model of '59 that didn't have the huge tail fins and bullet-shaped lights, which was built by coach builders Pininfarina in Italy, and cost a massive $13,000 – small wonder that only 99 made the transatlantic crossing this year. But underneath all the razzle-dazzle there were engineering improvements too, with better suspension, and revised power steering.

In May 1959, Motor Life compared the Cadillac to an Imperial and summed up with the following: "Cadillac's strongest claim to superiority is its unmatched feeling of luxury and quality. When riding in this car, the almost soundless operation coupled with rich materials and fine assembly produce the desired effect: you know that this is an expensive and luxurious automobile. One is never in doubt".

A smooth ride, luxury fitments, excellent performance and build quality – from almost any aspect, the 1959 Cadillac was a state-of-the-art prestige car of its day, but you cannot ignore the flamboyant body styling. Whatever your personal tastes, this is one car that it is impossible to be neutral about, you either love it or loathe it.

To its detractors, the '59 Caddy has all the glamor of a Las Vegas hooker, while others regard it as the ultimate expression of Fifties space age design. Its styling is unique and the obvious associations with rockets, missiles and aircraft are clearly visible – from the dual jet intake shapes of the parking lights in the massive front bumper to the bullet-like tail

# THE AMERICAN AUTOMOBILE

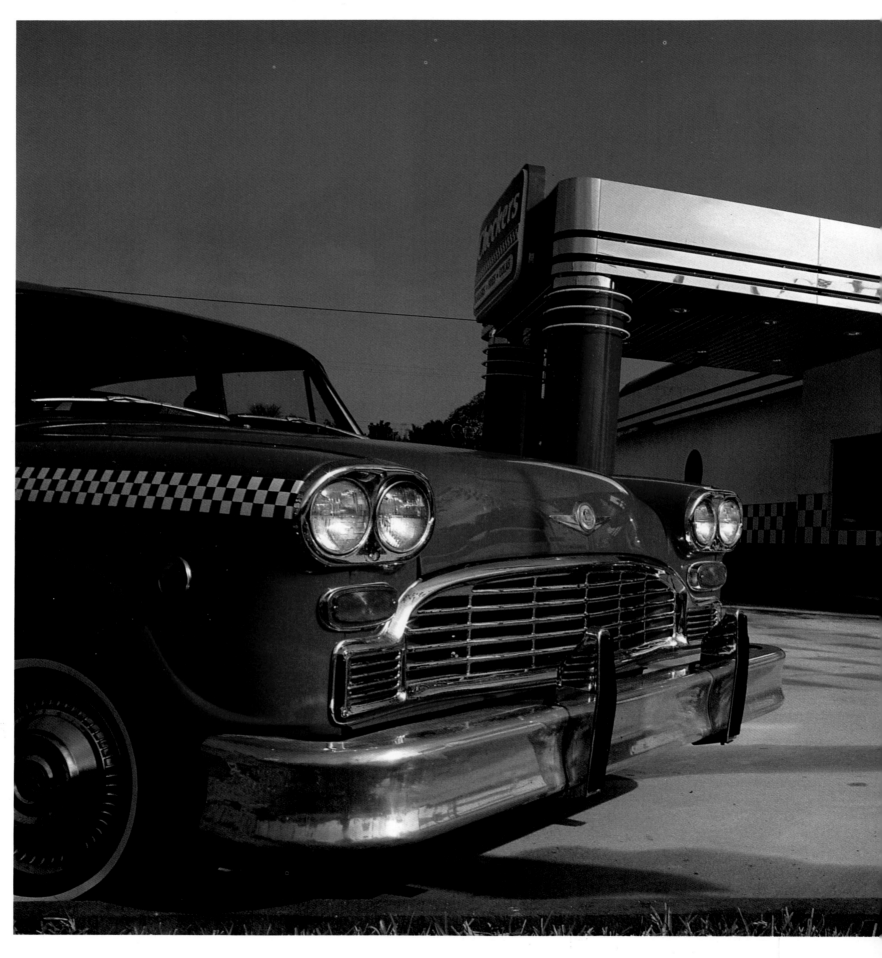

**Above:** The Fifties yellow Checker taxi is part of New York's image. There are now few working and many, like this one, have been relegated to static promotional tasks.

**Right:** The smoothly-styled '59 Buick Electra 225 convertible had fifty chrome rectangles in its grille, but this was about the only styling connection with preceding years' models.

product liability litigation was nothing like the rapacious industry of the Nineties so such small inconveniences as these would be tolerated for the sake of owning the newest shape of automobile.

The annual model change that ultimately spawned the '59 Cadillac was regarded as part of the process that would provide what the Detroit public relations machine called "better transportation tomorrows". A false promise if ever there was one because, as every child knows, tomorrow never arrives. We can look at these things with the condescension of hindsight, but caught up in the euphoria of the age it was hard to be completely objective. Without doubt, Car Life's Jim Whipple echoed popular opinion when he enthusiastically described the '59 Cadillac as "...one of the sleekest jobs that ever came down the pike".

But to many fans, 1959 marked the beginning of the end of rock 'n' roll, and the most significant event of the year happened on February 3 when a Beechcraft Bonanza light aeroplane crashed near Mason City, Iowa killing Buddy Holly, Ritchie Valens and J. P. "The Big Bopper" Richardson. However, if three stars had been extinguished from the pop music firmament, at least there were two new stars on Old Glory as Alaska and Hawaii became the 49th and 50th States. And NASA was also aiming toward the stars – besides launching satellites and two monkeys into orbit, it also named the seven astronauts who would take part in the space race.

Automobiles might be about to get their wings clipped and the raw energy of Fifties rock 'n' rollers seemed to be giving way to slushy music exploited by large record companies in pursuit of a quick buck, but there was still plenty to look forward to!

# 1960

The Fifties had been a great time for the American auto industry – a period of design excess, during which automobiles grew ever larger fins and literally dripped with chrome. But as the new decade of the Sixties dawned, things were changing, the emphasis would switch from overstated looks to more efficient performance, whether it be from smaller cars or bigger engines.

Changes in the auto industry were not the only news for 1960. In July, John F. Kennedy received the Democratic nomination for the Presidency, running against Republican Richard Nixon. Kennedy made it to The White House after a close race, but was tragically not to serve his full term. Meanwhile, relations with the Soviet Union received a major setback when a U2 spy plane was shot down over Soviet territory and its pilot, Gary Powers, captured. On a lighter note, Elvis Presley was discharged from his much-publicized spell in the US Army, while a young

boxer by the name of Cassius Clay won a gold medal in the Rome Olympics. He would become one of the most famous boxers of all time, who would ultimately be known to millions around the world as Muhammed Ali.

Lovers of speed had plenty to talk about, too. At the Daytona 500, Fireball Roberts, driving a '60 Pontiac, had set the pace during qualifying at 151.556mph, while the race proper was won by Junior Johnson in a 1959 Chevy. Pontiac products also featured prominently at the Bonneville Salt Flats in September, when hot rodder Mickey Thompson drove his Challenger streamliner to a speed of 406.60mph. The sleek projectile was powered by no less than four Pontiac V8s, but a broken driveshaft prevented him from making a return run that would have put him in the record books.

Back in Detroit, however, high-performance automobiles were not the latest innovation from the major manufacturers – they would come later in the decade. For 1960, the auto industry was looking in a completely different direction. Since the 1930s, American automobiles had grown steadily larger, particularly in the post-war years. But during that time, small imported cars had begun to make inroads on the market, particularly sporty

**Below:** The air-cooled, rear-engine layout of Chevrolet's Corvair was unfamiliar to potential buyers. Only when it was marketed as a sporty compact did it begin to succeed.

models. They were fun to drive and cheap to run. Concerned by the impact these foreign cars were making, the major auto makers began to take a serious look at building more compact cars themselves. By the late Fifties, two smaller manufacturers were already in this sector of the market – Studebaker with the Lark, and Rambler with the American. In 1960, they would be joined by compacts from the big three – Ford, GM and Chrysler – who launched the Falcon, the Chevrolet Corvair and the Valiant respectively.

Of the three, the Falcon and the Corvair were the main contenders and were pitted against each other from the outset. They were two very different cars, the Ford simply being a scaled-down conventional car, while the Chevy was very definitely a radical departure in terms of both design and powerplant. Both had their beginnings in the mid Fifties and, more by accident than design, they both arrived on the market at the same time.

One aspect that was common to the Falcon and Corvair was unibody construction, a relatively uncommon arrangement for American automobiles at the time which, in the main, relied on separate chassis to sup-

port the various mechanical components and body panels. In a unibody design, the bodyshell itself is strengthened to accept the loads of the engine and suspension, making for a lighter structure overall. However, that is where the similarities ended.

As mentioned, the Falcon was of a conventional design. It was powered by a liquid-cooled, straight-six ohv engine, with a cast-iron block and head, that displaced 144.3 cu.in. and developed 90 horsepower at 4200rpm. This drove through either a three-speed manual transmission or two-speed automatic to a live rear axle suspended on leaf springs. The Corvair was also powered by a six-cylinder engine, but it was a horizontally-opposed, aluminum, air-cooled unit mounted at the rear of the car and driving the rear wheels through a three-speed manual, or two-speed automatic, transaxle with coil-sprung, swing-axle suspension. The engine produced 80 horsepower at 4400rpm. Both cars had similar front suspension arrangements, making use of unequal-length wishbones and coil springing.

The cars were of similar sizes, although the Falcon was slightly larger and taller, and

**Above:** Ford's European experience of building small cars led to the Falcon compact, with its unibody construction. Later sporty versions provided the basis for the Mustang.

# THE AMERICAN AUTOMOBILE

both were intended as full six-seaters, being equipped with bench seats front and rear. However, the Falcon's transmission tunnel made it uncomfortable for anyone riding in the middle of the front seat, while the Corvair, with its virtually flat floorpan, was more comfortable, even though the manual transmission models had a floor-mounted shifter. This was curved to allow the center passenger leg room. Shifting was not a problem in the Falcon, since both manual and automatic transmissions had column shifters.

When first launched, the Corvair was offered in a 4-door body style only, while the Falcon came in a choice of 2- or 4-door models. The latter was conventional in appear-

ance, while the Corvair, with its lack of radiator grille and somewhat tub-like styling, was less so. Both lacked the fins and chrome that had characterized cars of the Fifties. They were intended as economy cars and they looked the part.

In terms of performance, the makers quoted very similar top speeds – 87mph for the Falcon; 88mph for the Corvair. But the Falcon could out-accelerate the Corvair; Road & Track magazine found that the former could reach 60mph in 17.7 seconds, while the Corvair was nearly a full two seconds behind at 19.5 seconds.

When the Corvair was launched, it was slow to gain acceptance; the unconventional rear-engine layout may have been okay in a foreign car, but it was downright un-American; the Falcon was a much more familiar concept, and it showed in the sales figures. Corvair sales were not helped by rumors that it tended to throw fan belts and that its handling was quirky. Indeed, if the tire pressures were not kept exactly as specified by the manufacturer and the car was pushed hard through a corner, it could switch from slight understeer to strong oversteer, kicking the rear end out with potentially disastrous consequences. Later in its life, a number of law suits were brought against GM for just this reason, although eventually the car was exonerated and would carry on in production

until the end of the decade.

Later in 1960, in an attempt to boost flagging sales, Chevrolet introduced a 2-door variant, the Monza. This was a much sportier-looking car, a look that was enhanced by fitting front bucket seats, full carpeting and better trim. Where the Corvair had failed as an economy car, it succeeded as a sporty model and sales took off at last. Eventually, it was to receive ever more powerful engines and became an excellent all-round performer. Not to be outdone, Ford uprated later models of the Falcon too, eventually fitting a new 260 cu.in. small-block V8 that was to have a significant effect on the company's efforts in the sporty compact field.

**Above:** Oldsmobile's Super 88 Celebrity sedan looks similar to Chevy's Impala but, mechanically, it differed with a choice of two V8s and a three-speed manual transmission.

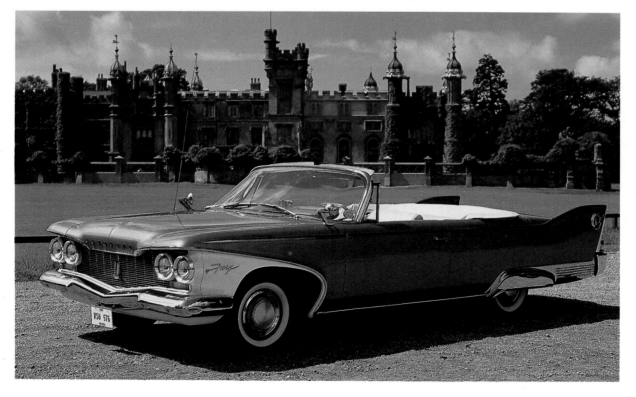

**Left:** Fins and chrome still featured on another Chrysler product, the Plymouth Fury. Although incorporating the modern unibody construction, the old "jukebox on wheels" style led to poor sales of their 1960 models.

# 1961

Recycling is a familiar theme of the 1990s, and many of today's manufacturers emphasize how much material in their cars can be re-used. However, nobody can approach the audacity of George Romney, the head of American Motors Corporation, who, when facing the economic recession of 1958, decided to recycle an entire automobile!

The plan was simple: dust off the tooling of the 1955 Nash Rambler 2-door sedan, slightly modify it to open up the rear wheel arches and simplify the hood design, add a mesh grille and a little chrome – and launch it as the new 1958 Rambler American. The experts said it wouldn't work, after all the Nash design actually dated back to 1950, but Romney had spotted a niche in the market for a US-built small car with a thrifty six cylinder engine at a rock-bottom price.

The Rambler American sold well, helping to put AMC in profit at a time when the competition was suffering losses. And, as frugal as the owners of the little car he was so enthusiastic about, Romney wasn't about to spend any more money on building the American than he had to. It continued almost unchanged until 1960, with increasing sales, establishing itself as the leader in the compact car sector at minimal cost.

Although he was careful to control spending, Romney appreciated that this virtual monopoly couldn't last forever. The popular

Volkswagen Beetle continued to dominate the import market, and the Studebaker Lark was the first American-made competition to arrive in '59. When GM, Ford and Chrysler entered the fray in 1960, George Romney knew it was time to act in order to protect AMC's hard-won customer base. Even then, chief stylist Edmund Anderson was only allowed to re-skin the ancient bodyshell.

Given these constraints, Anderson's achievement is remarkable. While the inner panels remained untouched and so the interior dimensions of the American were as before, the overall length was reduced by 5.2 inches and the width by over 3 inches giving a far neater package. Measurements aside, the squarer body now had a more modern Sixties shape and could stand alongside the competition without looking old fashioned.

The distinctive trapezium-shaped grille, sharp leading edge "brow" that flowed into a gradually flaring side indent and simple round tail lights weren't to everyone's taste. Critics have called Anderson's design "boxy and truncated" while supporters claim the car is "a little jewel". One feature that Anderson couldn't alter was the high beltline level, but this wasn't significantly detrimental. George Romney described the car as having "modern, enduring style".

Most customers were happy with the new look and, once again, AMC defied the detractors and sold 136,000 Americans in 1961, and a total of 370,600 cars, lifting the Rambler to an unprecedented third place in the charts behind Chevrolet and Ford (albeit a long way behind, by something like a million units!). Styling was no doubt important, but the American was more about economy than

**Above:** Restyled and modern-looking, the Rambler American for '61 was smaller than the '60 models, but kept its spacious interior. The 2-door sedan was the most popular model.

**Left:** The Rambler American 4-door station wagon was added to the model line-up for '61. Wagons could be ordered in all three trim levels: DeLuxe, Super and Custom.

**Right:** The 2-door convertible only came as a top-of-the-range Custom and was the most attractive of the American range. It was economical at under $2400 and 13,000 were sold.

# THE AMERICAN AUTOMOBILE

prestige and AMC used the slogan "the top resale value among the low-priced cars year after year" to reinstate that Rambler buyers could expect a better price than other owners when trading in their car for a new model.

By 1961, there was more choice for the Rambler American driver too. From the one model "plain Jane" 2-door sedan of '58, the range now featured three levels of trim – DeLuxe, Super and Custom – with a variety of bodystyles, including a new 4-door station wagon and a convertible. The top of the line Customs were also equipped with a modern overhead valve in-line six cylinder engine that produced 125bhp. This powerplant was available as a $59.50 optional extra on the lower specification models, otherwise you got the 90 horsepower antique flathead six. Both engines displaced 195 cu.in.

Not only was there a wider choice of models, Rambler American owners could now also specify extra creature comforts from an options list. You could jazz up the exterior with two-tone paint for $15.95, add front and rear DeLuxe foam rubber seat cushions at $19.90, or the ultimate has to be the Airliner Recliner Seats that folded down into Twin Travel Beds. If it was ease of driving you were after, there was the lever control Flash-O-Matic automatic transmission ($165), power steering ($72) and power brakes ($38). The most expensive add-on was undoubtedly air conditioning, which came with a heavy-duty cooling system and a hefty price tag of $359

**Below:** The Dodge Dart Phoenix was restyled for '61 with curious rear tapering tail fins whereas the rest of the industry was getting rid of fins. It was completely revamped for '62.

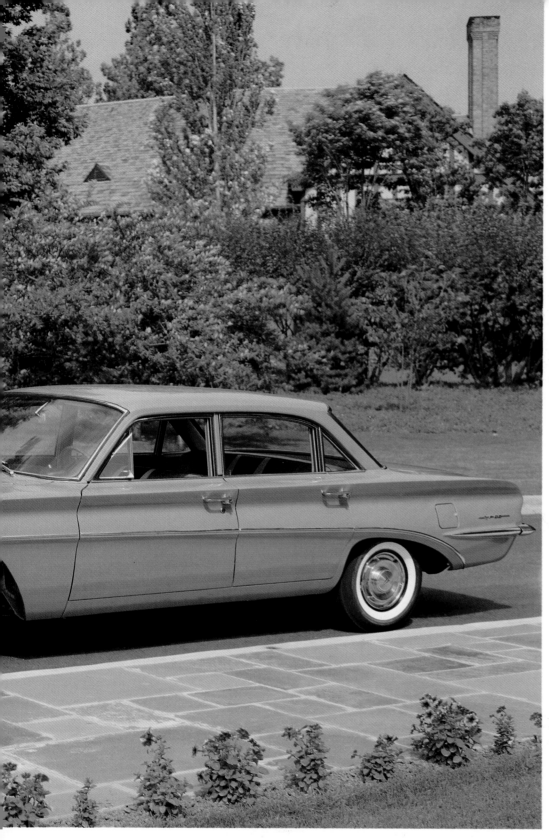

– almost 20% of the cost of the cheapest American model.

The best seller was the DeLuxe 2-door sedan at $1845, which compared favorably against $2230 for a basic Chevrolet, and 28,555 were produced. But if the Rambler buyer got carried away and opted for too many extras, the "cheap little compact" soon became as expensive as a full-size automobile. Mind you, the Chevy salesman wasn't going to let a customer out of the showroom without ordering a few extras either, so the price differential was pretty much maintained at the end of the day.

Away from the motor industry, President Kennedy was promising to put a man on the moon before the end of the decade and Alan Shepard became the first American in space on July 21. Less memorable was the failure of the CIA-orchestrated Bay of Pigs invasion of Cuba in April, and the decision to send 400 Green Berets to Vietnam. Also on the downside was an attack on the Freedom Riders in Alabama during a protest over segregation on buses, and a spate of airliner hijackings.

But there were plenty of winners to celebrate in 1961 too. Phil Hill became the first American to win the Formula One World Championship driving a Ferrari, A. J. Foyt took the chequered flag at the Indianapolis 500 (the first of four victories at The Brickyard) and Marvin Panch won the NASCAR Daytona 500 in a Pontiac. To compare the success of a cheap, compact, family car from an independent manufacturer based in Kenosha, Wisconsin with some of the great names in motor racing might seem a bit presumptuous. However, finishing third for Rambler was an amazing achievement given their limited resources. By beating the might of Detroit, AMC, George Romney, Ed Anderson and the Rambler American deserve to be included in the list of winners in '61.

**Above:** New to the compact market, the Oldsmobile F-85 came with 215 cu.in. aluminum V8 Rockette engine that produced 155bhp in standard form and 185bhp with the power pack option of a four-barrel carb, high compression heads and dual exhausts.

**Right:** A. J. Foyt won the Indianapolis 500-mile Race four times in his illustrious driving career. The first was in 1961 when he led for 71 of the 200 laps and his average winning speed was 139.130mph.

# 1962

By 1962, the Studebaker-Packard Corporation was in serious trouble and the end of the road was in sight for the once-proud names of two long-established marques who had merged in 1954. In fact, the last cars bearing the Packard badge were actually produced in 1958 and Packard was dropped from the company name in '62, marking the final sad ending of a history of building fine automobiles that stretched back to 1899.

But Studebaker still struggled on, and even in their death throes, they managed to produce some rather remarkable automobiles. Probably the most notable of these was the Grand Turismo Hawk which was a face-lift of a design dating back to 1956 (the '56 was actually a revamp of the body shell first introduced in '53!). The updated design was produced at record speed and with very little expenditure. The car enjoyed a favorable reception and its success can be gauged by the comments in Motor Trend who called it: "A bold new approach to luxury and power – a man's car all the way". Technical Editor Jim Wright described the response from other drivers by saying: "If the amount of interest generated in and around the Los Angeles area is any indication of what Studebaker-Packard can expect throughout the rest of the country, then we'd say their new Grand Turismo Hawk is definitely 'in'."

Other motoring magazines were equally supportive. Car Life stated: "In some ways, it was the most appealing car we've driven this year... It's very much the kind of car we'd be happy to own." Wheels magazine described it as "quick and handsome", while the reporter for Modern Motor magazine said about it: "...it's all motor-car, in the best sense of the term. The most advanced by far that I've driven." Judging from these reviews it would seem that Studebaker had created a triumph in spite of the prevailing doom, much in the same way as a conjuror pulls a rabbit from a hat. Unfortunately, Studebaker needed some magic of a more powerful kind to survive, and even the most skilled illusionist couldn't hide the enormity of the task facing the company which eventually folded in 1966 – after closing the South Bend, Indiana factory and moving its operations to Canada toward the end of 1963.

The foundations of the GT Hawk were laid by the studio of extrovert stylist Raymond

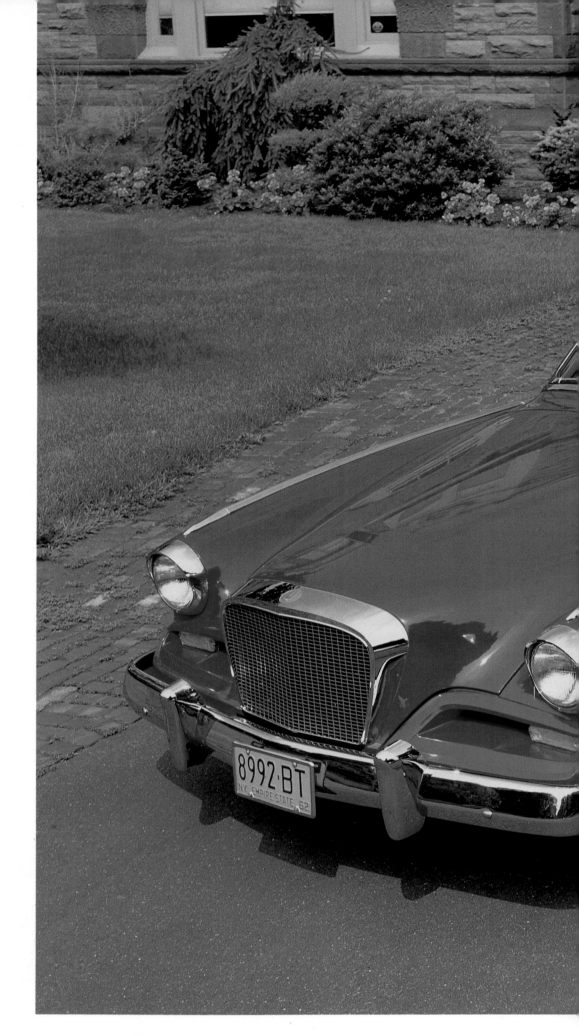

Loewy (whose long association with Studebaker resulted in some wonderful automobiles) with the new 1953 models which included the graceful Starliner hardtop and Starlight coupe – the work of designer Bob Bourke, assisted by Holden Koto. The Loewy

142

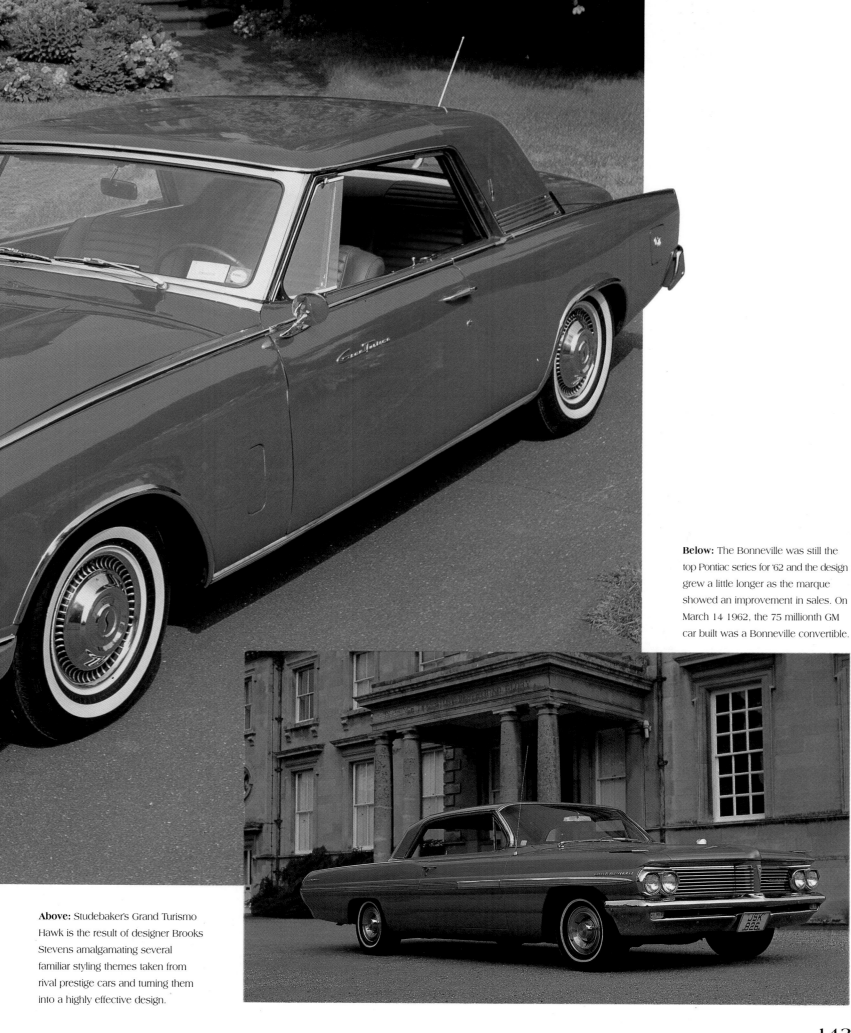

**Below:** The Bonneville was still the top Pontiac series for '62 and the design grew a little longer as the marque showed an improvement in sales. On March 14 1962, the 75 millionth GM car built was a Bonneville convertible.

**Above:** Studebaker's Grand Turismo Hawk is the result of designer Brooks Stevens amalgamating several familiar styling themes taken from rival prestige cars and turning them into a highly effective design.

studio also carried out the update for the '56 Hawk range, but this was to be a final collaboration and thereafter the relationship ended. The main reason for the split was one of cost. Strapped for cash, Studebaker couldn't justify the expense of the high-profile Loewy organization and started to seek out cheaper freelance designers.

The task of rejuvenating the Hawk was given to Brooks Stevens who has, over the years, accumulated many great designs in his portfolio, but who is probably remembered most often as the man behind the Excalibur automobile.

At a time when the development of a new model (or even a relatively straightforward face-lift) was usually measured in years rather than months, Stevens worked something of a miracle in just a few weeks. The first hand-built example was put together at his Milwaukee workshop in June '61 and finished versions were in front of Studebaker dealers by September! It was a truly remarkable turn round.

What Stevens did in essence was to take a good, if out-dated, design, refine it and add a quality of style and distinction that befitted a classic grand tourer. The rakish Fifties tail fins were quickly consigned to the rubbish bin to be replaced with far neater items, and the external re-skinning presented a flatter, more elegant body. Efforts were then concentrated on the roof section creating a squared-off, formal appearance which many people said was a direct copy of a Thunderbird, although Studebaker claimed it had been derived from the Packard Predictor concept car which had been built six years earlier.

Other styling elements that Stevens used to good advantage were altering the grille

**Above:** Described as the "projectile look" by designer William Boyer, the third generation Thunderbird had a pointed nose, razor-sharp lines, round tail lights with vanes in the trim and abbreviated fins. This was a land-locked missile, thanks to a 300 horsepower 390 cu.in. V8 under the hood.

**Below:** In an attempt to boost flagging sales, the Sport Fury model was announced four months after the rest of the Plymouth line. Available either as a hardtop sedan or convertible, and loaded with extras, the public still continued to shun Exner's designs and Plymouth sales plummeted.

which gave it a slight resemblance to the Mercedes (Studebaker was then the distributor for Mercedes-Benz cars) and adding a chrome strip along the belt line on top of the fenders which ran the whole length of the car in much the same manner as the Lincoln Continental.

This device of using styling features to bring an association with recognized upmarket automobiles could have been a disaster, but Brooks Stevens managed to bring all the elements together and made it work beautifully. The only item that looks out of place is the false, stick-on trunk lid "grille" which was used to disguise a virtually unchanged component. This was deleted for the '64 GT Hawks (the final in the series) and there's no doubt the smooth uncluttered panel works far better. The trunk lid apart, the decoration on the car is minimal and chrome trim is used in a restrained manner.

To back up the looks, a true GT needed some respectable performance, and here the Studebaker was able to take care of itself pretty well. The 289 cu.in. V8 engine might have been a touch on the heavy side for its capacity, but it was durable and, in standard form, it put out 210 horsepower which was sufficient to give a top speed over 100mph. For those who wanted to do some really "grand" touring, there was also a 225bhp option which included a four barrel carburetor and dual exhausts and, together with the four-speed manual transmission (three-speed was

standard and automatic was also an option), this provided sufficient performance for one magazine to label the Hawk "an enthusiast's car". In subsequent years there were even more powerful choices available, including a supercharged Avanti engine, but these are rare finds today.

Another highlight for Studebaker in 1962 was having the Lark Daytona chosen as the pace car for the Indianapolis 500 and, while Raymond Loewy's radical new Avanti would also provide the company with plenty of publicity, it couldn't halt Studebaker's slide into obscurity.

Studebaker's woes paled into insignificance compared to those facing the nation. The Cuban missile crisis saw JFK and Russian premier Kruschev bring the world to the brink of another war in October. Thankfully, everybody was able to breath a sigh of relief when the Soviet government backed down from the confrontation. A tragedy that was mourned by red-blooded men around the globe was the death of Marilyn Monroe on August 5 – an event that is still shrouded in intrigue today.

There was no such mystery over the demise of Studebaker. Poor management decisions following World War Two, inadequate investment for the future and difficulties with controlling the work force all contributed to the downfall. Even so, the company built some excellent automobiles and the Grand Turismo Hawk rates as one of the best.

**Below:** Introduced to counter the popularity of the Ford Falcon, the Chevy II arrived in '62. The no-nonsense economy model could be had with a four cylinder engine in the cheapest form, but a mid-level 300 like this 4-door sedan also came with choice of a 194 cu.in. straight six. Sales of all Chevy II variants reached over 326,000 in the first year.

# 1963

During the life of the Corvette there have been some highs and lows along the way, but ten years after the model's first introduction came one of the truly great ones – the 1963 Sting Ray.

What makes an automobile great? In this instance it is a perfect combination of styling and performance. And the plaudits for achieving such an outstanding example of the automotive art must go to two men – Bill Mitchell and Zora Arkus-Duntov. Mitchell, as vice president in charge of design for General Motors, regarded the Corvette (and especially the Sting Ray) as very much his own baby, even to the extent of warning off other in-house designers from attempting to come up with new ideas for styling the car. Engineer extraordinaire and successful racing driver, Arkus-Duntov was responsible for transforming the Corvette's handling and giving it the horsepower needed to perform.

Motor racing played a key role in the evolution of the '63 Sting Ray. To begin with, Bill Mitchell acquired the test vehicle from the abandoned Super Sport project (a factory-backed program developing a Corvette for endurance racing) and had Larry Shinoda design an open-top body for it. Shinoda took a lot of his inspiration from the Q-Corvette, an experimental rear-engined sports car that was the creation of Bob McLean – the designer who had laid out the very first Corvette. Mitchell christened his racer the Stingray

Special and got Dr Dick Thompson to drive it in the SCCA C-Modified class where it quickly proved to be a winner, taking the championship. At the end of the 1960 season, Mitchell decided he couldn't afford to keep funding the race car and so sold it back to GM, where it was rebuilt as a show vehicle.

By that time, progress was well in hand for what would become the sensational 1963 Corvette. Mitchell made no secret of his love for knife-edged styling and used it to great effect on the final production design which also incorporated the "triple hump" feature seen on the fenders and hood of the Stingray racer and Mako Shark concept car. But while the '63 Sting Ray was just about all new from the ground up (apart from engines and transmissions) Mitchell was careful to ensure some continuity of styling from the preceding years, and to this end had introduced the "duck-tail" rear on the '61 Corvette to give everyone the chance to get used to the theme.

At the Sting Ray's leading edge, the aggressive appearance was emphasized by the use of hidden headlights – the first time this device had been seen on a Chevrolet, and not used on any other US car since the 1942 DeSoto – but it was the rear window in the fastback boat-tail coupe model that would prove to be the most contentious feature of all. Bill Mitchell was adamant that the split rear window should stay and he argued long and hard to get his way saying "...if you take that off, you might as well forget the whole thing." Mitchell won the day, but criticisms in the press about restricted rear visibility and further pressure from people like Zora Arkus-Duntov saw the central spine removed for the '64 models, giving the 1963 Sting Ray a

**Right:** A split rear window was only used on '63 Corvettes, and has become an identifying feature of the model. But the boat-tail fastback coupe was much more than a styling exercise, giving superb performance. However, the duck-tail rear was a carryover from the preceeding model years to give continuity.

**Below right:** Hidden head lights were a rare concept on US-built cars in the Sixties, this Chevy sports car being the first since the 1942 DeSoto to use the idea. The knife-edge Corvette styling was a sensation at the time, and is as striking today as it ever was.

**Below:** After the disasters of '62, Plymouth models like this Sport Fury Hardtop had a hasty redesign but, although sales improved, the Chrysler division was still well behind Chevrolet and Ford in the race for customers. Top of the range Sport Fury models came with bucket seats, central console, de luxe steering wheel and interior trim, and special wheel covers.

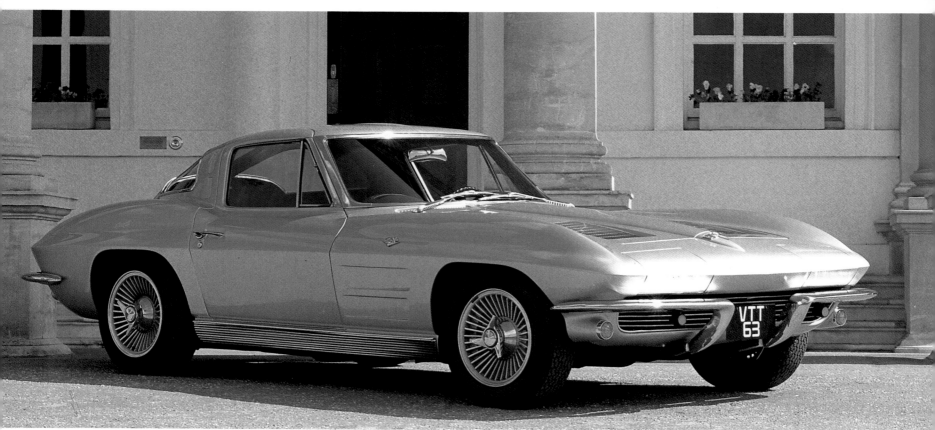

unique identifying feature and instantly turning it into a highly collectible item.

It has to be said, however, that some '63 models subsequently had their split rear windows replaced with a one-piece window and, after the 1964 model became available, Chevy dealers even offered a factory conversion – which immediately destroyed the car's value and it's certain that many Corvette owners today regret their actions.

As well as the split windows, Bill Mitchell also included several other non-functional styling ideas that met with disapproval and were dropped in '64. Dummy metal inserts in the hood copied lift-reducing vents used on Mitchell's Stingray race car and were deleted,

and fake ventilation outlets behind the coupe door pillars were replaced with functional grilles. Another feature removed after the first year was the stainless steel trim on the windshield pillar.

But apart from stunning looks, a sports car is all about performance and the Sting Ray had that too, thanks to Zora Arkus-Duntov who stated: "For the first time I now have a Corvette I can be proud to drive in Europe." His starting point was a simple, but highly effective, steel ladder chassis that proved so good it remained in Corvette production for 20 years with only minor alterations. Coupled to the channel section frame was an all-round independent suspension system which

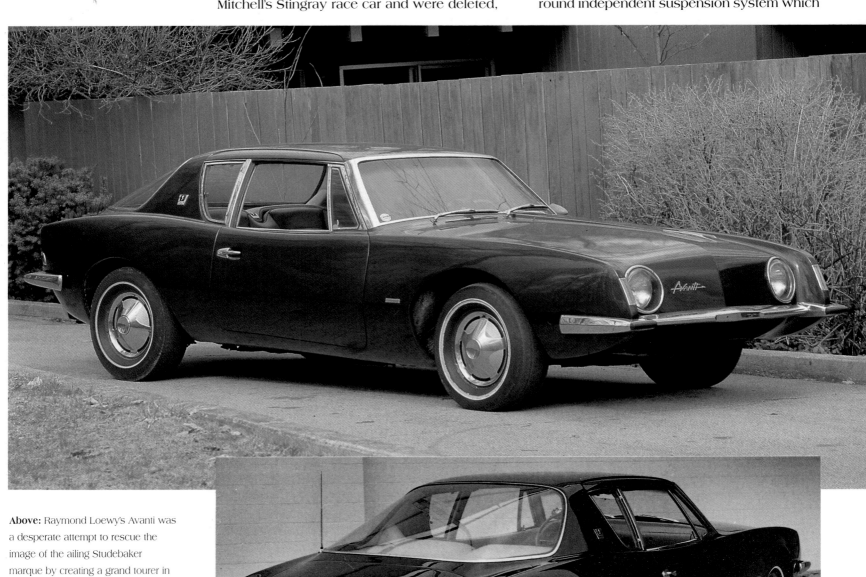

**Above:** Raymond Loewy's Avanti was a desperate attempt to rescue the image of the ailing Studebaker marque by creating a grand tourer in the classic mode.

**Right:** Avanti was powered by a supercharged 289 cu.in. V8 and gave a 0-60mph time of 7.3 seconds, but the 2-door coupe with fiber glass body suffered from production problems. European styling didn't appeal to everyone and less than 5,000 were built by Studebaker although Avanti continued under different owners.

endowed the Sting Ray with a cornering capability equal to the best of the competition. The most ingenious part of the suspension was the rear set-up which used a single transverse leaf spring and rugged, almost crude, construction to provide the equivalent of more sophisticated designs at a fraction of the cost.

Getting around corners efficiently is all very well, but the speed on the straights linking those bends is mighty important to the sports car enthusiast too. Once again, Arkus-Duntov had worked his magic and the Sting Ray could be had with horsepower aplenty. Standard was the 250bhp 327 cu.in. V8, but you could also order the optional 300bhp L75 version, 340bhp L76 or the fuel injected, 11.25:1 compression, Duntov cammed L84 specification which produced 360bhp at 6000 rpm. Car Life tested a 300bhp version with automatic transmission and recorded a 0-60mph time of 7.2 seconds which they reckoned compared favorably to the 5.9 secs achieved by Road & Track driving a 360bhp/4-speed manual car. Top speed was put at 130mph – fast enough for most, but there was potential for quite a bit more if needed.

From the start of the Sixties, Corvette sales had begun to climb from an average of around ten thousand a year, but so well was the '63 Sting Ray received that a second shift was taken on at the St Louis assembly plant to fulfil the growing demand. Even so, there was a two-month waiting list, and buyers could expect to pay the full sticker price as dealers weren't interested in offering any discounts. At the end of the model year, the Corvette Sting Ray had sold more than 21,500 units, split almost equally between the coupe and roadster, and virtually double the 1961 sales.

However, one event overshadowed 1963 and anyone who was alive back then can remember exactly where they were and what they were doing on November 22 when they heard the news that president John F. Kennedy had been assassinated in Dallas, Texas. Measured against such a tragedy, all other events pale into insignificance. It is impossible to say how differently things might have turned out had Kennedy not been shot, but the dynamic spirit of America survived and, in some small way, the Chevrolet Corvette can be viewed as a symbol of US determination to overcome all obstacles and produce something that is as good as anything manufactured elsewhere in the world – but at a price affordable by the majority. All Corvettes are great, but some are better than others and the '63 Sting Ray is undoubtedly one of the greatest.

**Above:** Typical of Sixties factory-supported drag racing machines is this Ford Galaxie 300 Club Coupe. Powered by a 427 cu.in. engine with 11.5:1 compression ratio and twin Holley four-barrel carbs that pumped out well in excess of a conservatively rated 425bhp, these machines were the terrors of the tarmac quarter mile.

# 1964

The first Ford Mustang is an automotive phenomenon that it would seem impossible ever to repeat. Just imagine suggesting that a new, but completely conventionally-engineered automobile based on an existing compact, economy model would sell nearly half a million in the first year and go on to set a trend affecting manufacturers for the next thirty years or more. Yet that's exactly what happened in 1964.

Ford certainly pressed all the right buttons with the Mustang, but had the good fortune to get some unintentional help from rivals Chevrolet and Plymouth. The Ford Falcon – introduced as a 1960 model following the success of the Rambler American and the demand for a cheap compact car – proved an immediate winner, taking up most of the spare production facilities left over from the Edsel debacle. The Chevy Corvair and Plymouth Valiant also entered this market sector, but a combination of radical rear-engined configuration (Corvair) and quirky styling (Valiant) gave the Falcon a distinct advantage. Ford were also able to utilize the compact's underpinnings in such a way that was impossible for Chevrolet to do with the Corvair, and although Plymouth had a similar idea with the Valiant-based Barracuda their offering lacked the Mustang's glamor.

As the US economy started to improve in the early Sixties, customers began to ask for better performance from the smaller models and the auto makers were happy to oblige – after all, luxury and extra horsepower options meant more dollars! But though the uprated Falcon Futura Sprint and Corvair Monza models were acceptable, they didn't really satisfy the younger generation of affluent car buyers' demands for a true sporty compact that was just that little bit different from the usual run-of-the-mill Detroit products.

Whenever the history of how the Mustang came into being is discussed, one name always gets top billing – Lee Iacocca. Described as "The Father of the Mustang", Iacocca had the energy and foresight to get the project underway and the determination to see it through, even when Ford's top management kept refusing to approve the construction of such a car. Several Ford concept cars came under consideration for inspiration when the design parameters were being set,

but the most logical choice seemed to be for a snappy little four-seater based on the Falcon platform.

Before this, Ford stylists John Najjar and Jim Sipple came up with a sleek two-seater roadster body that was dubbed Mustang I and, powered by mid-mounted V4 engine, was demonstrated by Dan Gurney at the 1962 US Grand Prix. Although an interesting vehicle which contained several styling cues that would find their way onto the production

**Above:** The Ford Mustang established a new class of automobile called the "pony car" and set sales records that are unlikely to be bettered. The early ragtop has a 260 cu.in. V8 which gave lively performance in a smart, reasonably-priced package.

version, Mustang I didn't really fulfil the requirement that Iacocca and his committee had laid down. Further design development work was needed and this culminated in an internal competition between the Ford Studio, Corporate Advance studio and Lincoln-Mercury. The proposal presented by the Ford Studio team headed by Joe Oros, Gail Halderman and David Ash, was unanimously chosen as the winning design, and this was eventually turned into a running prototype in

151

# THE AMERICAN AUTOMOBILE

**Above:** Elwood Engel had replaced Virgil Exner as head of styling at Chrysler and one of his first designs was the '64 Imperial Crown which carried several styling cues from the Lincoln which Engel had worked on. Similarities of slab sides, sharp-edged fender lines and even the hint of the Continental's spare wheel hump in the trunk lid are apparent.

**Below:** The Chevrolet El Camino re-appeared after a four-year gap, but was now based on the mid-sized Chevelle, rather than a full-size car as before. Dubbed a "personal pickup" by Chevy, the '64 El Camino came in two trim levels, with six cylinder or V8 engines and a wide variety of passenger car type options.

1963 called Mustang II which is generally acknowledged as being the forerunner of the production Mustang.

Iacocca set the launch date for the Mustang as April 17 1964 at the New York World's Fair but, just over a month before that, the Motor City press were allowed an "accidental" sneak preview when Walter Ford (Henry Ford II's nephew) drove a pre-production Mustang convertible to a lunchtime meeting in downtown Detroit. The photos were quickly circulated to other magazines and newspapers and the corporate publicity machine swung into action to keep interest at a fever pitch until the official debut.

Pandemonium broke out wherever the Mustang went on sale and there are many stories of the chaos caused by Ford's new car – some of which had little foundation in fact, but it all added to the hype. Not that the Mustang needed much hyping – dealers couldn't write up the orders quick enough and it took only four months to reach 100,000

sales – a total which had been earlier forecast for the first twelve months! Demand was at such a pitch that the Ford assembly plants at Dearborn, Michigan and San Jose, California were working flat out to keep pace. Early in the summer, a third plant at Metuchen, New Jersey was brought on-stream and ran around the clock pumping out Mustangs.

While it was clear that the Ford designers had created a car totally in tune with the times, a major contribution to the Mustang's popularity was the extraordinarily low base price of $2,368 f.o.b. Detroit for the coupe model. This was the price that Ford pushed in its advertisements, but it only bought the standard straight six engine with three-speed manual transmission – the big news was the lightweight V8 available at extra cost.

And it was the extensive options list that provided the opportunity for each owner to transform a docile, if stylish, standard specification automobile into anything from a grand tourer in the classic mold to a tire-shredding

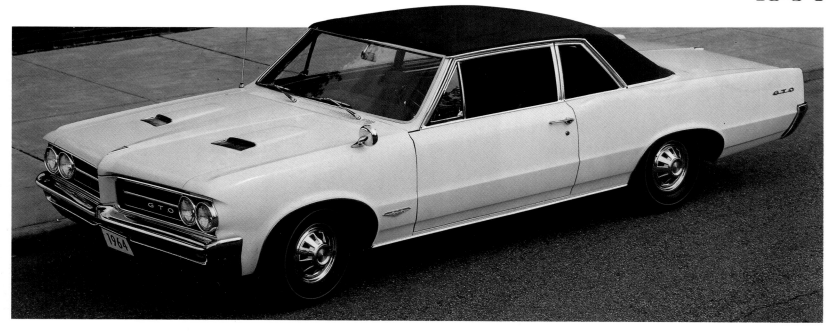

hot rod. This incredible variety of choice was even more surprising when you remember that, underneath the bodywork, most of the mechanical components came directly from the old Falcon. It also meant that although the Mustang was aimed at younger drivers, ownership was opened up to anyone – there was no such thing as a typical Mustang buyer. They ranged from eighteen to eighty, and the car was equally welcome at the country club, fashionable restaurant and church as at the local drive-in or drag strip. That remains as true today as it ever was.

What achieved such a broad spectrum of appeal? There's no doubt that the classic sports car "long-hood, short-deck" proportions set the right image, and the Mustang name evoked connotations of everything positive about the American way of life — but most of all it was about timing. The Mustang was simply the right car at the right time. Arriving at the precise moment when speed and performance were becoming major selling points

as the "muscle car" era took off, even parked by the side of the road, a Mustang had the look of motion that Lee Iacocca had appreciated when he first saw the clay mock-up presented by Joe Oros.

The term "pony car" came to represent a new class of automobile, which Ford called "the family man's sports car" in its adverts, and one that remains in use even today. And although the Mustang is still in production, the "Mustang generation" (a description first used by a California real estate developer in a sales brochure promoting apartments for young singles) belongs to the Sixties.

The Beatles brought pandemonium to the streets of New York when they arrived in February, and Lyndon Johnson's landslide victory to retain the presidency over Barry Goldwater in November was seen as a vote to unify the nation but, in 1964, the one thing that all generations of Americans were united about was their love of the Mustang. And the streets and highways were filled with them.

**Above:** Shoehorning a large engine into a small car and giving it a fancy name cribbed from an Italian sports car might not sound too inspiring, but John Z. Delorean had the right idea when he came up with the Pontiac GTO. Actually a Tempest Le Mans option, the GTO spec included 389 cu.in. engine, floor shifter, uprated shocks and dual exhausts and is regarded as the first of the Sixties "muscle cars".

**Below:** Introduced as a '63 model, the Buick Riviera had only small detail changes for 1964 and remained a stunning sports luxury car in the classic mold. The most expensive Buick, it was both fast and elegant, thanks to a 425 cu.in. engine and crisp lines from stylist Bill Mitchell.

**Above:** Ford's big Galaxie was completely updated for 1965, having new body styling on a new perimeter frame with coil-spring suspension front and rear. The squared-off styling included vertically-stacked dual head lights and matching tail lights. This 4-door sedan was one of several body styles offered.

426 cu.in. and had a four-barrel and developed 365 horsepower. The amount these engines added to the cost of the car ranged from $31 to $545, depending on the engine. For those with deep pockets and an urge to burn rubber, however, there was the 425 horsepower, 426 cu.in. Hemi engine with dual four-barrel carburetors and a price tag of either $1150 or $1800. This included the cost of a four-speed manual transmission. There were two prices because the engines were retrofitted at the factory, and the higher figure applied to cars that had originally been equipped with automatic transmission. The same arrangement applied to the wedge-head engines, with two prices being quoted. Given that the base price of a Satellite 2-door hardtop was $2612, the hemi represented a substantial investment and, in truth, these engines were really intended for competition use.

Although the four-speed came as standard with the 426 engines, it could also be specified with the 361 and 383 engines, while a positive-traction rear axle was also available for an extra $39. Other performance options included a choice of rear axle ratios (3.23 or 2.93:1) and a tachometer.

Not many Satellites had the monster 426 wedge-head or hemi engines. Most buyers opted for the more tractable 383 V8, which

had power and torque aplenty and was much more user-friendly on the street. But the big engines, particularly the Hemis, were in keeping with Chrysler's interest in NASCAR and drag racing. In the former, the Hemi would be fitted to full-sized Dodges and Plymouths run on tracks of over a mile in length, while on shorter tracks, Dodge Coronets and Plymouth Belvederes would use it. In drag racing, too, the Hemi-engined Belvedere was legendary, being campaigned by the likes of Ronnie Sox and Buddy Martin and the "Drag-On-Lady" Shirley Shahan, who used it to set a National S/SA record of 127.30mph with an elapsed time of 11.21 seconds. Such was the company's interest, that they produced an altered-wheelbase drag package for Dodge and Plymouth automobiles so that they could compete in the NHRA Factory Experimental class.

The actual body styling of the Belvedere models had been carried over from the previous year, when it had been common to all intermediate Plymouths. For 1965, it was changed by replacing the previous dual head lights with single lights, while the grille was given a cruciform trim with mesh background.

The sporting image of the Satellite that resulted from the company's NASCAR and drag racing activities, plus the undoubted performance of the car, helped boost sales and just over 25,000 of the 1965 models were built, most of them hardtops (only 1,860 convertibles left the factory). The car continued with this image for some time, and in 1966 was restyled with a swoopier roofline and more slab-sided contours. The big news for that year, however, would be a more refined 426 Hemi engine that was intended for street use. The Street Hemi had cast-iron cylinder heads rather than aluminum (although these were available as an option), while the inlet manifold was aluminum rather than magnesium. A wilder cam was available, and although compression was down to 10.25:1 from 12.5:1, output was still 425 horsepower. With this came a Sure-Grip axle, whether a four-speed or Torqueflite automatic was fitted.

The Street Hemi turned out to be a real winner, offering tractability as well as high performance. Car and Driver said that the car offered the "best combination of brute performance and tractable street manners" that they had ever come across. In their test of the car, they recorded a 0-60mph time of 5.3 seconds, with a 13.8 second quarter mile time and terminal speed of 104mph. Stopping such a projectile needed substantial brakes, of course, and while front discs were not an option, 11 inch police-specification drums were.

Although it never looked particularly like a muscle car, Plymouth's Belvedere Satellite was definitely a force to be reckoned with. It would go on in this vein, eventually spawning the famed GTX and Road Runner.

**Above:** Oldsmobile's 4-4-2 muscle package had appeared as an option on the F85/Cutlass series in 1964. Then the figures had stood for four-barrel carburetor, four-speed manual transmission and dual exhausts. For 1965, the package gained a 400 cu.in. engine in place of the previous 330 cu.in. unit. So they now stood for 400 cu.in., four-barrel carb and dual exhausts.

**Below:** The Galaxie hardtop was a particularly good looking car with sharp styling. In total there were six main series of Galaxie, giving 17 models. Engines comprised six and five V8s, the most powerful producing 431 horsepower.

# 1966

If you're involved with the decision making process at the upper end of management for a division of a large auto corporation, it is accepted that there will be a great deal of give and take. In all probability, you do not wield enough influence to insist on your division being able to produce a brand new model from the ground up – you have to share the basic corporate platforms with the other divisions and make as many alterations as is allowed within the constraints of the budget available. In this respect, Chrysler in the Sixties was no different from the many other large companies leading the automobile industry.

However, just once in a while, restrictions such as these engender creativity which produces something very special and the 1966 Dodge Charger is an outstanding example of what the art of compromise can achieve.

Around the mid-1960s, the fastback body style enjoyed a period of popularity as the result of the rest of the auto industry rushing to come up with their own versions of the ultra-successful Ford Mustang. Dodge were offered the opportunity to share the Plymouth Barracuda platform with this in mind but, instead, they decided to go their own route and use the larger Coronet model as a basis for an entry into the burgeoning muscle car market.

The leading lights at Dodge behind this policy were product planner Burt Bouwkamp and stylist William Brownlie – both newcomers to the division and both self-confessed performance car buffs who simply loved the work they were doing.

Even so, the merits of the Sixties fastback are hard to define from a practical point of view. Rear seat passengers had restricted headroom and minimal leg space, the large area of glass created a greenhouse effect causing the interior to heat up rapidly in the sunshine and, to cap it all, luggage space was abysmal. On the plus side of course, the fastback Charger does look great. Even when it is standing still, it seems ready to spring into tire-blistering action – and, when talking about muscle cars, that counts for a whole lot more than how much shopping can be accommodated in the trunk or the niceties of passenger comfort.

The starting point for the Charger actually came about almost by chance rather than

being attributed to part of some grand corporate marketing strategy. Facing the lack of an attention-grabbing exhibit for an auto show in the summer of '65, Bouwkamp asked Brownlie to come up with an idea for a show car that could not only be built quickly, but at minimal cost. It was a tall order, but the

**Below:** The Comet Cyclone GT adopted the Ford Fairlane body shell and had a 335 horsepower, 390 cu.in. engine plus twin hood scoops, heavy duty suspension and dual exhausts. Only 2,158 GT convertibles were built in '66, making it highly-collectible.

**Above:** Hidden head lights and a full-width grille give the Dodge Charger an aggressive look, matched by ground-shaking acceleration thanks to the brutal horsepower of a 426 cu.in. Hemi engine. This was the car described as "...the hot new leader of the Dodge Rebellion".

designer rose to the challenge and suggested putting a fastback roof on the popular Dodge Coronet model. Following Brownlie's specifications, a 2-door hardtop was speedily modified and readied for the show.

Dubbed "Charger II" (Dodge had used the Charger name before on another show car a year or two previously), this car was not, as is often supposed, intended as an official prototype for a proposed new model but was simply created as a last minute showpiece. However, public reaction to the fastback was

so enthusiastic that plans were immediately rushed through to put the Charger into production.

Brownlie's show car had, naturally enough for something designed to attract attention, several rather exaggerated styling features and it was deemed necessary to trim these excesses back for the version intended for sale to the public. Nevertheless, the production Charger retained all the good points of the original concept. The sloping fastback roof remained unaltered, and the full-width

**Above left:** The finely-sculpted Charger has a sweeping fastback roof line which was popular in the late Sixties, but the Dodge hardtop coupe was one of the most attractive versions. This model sold 37,300 in its first year but this halved in '67 when the body style remained virtually unchanged.

# THE AMERICAN AUTOMOBILE

tail lights were incorporated in a flat rear panel with the slab-sided fenders neatly squared off at the back and a razor-sharp top edge picked out with a bright metal strip.

But it was the front end that provided the most radical departure from the show car's original appearance. In place of the simple grille with five thin horizontal bars and single rectangular head lights, the Charger presented a blank face made up of fine vertical lines interrupted only by the round medallion in the center. Hidden head lights, another Sixties styling fad, were in vogue and the use of them on the Dodge represented the first time that they had been seen on a Chrysler Corporation car since the 1942 DeSoto. When turned on, the four round head lights rotated into view but there was an override switch allowing the lights to be left exposed without being on. This feature was a clever Dodge engineer's solution to the problem of head light mechanisms being frozen shut in harsh winter conditions, which had blighted this feature on other makes.

The interior of the Charger, especially the dashboard and instrument layout, was taken almost directly from the show car and used unaltered, providing one of the most comprehensive packages on offer at that time. Elsewhere, it was luxury all the way with deep plush carpets and foam-padded bucket seats, plus a fake wood rimmed steering wheel as the final touch. In addition, the rear seats folded flat to give increased carrying capacity but, without a full hatchback, it didn't really help much on a practical level.

Because of the low budget allocated, the Charger II show car had a meek 318 cu.in. V8 under the hood, but the majority of '66 Chargers were ordered with the 325 horsepower 383 cu.in. engine. Thus equipped, the

**Above:** The arrival of the Ford Bronco Sports Utility pickup showed a new market was opening up for a 4x4 leisure vehicle that could "go nearly anywhere and do nearly anything". "Neither a car nor a truck, but a vehicle which combines the best of both worlds", the Bronco closely resembled the International Scout which had debuted in '61.

**Right:** The Oldsmobile Toronado was an ingenious piece of engineering which successfully used a big V8 engine mounted in the conventional position with a front-wheel-drive system. The first front-wheel-drive American car since the Thirties Cord, it was designed to give sports car handling on a roomy six passenger sedan, and proved its worth when Nick Sanborn won the stock car class of Pikes Peak hill climb in '66 driving one.

hefty fastback could reach 60mph in eight seconds, cover the quarter mile in sixteen at over 90mph and run on up to reach a 120mph top speed.

But for the serious performance devotee, there was only one powerplant – the mighty 426 Hemi. Fed by dual Carter AFB four barrels and rated by the factory at a very conservative 425bhp, this engine gave the Charger a 0-60mph time of six seconds, and quarter miles in the 13 second bracket. As befits a road-going race car, underneath, everything about the Hemi Charger was heavy duty, from the vented four-pot front disc brakes, massive torsion bars and anti-roll bar to extra rear springs and Dana 60 axle.

There was one thing that the Hemi Charger didn't come with – a factory warranty. Instead, there was a bright yellow sticker which stated: "This car is equipped with a 426 cu.in. engine (and other special equipment). This car is intended for use in supervised acceleration trials and is not intended for highway or general passenger car use. Accordingly, THIS VEHICLE IS SOLD "AS IS", and the warranty coverage does not apply."

Driving a Hemi-powered Dodge Charger could undoubtedly be a very exciting experi-ence, but the year's ultimate piece of steering must go to astronaut Neil Armstrong who, when piloting the Gemini 8 space craft, performed the first docking manoeuvre and described it as "Just like parking a car". Other people on the way up were Ronald Reagan who was elected as Governor of California, and The Monkees pop group who were launched into the limelight through a madcap television series. Also riding high were the hems of women's' dresses and skirts across the nation as high fashion saw the mini skirt become all the rage.

Dodge used the success of the Charger to launch a campaign called "the Dodge Rebellion" and the new fastback sold well on the back of some heavy media promotion and race-winning results, but the '67 body looked identical and sales halved in the following year. A completely new shape arrived in 1968, making the first Dodge Charger very much a child of its time.

1966 was the year that civil rights movement leader Stokely Carmichael brought the term "Black Power" into the forefront of the American political debate, but for an automotive enthusiast it was the year of "Hemi Power" and the Dodge Charger.

**Below:** This was to be the final year for Studebaker, with cars like this Daytona 2-door Sports Sedan being built in Hamilton, Ontario, Canada. Only 2,321 Daytona models were built (out of a total of just under 9,000 units) before production was closed down in March 1966 and the Studebaker name disappeared.

# 1967

Coming second to Ford is something that Chevrolet has never liked and, when the Mustang proved to be such a runaway success in 1964, the heat was on to find a way of redressing the balance. Chevy supporters will tell you that there were all manner of reasons why the GM division didn't have an equivalent to Ford's pony car – the Corvair Monza was selling well, they had too many different models already on offer – but the plain fact of the matter is that Ford had got there first, and so it was down to Chevy to play catch up.

Wisely, the Chevy hierarchy appreciated that arriving second in the market place meant that they had to produce more than just a Mustang clone – a new model had to be perceived as something better. Ford and Chevrolet fans will debate forever about which is best, but there is no doubt that the Camaro provided a more than adequate riposte to the Mustang and, even if it did take until 1977 to outsell the Ford, the Chevy Camaro was definitely here to stay.

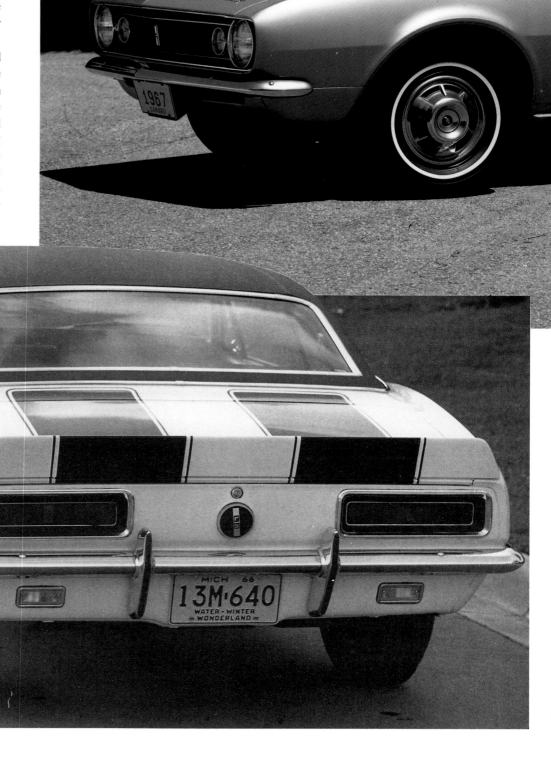

Taking advantage of the example provided by Ford, Chevy abandoned the rear-engined layout of the Corvair and returned to the conventional front engine, rear-wheel-drive arrangement for their new car. Henry Haga was put in charge of the styling and, in addition to the Mustang, his influences came from a clandestine 1962 project by Chevy design director Irwin Rybicki that used a Chevy II as the base. Certain similarities can also be seen with the Corvair Monza. Due to a management reshuffle, David R. Hollis took over as chief designer and, after four months intensive work, in December 1964, a full size clay model was constructed and photographed against a Mustang for comparison.

Initially, the "Chevy Mustang" project was given the Experimental Project code number XP-836. Later on it got christened the "F-Car" (the "F" supposedly referring to Ford), and subsequently carried the name Panther, which many assumed would be the final model name. However, General Motors was locked in a battle with Ralph Nader and his safety crusaders during this period, and it was decided that using the Panther name was too provocative, and so a search began for an alternative. Chevrolet's head man, Elliot M. "Pete" Estes reckoned that the name should start with a "C" and, for a while, the name "Chevette" was under consideration,

**Above:** The Chevy Camaro was available with everything from an economical six cylinder up to one of the hottest small block V8s on the market. The basic version here has simple round head lights and turn signal lamps mounted in the grille. Only 2-door hardtop coupe and convertible body styles were offered, with the Camaro roof line being such that a fastback was not deemed necessary.

**Left:** The Camaro Z-28 was the hottest option, intended mainly for Trans Am racing, and included a special 302 cu.in. V8 rated at 290 horsepower although it was actually capable of well over 425bhp in racing trim. Only 602 Z-28 specification cars were built in 1967.

**New Camaro**
BY CHEVROLET

**Left:** The Super Sport 350 Camaro has bumble bee stripes around the nose and a 350 cu.in. V8, but the grille with electrically operated head light covers actually forms part of the Rally Sport option which were often ordered together to make a stunning combination.

163

but merchandising manager Bob Lund and vice president Ed Rollert searched through Spanish and French dictionaries and picked out the word Camaro in one of them. Estes liked the name and it was announced to the press in June '66, well in advance of the car itself being previewed. Chevy publicists said Camaro translated from French as "comrade" or "pal", but other researchers noted that in Spanish it could be interpreted as a type of shrimp or even "loose bowel movement" – but the fuss soon died down and the name became established as quintessentially Chevrolet.

When the Camaro was announced, on September 29th 1966, it was immediately apparent that Chevrolet's designers had taken the Mustang concept to heart and yet had added their own distinctive ideas. Where the Mustang's body lines were straight and aggressive, the Camaro's were curved and flowed ("fluidity" was a term used a lot by GM's designers) and the Chevy shape had been the subject of wind tunnel testing to prove its superior aerodynamic performance.

But it wasn't only in the bodywork design that the Chevy differed from the Ford. The basic understructure consisted of a front sub-frame attached to a unitary bodyshell, instead of the complete unitized construction used on the Mustang. In many ways this configuration gave the Camaro an advantage and, because the front chassis could be isolated from the rest of the body with rubber bushings, the ride quality was improved. In addition, the design had better space utilization, improving the room allocated for rear seat passengers and the trunk capacity.

But despite these improvements, the Chevy Camaro was not without its teething problems. While the attractive 2-door coupe body could happily rival both that of the Mustang notchback and fastback models, the convertible suffered from body flexing, door sagging and rattles all of which required fixing. Also, the single leaf Mono-Plate rear springs used were okay with the base six cylinder engine and Powerglide automatic transmission, but the more powerful V8 cars suffered from axle tramp and all '67 Camaros

**Above:** The Cadillac Eldorado used a front-wheel-drive system and combined roadability with superb styling. The Cadillac 472 cu.in. V8 could give 125mph top speed and nearly 18,000 were sold in '67.

**Below:** Pontiac adapted a Chevrolet Camaro bodyshell for their entry into the pony car market in '67 with the Firebird. Pontiac engines and firmer suspension gave improved handling.

would bottom out on the rear suspension with alarming ease.

Like the Mustang, the Camaro could be specified with any number of additional options selected from a huge list. In fact, the list was so comprehensive and so complicated that it was suggested that few people really understood all the available possibilities. Apart from the bewildering array of engines, transmissions, colors, interior trim and special packages on offer for the standard specification car, the potential Camaro owner could also select from some serious high performance options – notably the Super Sport (SS), Rally Sport (RS) and the now legendary Z-28.

Once you got into the SS and RS models (which, to add to the muddle, could also be combined together on one car), the Camaro came with hidden head lights and a special paint stripe around the nose plus various other items. But the "bumble bee" stripe proved to be so popular that it was quickly made available on any Camaro model. Then, when the big block V8s were introduced, the SS package came as a mandatory part of the deal. Confusing? You bet!

Despite this apparent minefield of choice, nearly 65% of the 220,906 '67 Camaros produced were base model V8 Sport Coupes and there can be few people who would argue that this was, indeed, a pretty shrewd selection for just about any form of motoring. Whether cruising down to the corner drive-thru burger joint or high speed touring cross-country on the Interstate, it was all the same and the Chevy proved a match for the Mustang in just about every department.

"Long-awaited and much-speculated, the youthful Chevrolet Camaro has arrived on the domestic automotive scene with a fine pedigree and high promise", wrote Car Life magazine in October 1966, continuing: "Though a follower in a field pioneered by others, the Camaro nonetheless seems exciting in looks and performance, is particularly well-suited to its intended market and will be sold and serviced by the world's largest dealer body". This emphasis on youth and excitement reminds us that these were indeed the heady days of the Sixties – 1967 being the so-called "Summer of Love" when everything went psychedelic and the Monterey Pop Festival heralded the hippie culture taking over San Francisco.

There were plenty of dark clouds in the purple haze, what with continuing Vietnam War protests, race riots in the Motor City of Detroit and the tragic deaths of three astronauts – Virgil Grissom, Edward White and Roger Chaffee – when their Apollo spacecraft caught fire on the launchpad at Cape Canaveral. Despite the harrowing events of this year, however, memories of '67 will, for most people, be of a highly colorful and supercharged period that welcomed the arrival of the Camaro as a small part of the more positive trends in society.

**Above:** The Mercury Cougar was a cousin of the Ford Mustang and a de luxe entry in the pony car-market, priced about $200 higher, but with a 200bhp 289 cu.in. V8 as the base engine. Riding on a 111 inch wheelbase (3 inches longer than the Mustang), the Cougar was easily identified thanks to its grille; 123,672 were sold in '67 – its debut year.

# 1968

By 1968, the United States was heavily involved in the Vietnam war. The conflict had cost billions of dollars and, subsequently, American taxpayers were saddled with a 10% rise in their taxes. Harder to swallow still, was the number of American lives lost, and there seemed no end in sight. Despite putting out peace feelers in the previous year, the North Vietnamese together with the Vietcong, launched a massive new offensive at the end of January, during the sacred Tet new year holiday, penetrating the grounds of the US embassy in Saigon. In fact, the Tet offensive was a desperate gamble for the North Vietnamese, who had suffered considerable losses in both men and equipment as a result of US bombing, particularly in the north of the country, but it paid dividends. Stung by the speed and success of the attack, and by the ever-growing peace protests at home, President Lyndon B. Johnson ordered a halt to the bombing of North Vietnam. The demoralized Johnson did not seek re-election later that year and was succeeded by Republican Richard Nixon, whose Presidency was to be less than trouble-free.

Along with the relentless grind of the Vietnam war, there was more bad news that year: civil rights activist Martin Luther King was assassinated, and attorney general Robert Kennedy shared his fate a short time after. The one bright piece of news was that Apollo 8 became the first spacecraft to orbit the moon, paving the way for a manned landing in the following year.

In Detroit, the car makers were still caught up in the muscle car business. All had at least one horse in the race, which was fast becoming a contest to see who could cram in the biggest engine and out-accelerate the rest. Straight-line performance was the main criterion and, in the process, handling, braking, ride, build quality and levels of trim often left a lot to be desired.

For 1968, Buick's entry in the pony car wars was the Gran Sport, which became a model in its own right that year. Prior to that, the Gran Sport had been an option package that was available on the company's 115 inch wheelbase compact model, the Skylark.

When Ford announced the Mustang in 1964, they had caught everyone on the hop. A mad scrambling ensued among the other manufacturers to produce a comparable car

and take advantage of the lucrative pony car market. Unable to develop a completely new model in time, Buick reworked the relatively mundane Skylark in 1965, offering a package that included a 400 cu.in. big-block V8 engine, three-speed manual transmission, uprated chassis, rear axle and suspension, wide wheels and revised exterior trim. Despite the prissy Skylark name, the Gran Sport offered some genuine muscle, cranking out a 0-60mph time of six seconds, while on the drag strip it ran the quarter mile in 14.7 seconds with a terminal speed of 100mph.

**Right:** AMC's pony car was the AMX. Featuring unibody construction, the standard car had a 290 cu.in. V8, but 343 and 390 cu.in. V8s were among the options.

**Below:** The Buick Gran Sport had GM's new "B" body with its distinctive sweeping side molding and had big-block 340 and 400 cu.in. engines that delivered astounding acceleration.

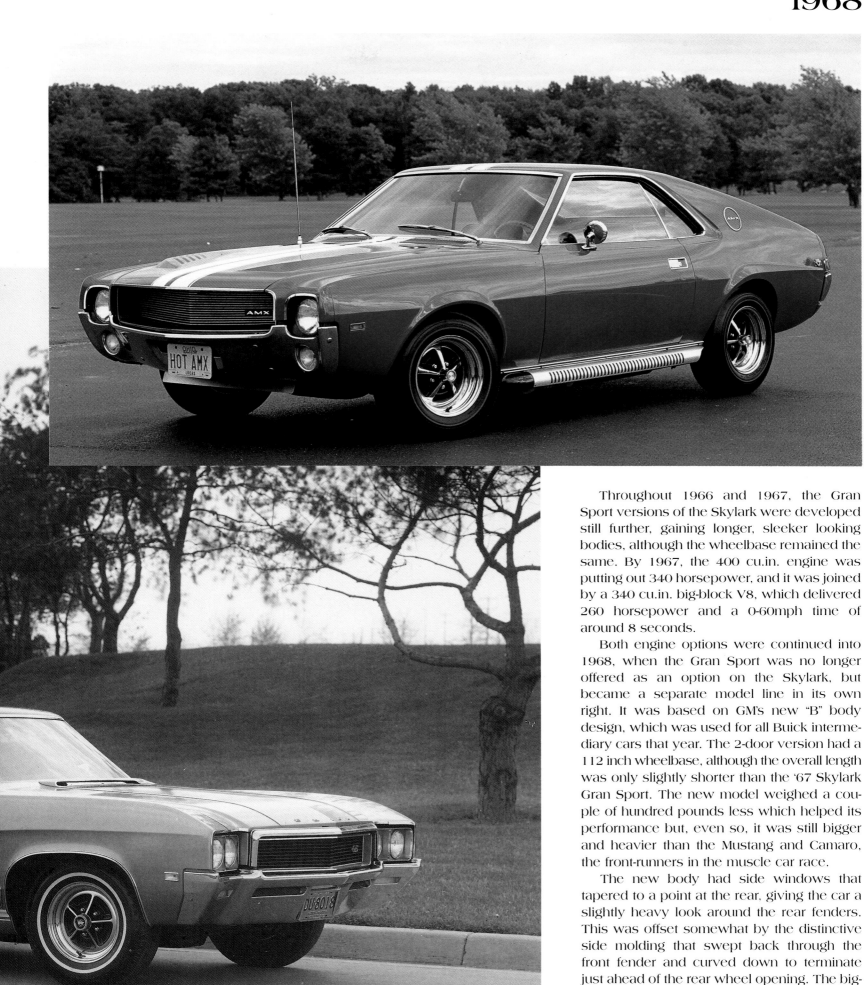

Throughout 1966 and 1967, the Gran Sport versions of the Skylark were developed still further, gaining longer, sleeker looking bodies, although the wheelbase remained the same. By 1967, the 400 cu.in. engine was putting out 340 horsepower, and it was joined by a 340 cu.in. big-block V8, which delivered 260 horsepower and a 0-60mph time of around 8 seconds.

Both engine options were continued into 1968, when the Gran Sport was no longer offered as an option on the Skylark, but became a separate model line in its own right. It was based on GM's new "B" body design, which was used for all Buick intermediary cars that year. The 2-door version had a 112 inch wheelbase, although the overall length was only slightly shorter than the '67 Skylark Gran Sport. The new model weighed a couple of hundred pounds less which helped its performance but, even so, it was still bigger and heavier than the Mustang and Camaro, the front-runners in the muscle car race.

The new body had side windows that tapered to a point at the rear, giving the car a slightly heavy look around the rear fenders. This was offset somewhat by the distinctive side molding that swept back through the front fender and curved down to terminate just ahead of the rear wheel opening. The bigger-engined GS400 was available either as a hardtop or a convertible, while the GS340 was available as a hardtop only. Bench seats were standard in all versions (front buckets

**Left:** The 1968 Chrysler Dodge Charger was restyled with a sleek body to match its high performance. A 440 Magnum or 426 Hemi V8 was offered, the latter propelling the car to 60mph in under five seconds.

**Right:** Also new in '68 was a restyled Corvette Sting Ray, with a body reminiscent of Chevrolet's Mako Shark II show car of 1965.

**Below:** The long, sleek Chrysler 300 sedan had used the same basic body style since 1965, but for 1968 it was revamped with hidden head lights, a new grille and powered by a 440 V8.

were optional), but both GS models could only be considered four seaters. Like most muscle cars, they sacrificed refinement for performance, and this was not helped by the poor quality of build prevalent at the time.

Among the options offered with the Gran Sport was a choice of transmissions. As standard, the car came with a three-speed manual with floor shifter, but the buyer could order a four-speed manual transmission instead, or an automatic.

Like so many other muscle cars, the Gran Sport was not a comfortable car for long-distance touring. With its stiff suspension, the car's ride left a lot to be desired, while either big-block engine made it nose heavy with a detrimental effect on the handling.

Where the Gran Sport really scored was in its blistering straight-line performance; for anyone who wanted to burn rubber, neither the GS400 nor GS340 would let them down. The gutsy, big-block Buick V8s churned out gobs of horsepower, but the gearing was such that top speed was only about 110-115mph, and they would only get about 11-14 miles on a gallon of gas.

The major problem was that, even as early as 1968, all the manufacturers were chasing a muscle car market that was already beginning to disappear. The hullabaloo that followed the launch of the Mustang had died down and emissions controls were beginning to hamper the cars, increasingly emasculating their performance. Interest was on the wane and the potential buyers were starting to look for more traditional features in a car. Although the bubble had not burst, it was beginning to deflate. In 1965, when Buick introduced the first of the Gran Sport options on the Skylark series, they sold over 69,000 examples of the sporty car. Despite the new body styling, for 1968 the sales of the Gran Sport totaled only 21,514.

Although sales figures continued to fall, Buick persevered with the Gran Sport, keeping it in production until 1972 but, by that time, it had returned to being a version of the compact Skylark. Along the way, it received trim changes, a 455 cu.in. engine in place of the original 400 cu.in. unit, and a 350 cu.in. V8 instead of the 340. Other options included hot camshafts, revised valve trains, positraction rear ends and dual exhaust systems. For the hot rodder who wanted to drag it out, these may have been very welcome, but they were not enough to keep the breed alive.

# 1969

As the Sixties came to a close, America still found itself enmeshed in the Vietnam war, although the number of US troops there was being reduced and efforts were being made towards the Vietnamization of the war by providing material and air support to the indigenous forces of South Vietnam. The anti-war rallies continued and home-coming troops who had served in South East Asia often returned to find that they were looked upon with disgust by many of their peers, despite the fact that most of them had been drafted. Later in 1969, news of the massacre of innocent civilians in the village of My Lai by American troops stirred up the anti-war sentiment all the more.

It was a year of mourning, not just for the thousands who had died in Vietnam, but also for one of America's great heroes of the twentieth century. On March 28, the country was shocked by news that Dwight D. Eisenhower, former President and Commander in Chief of the Allied forces in Europe during World War II, had died.

If many Americans were not proud of what was being done in their name in Vietnam, all had reason to be proud of their country's achievements in space. Following successful orbital missions to the moon, NASA carried out a successful landing in July, and Neil Armstrong became the first man to set foot on its dusty surface, quoting the now immortal phrase: "One small step for man; one giant leap for mankind".

The auto industry, however, took a slightly shorter step that year, with new car sales being a little below those of the previous year. It was not the easiest of times for manufacturers. With increasing pressure to improve the exhaust emissions and safety aspects of cars, production expenses increased. By this time, the industry's flirtation with the compact had just about come to an end, and the future seemed to lie with intermediate-sized cars. Some, however, continued to build big cars, among them Chrysler – a company that was rarely known for styling innovation, although they often led the field in engineering. The real luxury models in Chrysler's line-up came from the company's Imperial division which, for many years, had sought to compete with Cadillac for the prestige end of the market. For 1969, the Imperial range comprised of 2-

and 4-door hardtops and a 4-door sedan. In addition, a custom-built limousine was also available to special order.

Imperial had been a name associated with Chrysler for decades but, until the mid -fifties, it had simply been applied to the most luxurious models sold under the Chrysler badge. The company built long wheelbase sedans

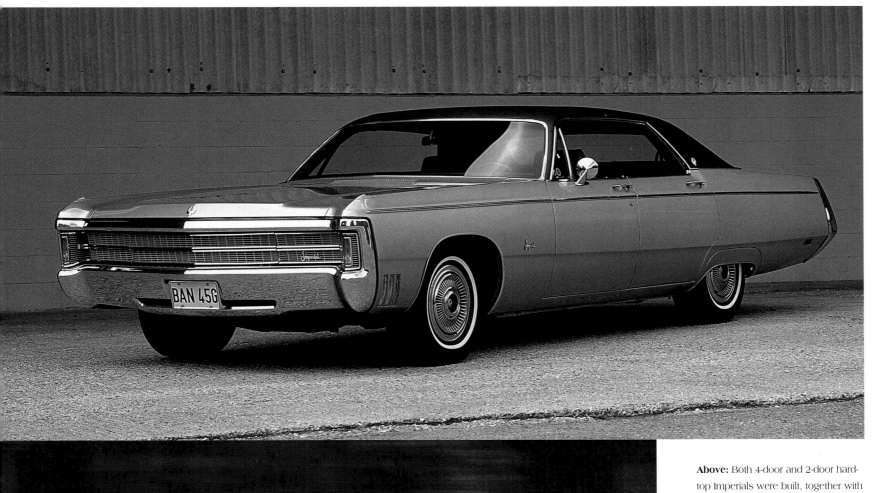

**Above:** Both 4-door and 2-door hard-top Imperials were built, together with a 2-door sedan. Although originally intended to compete with Cadillac, the Imperials could never quite make the grade.

**Right:** For 1969, Lincoln's Continental Mark III remained pretty much unchanged from when it was announced in 1968. The 2-door body was based on the Ford Thunderbird, although this was by no means obvious. It was given a Rolls-Royce-like grille, which was flanked by fold-away head lights. Powered by a 365 horsepower, 460 cu.in. V8, the Mark III was an instant success.

**Below right:** Many manufacturers were still playing the pony car game in 1969. Chevrolet not only had the Camaro, but also the Chevelle SS 396, a high-performance version of its standard Chevelle intermediate-sized automobile.

**Below:** Oldsmobile's 4-4-2 was another tire-burning muscle car that shared the GM "B" body with Buick's Gran Sport, among others. Powered by a 400 cu.in. V8, the car was offered with a range of options, including forced-air induction and a variety of rear axle ratios.

and limousines as well as other luxury models under the Custom Imperial and Crown Imperial names. However, these were obviously Chryslers and could be associated with more mundane company products. It was not good marketing for a company that wanted to do well in the luxury market, dominated by Cadillac.

If Imperial was to make it, the image of the cars had to improve; they needed to be less obviously part of the Chrysler empire, with a mystique of their own. As a result, in 1955, a separate Imperial division was formed and a new range of Imperials launched. Sadly, one of the new cars – the 2-door hardtop – looked very similar to the Chrysler C300, a popular high-performance automobile that had done well in competition. This undoubtedly affected the sales of the Imperial range, but even so their total sales doubled compared to the year before.

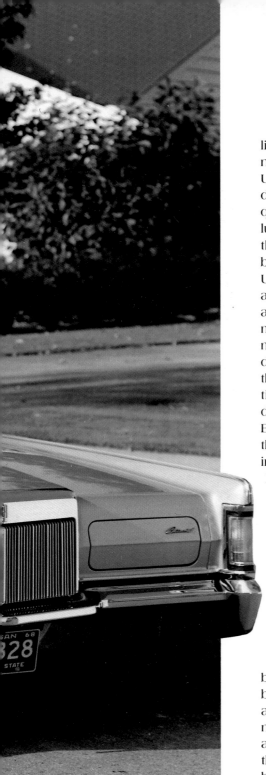

However, Imperial had become established as a maker of luxury cars, and the name became more familiar with buyers. Until the mid Sixties, many Imperials were designed by Virgil Exner, who had some quirky ideas of what made a good-looking luxury car. As with most other automobiles of the late Fifties, Imperials grew fins that became ever-larger with each new model. Unfortunately, because the company had relatively limited resources, new models appeared less frequently than those of other manufacturers and, towards the end of each model run, the cars were beginning to look decidedly dated. This is particularly true of the '62 models which had outlandish fins at a time when all other manufacturers had dropped the idea. Lights were another of Exner's foibles. Wanting to give his designs the classic look of Thirties automobiles, he incorporated freestanding head lights and tail lights that looked as though they had been stuck on as an afterthought. If nothing else, Imperials were unique in appearance.

Exner was eventually replaced by Elwood Engel, who had worked at Ford, and he brought a considerable degree of Lincoln influence to the '64 Imperials, which were big slab-sided automobiles.

From this point on, Imperials tended to reflect design trends within the industry, rather than setting standards of their own.

However, with falling sales, costs had to be cut so, for 1967, the Imperials used the basic Chrysler New Yorker body shell, although different front and rear end treatments gave it a distinctive appearance. It was a unibody design fitted with a 440 cu.in. V8 that developed 350 horsepower and was backed by a three-speed TorqueFlite auto-

matic transmission; this was the same drivetrain that had been used in previous models. Imperials were back where they started, being uprated versions of existing Chrysler models. Things would stay that way until all production ceased in 1975.

Although featuring a completely new 127 inch wheelbase body, when the '69 Imperial models were unveiled, the similarity with the New Yorker was even more pronounced. The body had gently rounded sides and was referred to by Chrysler as having "fuselage styling". The drivetrain was the same as that used previously, while power steering and brakes were standard equipment. Two series of Imperial were built: Crown and LeBaron. The latter was the more luxurious of the two and was available on both hardtop models, while Crown versions of all three body styles were available.

There is no doubt that all the Imperial models were luxury cars – for Chryslers. But the company had slipped out of the market they had long wanted to be a part of. Moreover, they would never return.

Despite its obvious Chrysler parentage, the 1969 Imperial sold well compared to previous years. In total, just over 22,000 examples were built; the last time sales had been above 20,000 was at the launch of the new 1964 model. Sadly, that was the highpoint for, thereafter, sales dropped quite alarmingly (by almost 50% in 1970 and 1971). Minor changes were made until 1974 when, again, it shared the latest New Yorker body shell. By this time, Imperial no longer existed as a separate division of Chrysler. However, the oil crisis of 1973 had sounded the death knell for big gas guzzlers and, after 1975, production of Imperials was brought to a halt.

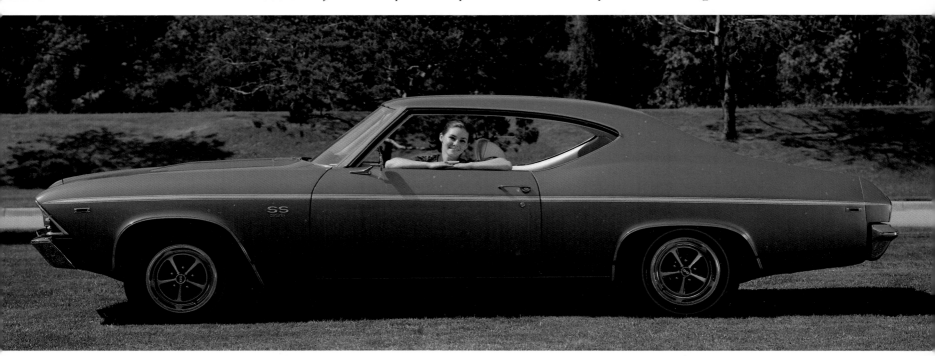

# 1970

Imagine taking a chainsaw and hacking off the back of a compact family sedan to produce a sub-compact model, giving it a whacky name and introducing it on April 1! Bizarre? Well, this was how economy-minded American Motors Corporation (formerly Rambler) chose to compete with the rising tide of imported four cylinder small cars and, at the same time, beat the Ford Pinto and Chevy Vega models into the market by six months.

Well, maybe the chainsaw was a bit of an exaggeration but, by reducing the wheelbase of the Hornet by a foot and using most of the same front panels, interior and underpinnings, AMC were able to bring the Gremlin to production with incredibly cheap tooling costs. Not that the original Hornet hadn't been designed by Dick Teague with some ingenious money-saving features to begin with. For a start, front and rear bumpers were interchangeable, 2- and 4-door models shared the same roof pressing, and costly versions like the 2-door hardtop and convertible were deliberately omitted from the line up.

Chopping the Hornet off short to make the Gremlin wasn't a new idea for AMC – they'd done just the same thing a couple of years earlier with their Javelin pony car in order to produce the AMX two-seater sports coupe. And, to keep the Gremlin base price to a bare minimum, it was introduced as a two-seater with just a rubber mat in place of the rear seat. Actually setting the price caused AMC a few headaches as, being the first of the US

**Left:** The basic Gremlin was pretty spartan, but options could be added such as a roof rack, body stripes, wheel covers and whitewall tires – and this also helped AMC profitability. The hatch-style opening rear window was only used on four-passenger models. 28,500 Gremlins were sold by the end of 1970.

**Right:** The Gremlin was identical to the larger Hornet model from the doors forward, saving on tooling costs. It used the same six cylinder engines, transmissions, and suspension components to further reduce production expenditure. The wheelbase of 96 inches was a foot shorter than on the Hornet, but the Gremlin was only 3.5 inches longer than the VW Beetle.

manufacturers into the sub-compact field with a home-produced car, they didn't have any competitors to gauge their offering against. In the end, the cheapest Gremlin was set at just $1,879 – aimed right at the P.O.E. price of the cheapest Volkswagen Beetle.

But, exactly as anticipated by AMC chairman Roy Chapin, very few of these base model Gremlins were sold and, instead, customers went for the four-seaters with extra options which all helped to push the price (and profitability) up. Advertising for the Gremlin emphasized the fun aspect of the car, with its practicality and economy being an added bonus. This struck a chord with many of the younger generation who also liked the fact that the quirky styling didn't appeal to their parents.

Market research had shown AMC that there was a youthful market with considerable purchasing power for cars like the Gremlin, and predicted that the demand for new small cars would exceed the combined sales of standard size, medium and luxury cars in a few years time. Their studies showed that a typical Gremlin purchaser would be in his or her early 30s and have an annual income of $10,000. A high percentage would be women, and single people would make up a quarter of the total. It was forecast that by 1975, persons under 34 years of age would buy 40% of all cars in the USA and 60% of all compact and sub-compact models.

At the press launch in Palm Springs in February 1970, president of American Motors, William V. Luneburg, announced the car with the following statement: "The Gremlin is the first domestic car specifically designed to meet the foreign car challenge and halt its domination of a sizable segment of the American market. We believe the reason more and more buyers have turned to imports is that they did not have an acceptable alternative among US cars for the combination of features they were seeking in a smaller car. The Gremlin includes not only the desirable features of import-size cars but also provides the handling and roadability charac-

**Above:** The Ford Maverick was billed as the "first car of the '70s at 1960s prices". The Economy model was introduced on April 17 1969, exactly five years after that other popular equine Ford, the Mustang. Powered by a 170 cu.in. six cylinder, the Maverick proved to be in such demand that it remained unchanged throughout the 1970 model year too. With a 103 inch wheelbase, it wasn't really in the sub-compact class, but still sold over 450,000 units in its first full year.

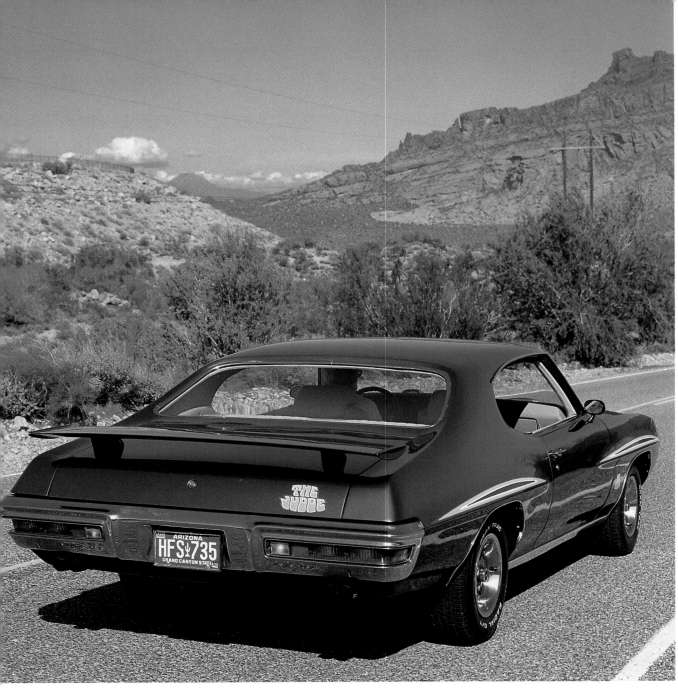

teristics most US buyers want."

Although all the other sub-compact cars had four cylinder engines, this was one item that AMC couldn't offer and the Gremlin came with a 128hp, 199 cu.in. straight six as standard (a 232 cu.in. 145hp six was optional). Somehow this didn't matter in 1970, as quite a few people looking at a smaller car for the first time were a bit unsure about durability and found a smooth, torquey six more comfortable than a high-revving four. In following years the Gremlin also acquired a 304 cu.in. V8 under the hood – some were even drag raced with the 401 cu.in. engine – and it wasn't until towards the end of its life in '77 that a four cylinder VW/Audi powerplant was used.

Another advantage that the Gremlin had over the smaller imports was the list of extra convenience equipment that could be specified. For American drivers unused to manual gear shifting, the Shift-Command automatic transmission was a plus, as were the power brakes and Variable-Ratio power steering and, of course, there was also air conditioning. For the more performance-orientated, there was a handling package including heavy-duty springs and shock absorbers and front sway bar, and Twin-Grip limited slip differential and special axle ratios. All told, more than forty items were available as factory installed options and, naturally, many dealer installed accessories could be had as well.

Offbeat it may have been, but the Gremlin fitted right in with the needs of AMC in the early 1970s to create positive media coverage, promoting interest and thereby sales. After the Rambler name had been dropped, Roy Chapin faced an uphill battle to establish the identity of American Motors with the public and there's little doubt that bringing out such an unusual shape as the Gremlin on April Fool's Day guaranteed widespread publicity. Chapin was nobody's fool, however, and the Gremlin sold well – over 671,000 between 1970 and '78 – with just an occasional face-lift, making millions of dollars for the company and helping it to survive.

The design of the Hornet/Gremlin can be traced back to the experimental Cavalier unveiled in 1966. On a nationwide tour, the Cavalier generated a good response, particularly for the use of interchangeable components – for instance, left front and right rear fenders were identical. Several styling cues from the Cavalier were carried through to the

Gremlin, including wide wrap-around grille, flared wheel arches and ventless side windows. Another associated design study was the AMX/GT, a two-passenger show car using the abrupt chopped-back configuration.

Something like a Gremlin is bound to be full of surprises, but how many people would have described it as a 2-door sedan? That's what AMC chose to call it, saying quite straight-faced, "Diminutive in an automotive sense, it is not a scaled-down version of any American Motors passenger car". But the point they were trying to make was that the extra width inside the Gremlin gave more shoulder and hip room when compared to any other import in the sub-compact category.

The Gremlin might have looked weird to some, but generally it could be relied upon to raise a smile for daring to be different in what were difficult times. 1970 saw four students killed at Kent State University in Ohio by the National Guard during an anti-war demonstration and women protesters marching for equal rights in New York – unrest was everywhere. Maybe only AMC could have gotten away with the Gremlin but, coming from a year when smiles were a bit thin on the ground, the sawn-off little car deserves to be remembered with affection.

**Above:** The Plymouth Road Runner Superbird was developed in a wind tunnel to win NASCAR stock car races, and qualifying speeds of over 190mph were recorded at the super speedways like Daytona and Talladega. Around 1,935 road-going versions were sold, although prices were heavily discounted towards the end as demand didn't live up to Plymouth's expectations. When powered by the legendary 426 cu.in. Hemi V8 engine, this is an awesome street machine!

# 1971

Following the success of the Disneyland theme park in Anaheim, California, 1971 saw the opening of the much larger Disneyworld in Orlando, Florida. No doubt, this was well received by kids all over the States, but young people in their late teens would probably have been more interested in the fact that henceforth, from age 18, they would be eligible to vote in all political elections.

People in the news that year included the boxer Muhammed Ali, who was cleared of draft dodging after his earlier refusal to join the army, which inevitably would have resulted in him being sent to Vietnam. The pardon allowed him to resume his successful boxing career. One person who would not receive a pardon, however, was cult leader Charles Manson, who was sentenced to death for the murder of actress Sharon Tate in 1969.

Meanwhile, NASA had sent men to the moon again, but this time they had taken along a set of wheels for exploring the lunar landscape. The Lunar Rover gave the astronauts mobility, but it was not the swoopy space vehicle of science fiction. Little more than a bare frame, it was fitted with a pair of seats and equipped with special wire-mesh wheels driven by electric motors. However, it did the job, although it had to be left on the moon, as the astronauts' spacecraft did not have the capacity to bring it home.

Back on earth, towards the end of the year, GM recalled a record 6.7 million cars to rectify a problem with faulty engine mounts. It was not their most memorable achievement that year, but one that was more notable was the launch of Buick's new Riviera. Although not to everyone's taste, the Riviera had eye-catching styling teamed with luxurious appointments and plenty of power.

By 1971, the styling of most Detroit products was becoming a little subdued compared to previous years. While many of the designs were good, few could be considered head-turners. One automobile that did turn heads, however, was the Riviera.

Since the introduction of the 1963 Riviera, GM's design department, under the leadership of Bill Mitchell, had been turning out elegant designs for Buick's personal luxury car. All stood apart from the run-of-the-mill models, and the '71 was the most outstanding yet. Mitchell had been the driving force behind a number of unique designs for GM, among

them the 1963 Corvette Sting Ray, which shared one important feature with the new Riviera: the tapering, boat-tail shape of the rear roof and deck. It was this aspect of the design that caused the most comment from magazine road testers and potential buyers alike. Some loved it; others hated it.

Like the earlier models of the Riviera, the 1971 version was a 2-door hardtop coupe. It was based on a new 122 inch wheelbase perimeter frame, which was longer than the previous model by some 3 inches. This helped emphasize the long, sleek shape with overtones of an earlier era that designer Jerry Hirshberg had penned for the body. When viewed from the side, the line of the front

**Above:** The rakish looking '71 Riviera was slightly longer than its predecessor, which helped the sleek design. However, the optional vinyl-covered roof detracted from the design somewhat, breaking up the clean lines.

**Right:** The most distinctive feature of the design was the tapering boat-tail, which projected beyond the rear deck and was mirrored by the shape of the inset bumper. The trunk lid incorporated louvers on '71 models, but these were dropped for 1972, as was the boat-tail itself in 1973.

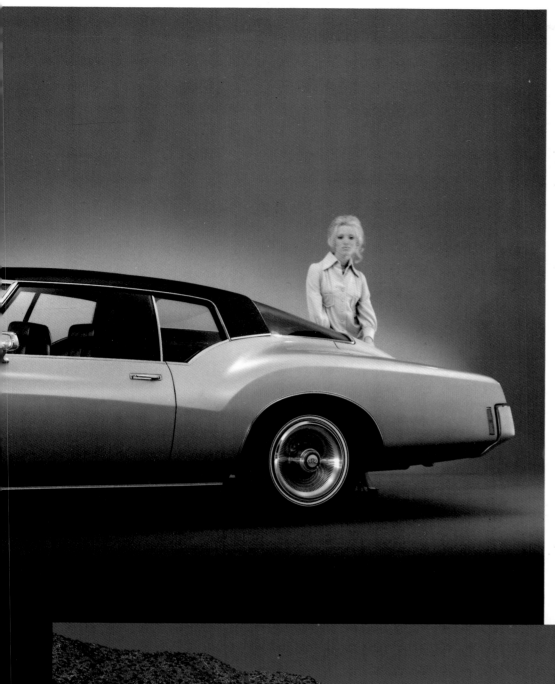

fender swept back and curved gently down-ward, continuing well into the door, the top of which also ran downward slightly towards the rear. Immediately behind the door, the line kicked up quite sharply to match the prominent curve of the rear fender. The shape of the latter was quite pronounced, bulging slightly out of the body, much like the rear fenders of a Forties Roadmaster although, in this case, the fender itself tapered downward to the rear.

The overall effect was that of the classic "leaping cat" shape found in so many sports and luxury cars of the Forties and Fifties. The line through the fender and door emulated the outstretched front limbs, while the rear fend-er echoed the powerful haunches, pushing the body forward. It was unlike anything offered by any other US manufacturer at the time.

On top of this traditional outline was the unique roof treatment. From the steeply raked windshield, the roof curved down to the tapering boat-tail. This swept across the deck and came to a rounded point that pro-jected out from the rear of the car. This pro-jection was emphasized by the trailing edge of the trunk lid, which tapered inwards slight-ly from the rear fenders in a shallow V-shape. The inset bumper mirrored the shape of the trunk lid and boat-tail. The latter was flanked by two narrow rectangular tail lights, while the license plate was sent into the bumper on the left side.

The roof treatment was pure '64-67 Sting Ray, only wider. The rear window was of the

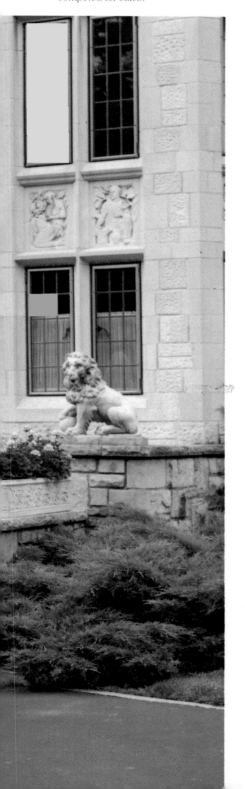

same shape, while the same raised molding ran down the center of the roof and continued beyond the rear window, right down to the tip of the tail. The window itself proved a problem in more ways than one. Because of its size and position, it had to be specially tempered to withstand the stresses imposed on the body when the car was driven over extremely harsh road surfaces. This resulted in a slight distortion of its optical qualities. Moreover, the large area of glass exposed to the sun could turn the interior into an oven quite rapidly, so air conditioning was an essential option for cars that were destined to spend their lives in the sunnier states.

At the front, dual head lights flanked a simple grille of horizontal bars, while rectangular parking lights were incorporated in the lower bumper. Although there was a degree of peaking to the hood, the front end styling was somewhat subdued compared to the rear.

Inside, the car was well trimmed with the dashboard taking on a dual binnacle form, with the triple-faceted instrument panel designed so that all controls and instruments directly faced the driver. Despite the car's size, the interior was not exactly roomy, and it would be better described as a 2+2 rather than a full four seater.

Mechanically, the new Riviera was similar to its predecessor, having coil spring suspension all round and front disc brakes as standard (although these had been an option of the previous model). However, the earlier models had demonstrated quite poor handling, so Buick engineers redesigned the suspension to good effect, producing a car that

rode and cornered well. Moreover, the Riviera could be ordered with the Max Trac option – a computer-controlled system that prevented wheelspin and fish-tailing under hard acceleration on slippery surfaces by restricting the amount of power fed to the rear end.

Only two models of Riviera were available: the base version and the Gran Sport (GS). Both were powered by a 455 cu.in. V8, which produced 315 horsepower in the former. However, the engine of the latter was equipped with a modified carburetor, a different camshaft and other bits and pieces that bumped output to 345 horsepower. In both cases, the engine was backed by a Turbo 400 three-speed automatic transmission, with a choice of column- or console-mounted shifter.

With the big 455 engine, the Riviera offered performance to match its striking looks, and was capable of reaching 60mph in around 9 seconds with a top speed in the region of 125mph. However, with such a large engine and weighing in at 4500 pounds, gas mileage was not outstanding, although the car had never been designed with economy in mind. It had a very well-defined, but limited, market, being aimed at junior executive types who were moving up the income scale and wanted to say to all and sundry: "Look at me; I'm going places". Within this market, the Riviera sold well and steadily. It continued in production through 1972 and 1973, although in the latter year it lost the distinctive boat-tail and received the federal "5mph" bumpers. After that came another restyle, but never again would the Riviera be the head turner or performer it once was.

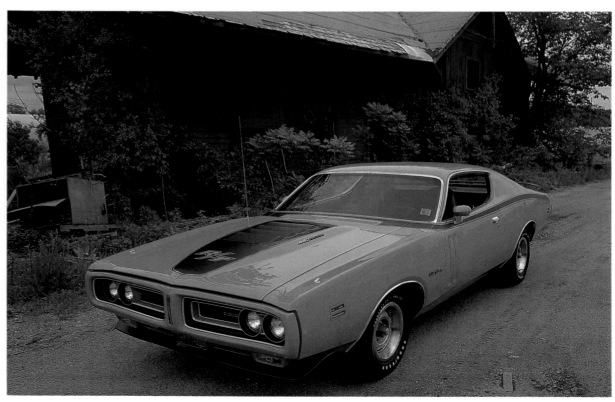

# 1972

With every move geared towards securing a second term in The White House, in many respects, 1972 was a good year for Richard Nixon. He got off to a good start by visiting communist China in February; in June he had a summit meeting with Soviet leader Brezhnev; and he was pulling American troops out of Vietnam. However, in June an event came to light that no doubt Nixon would have preferred to remain secret. It was some time before he was directly linked to the burglary of the Democratic Party's headquarters in Washington's Watergate Building and, in the meantime, he had won the sought-after second term. But when the truth came out, he had no choice but to go. Out of office and in disgrace, he retired to his home in California, but eventually he would bounce back, becoming a venerated elder statesman.

The Watergate scandal would rumble on for many months but, in September, Americans had good reason to be proud. At the Munich Olympics, swimmer Mark Spitz picked up seven gold medals, while Bobby Fischer beat Boris Spassky to become the first American World Chess Champion.

In Detroit, Ford's Lincoln division also had reason to be proud. 1972 saw the launch of the Continental Mark IV, replacing the Mark III, which had been introduced in 1968 as a direct competitor to the Cadillac Eldorado, achieving immediate success. The luxurious 2-door coupe was originally conceived on the 117 inch wheelbase Ford Thunderbird perimeter frame. It utilized portions of the T-bird's cowl and roof but, for the Mark IV, designer Wes Dahlberg used a new 120.4 inch perimeter frame, giving the car greater luxury and style.

The styling clues of the Mark III were continued, however: the classic long hood/short deck proportions; the prominent Rolls-Royce-like grille flanked by fold-away head lights; the tall, slightly rounded sides; the low roofline and Continental spare hump in the trunk lid. Because of the longer wheelbase, the rear roof pillar was wider than that of the Mark III, and Dahlberg put this to good use by incorporating an oval opera window.

In keeping with the car's luxury status, the Mark IV was richly upholstered with "loose cushion" seats, while the dashboard was designed to reduce injury in an accident. As an added safety feature, sturdy crash rails were incorporated in the doors.

**Top & above:** The Lincoln Continental Mark IV exhibited sharp styling from every angle. With a new, longer frame and a completely new body, it incorporated many features of the successful Mark III, including the

182

Power for the Mark IV came from the same engine used in the Mark III: a 460 cu.in. big-block V8 that was rated at 212 horsepower; an engine also used in the Continental sedan. The Mark IV also shared the sedan's drive-train and coil-spring suspension.

It was an immediate success; the Mark III had sold well against the Eldorado, but the Mark IV outsold it, and continued to do so for the next two years. The car's popularity generated intense owner loyalty, many remaining with the same owners for years, providing a degree of luxury and style that American manufacturers eventually ceased to offer.

The Mark IV would remain in production until 1976 but, as the years passed, exhaust emissions equipment would strangle the engine and heavy energy-absorbing bumpers would add to the car's weight, reducing performance. Even so, the Mark IV remained a winner until the end. Production peaked at 69,437 in 1973, and reached 56,110 in 1976, indicating just how popular the car was.

**Above:** For 1972, Chrysler continued with the "fuselage" styling introduced in 1969, as this New Yorker Brougham 4-door hardtop illustrates. The smooth rounded sides accentuated the car's length, while a massive expanse of hood did the same for its width.

**Below:** Ford restyled its dual-purpose, car-based pickup, the Ranchero, for 1972, adopting the Coke-bottle shape that was prevalent in standard automobiles at the time. As always, the Ranchero provided the comfort of a car with the load-carrying ability of a truck, but its days were numbered by the arrival of the much cheaper Japanese mini-trucks that had almost as much load space.

large chromed grille, fold-away head lights and the Continental spare hump on the trunk. The Mark III had sold well, but the Mark IV did even better, outselling the rival Cadillac Eldorado for the first time.

# 1973

By just about any yardstick, 1973 wasn't exactly a vintage year – although the signing of the Vietnam War ceasefire agreement on January 27 seemed to indicate that there was some cause for optimism. Unfortunately, the aftermath of the Watergate break-in was about to engulf The White House and both President Nixon and Vice President Spiro Agnew resigned following a tax evasion scandal. And, if this upheaval wasn't demoralizing enough, there was the oil crisis caused by the OPEC embargo which resulted in long queues at gas stations. The automobile industry was further hampered by the imposition of a nationwide 55mph speed limit.

Given those circumstances, it would seem unlikely that a car born in the youth-driven Sixties – when performance was everything and fuel economy didn't matter – could even survive, let alone nearly double its sales. But the Pontiac Firebird has always been a rather special automobile and, anyway, nobody ever said there was much logic in the reasons people had for choosing which car to buy.

In many respects, it is actually quite remarkable that there was a '73 Firebird at all, given the situation in 1972. Pontiac faced problems on several fronts, the most damaging for the Firebird line being a five month-long strike by the United Auto Workers union at the Norwood, Ohio, plant where the cars were built. By the time the stoppage ended in September, the losses amounted to thousands of cars representing millions of dollars that the company could ill-afford. With the situation as it was, there is little wonder that there was considerable pressure from the GM boardroom to drop the model from the catalog altogether.

Further complications arose from the increased number of Federal safety regulations being introduced and the power-sapping emission control systems required – all of which tended to work against the pony car brigade. It was as if the fun had been taken out of driving and, as a result, many of the cars being produced lost their individuality as the design and engineering teams struggled to incorporate the new changes dictated by legislation.

It is no surprise to learn, therefore, that the '73 Firebird showed few obvious alterations from the previous year. Well, unless you look at the hood of the Trans Am that is! Nobody

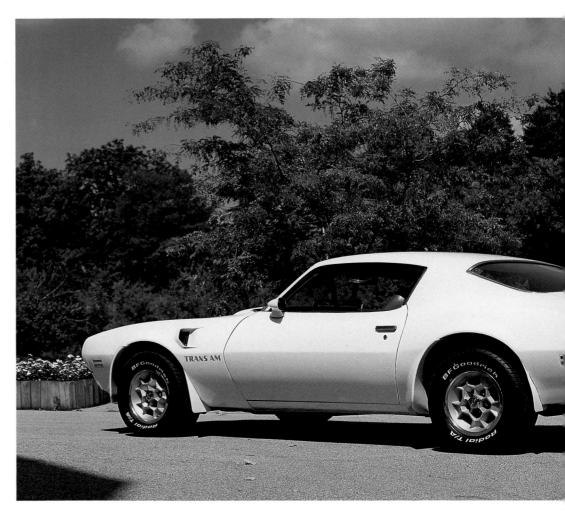

could possibly miss that huge "screaming chicken" decal which has since become the enduring symbol of the Firebird. The idea for the gigantic stick-on had originally come from chief designer Bill Porter and his assistant Wayne Vieira for a pair of show cars being prepared in 1970. However, GM's tyrannical head of styling, Bill Mitchell, took an instant dislike to the big bird and put a stop to it being used.

Bill Porter was promoted in '71 and in his place came young designer, John Schinella, who set about resurrecting the huge hood motif and managed to persuade Mitchell to accept it. Schinella redesigned the decal so it differed from the smaller version that had appeared on the nose of earlier cars and the Porter/Vieira design that Mitchell objected to. The name of the artist responsible for the very first rendition of the Firebird logo remains unknown, simply for the fact that it was copied from a mural on the wall at the airport of Phoenix, Arizona! But that initial design was far more traditional in execution and was only used as a small decorative feature on the fenders and rear of '68 and '69 models.

For a model that started out in 1967 as basically a Chevrolet Camaro with a nose job and a different rear end, the Firebird quickly developed its own separate identity, partly

**Above:** The Pontiac Firebird Trans Am came bedecked with spoilers, air dams, scoops and flares for '73, but in its best form – the SD-455 – it was capable of over 130mph and could handle corners well too. However, its braking capability was deemed to be rather marginal for such a high performance car.

thanks to some clever styling work – initially by Pontiac's head of design, Jack Humbert, followed by Bill Porter. Skillful engineering of the suspension and drivetrain, and the use of Pontiac's own range of engines helped to establish this identity all the more. However, the Pontiac powerplants did face one drawback when it came to calling the model, Trans Am, after the race series of the same name – the V8s were all of too big a capacity to run in the championship.

The highly successful Trans Am series was organized by the Sports Car Club of America (SCCA) and, in the 1960s, it attracted a lot of media attention and factory-backed entries of Ford Mustangs, Chevy Camaros, Mercury Cougars, AMC Javelins and others.

**Right:** The Trans Am's giant "screaming chicken" hood decal appeared for the first time in '73 and quickly became the trademark of all Firebird models. Designer John Schinella was responsible for getting the motif approved by GM's head of styling, Bill Mitchell.

But the 303 cu.in. maximum limit on engine size presented Pontiac with a problem in that their smallest production V8 displaced 350 cu.in. In a bid to get round the regulations, Pontiac co-operated with the T/G Racing Team of Jerry Titus and Terry Godsall who entered "Canadian" Firebirds (actually Camaros with Pontiac front sheet metal) equipped with Chevy 302 cu.in. engines. After a while, Pontiac produced a special destroked version of the 400 cu.in. engine and managed to convince SCCA officials that

this was going into series production, and so allowing them entry to the series. However, with this hurdle overcome, winning was to prove elusive.

As it happened, track success wasn't necessary for the Firebird Trans Am to be triumphant on the street and, after its low key introduction in '69, the model went on to evolve into a great American sports car. Bedecked with spoilers, air dams, hood scoops and flares, the Trans Am looked just like a race car should, and handled better

**Right:** The first major styling change to the Sting Ray came in '73 but the rear view of the Chevy didn't look much different from previous years. The famed LT1 high performance engine was dropped, and new top spec was a 454 cu.in. LS4 that produced 275bhp.

**Below:** The Sting Ray had urethane plastic covers over steel bumpers to comply with federally mandated "5mph" bumpers. The extra two inches in length was more acceptable than the 35 pounds in weight. Extra insulation reduced noise as the Corvette became more of a long-distance freeway cruiser.

than most of the competition too. From 1971 onwards, the only engine available was the 455 cu.in. V8 and, if by '73 its power had been strangled down to a meek-sounding 290 horsepower for the optional Super Duty version (250hp was standard), there was still sufficient "grunt" to give some seat-of-the-pants excitement when the right hand pedal was pushed to the floor in anger.

Exactly how well the people at Pontiac had preserved the Trans Am's performance in the face of the ever-increasing restrictive legislation can be judged by contemporary road test reports. Hot Rod magazine cranked out a 13.54 second quarter mile at 104 mph, while Car & Driver were only a fraction slower at 13.75 secs and 103 mph. These were impressive numbers by any standards, and Car & Driver also made the point that the '73 Trans Am was actually quicker than the 1970 version with 340 horsepower on tap. It is no wonder that the SD-455 has become something of a legend among Firebird enthusiasts ever since.

And it wasn't just the car's capability to go fast in a straight line that C&D liked; the Trans Am was just as quick off the mark when going round corners: "...the Trans Am's second most endearing quality – next to its ability to out-accelerate anything not assisted by a rocket motor – is handling". They were less than happy with the brakes on a car timed at 132 mph though, and suggested that the semi-metallic front brake pads from the heavy duty Police Package were a must. The report concluded: "The Firebird Trans Am is a genus of an automotive species approaching extinction. It could be the last of its kind. Just the car you need to carry you through the upcoming years of automotive sterility..." With the benefit of hindsight, perhaps it is only now that we can fully appreciate that this statement was really quite an amazing piece of prophetic writing.

The 1973 Pontiac Firebird Trans Am was virtually the final fling of the mass produced, cheap, high performance car for a couple of decades. And, even over twenty years later, it remains as an exceptional example of just how good an American sports coupe can be, no matter what obstacles are imposed by the law makers.

**Above:** In '73, full-sized cars like this Ford LTD 2-door hard top were pretty hefty animals, stretching to over 17 feet long and tipping the scales at nearly two tons. In retrospect, it's hard to believe that LTD was voted Car of the Year by Road Test magazine, but with over 941,000 full-size Custom/Galaxie/LTD models sold in 1973, there were obviously plenty of willing customers.

# 1974

In politics, 1974 was a year of change. Watergate had finally caught up with Richard Nixon, who resigned from the Presidency on August 8. His replacement, Vice President Gerald Ford, pardoned him a month later.

Another event of that year was the kidnapping of heiress Patty Hearst, who promptly joined her kidnappers to take part in a bank robbery. There was violence in Boston over the bussing of black students; and pioneer aviator Charles Lindberg died.

There was good news on the automotive front in that OPEC had lifted their oil embargo of the United States, but sadly it came too late to save the big-bodied, big-engined, gas-guzzling American automobile that so many had come to love. Faced with stringent exhaust emissions regulations and the rising price of gasoline, Detroit had no choice but to turn its back on the type of cars it had traditionally built. Intermediate models, compacts and sub-compacts with cleaner, smaller, more economical engines were the order of the day. While the majority of them would prove to be efficient means of transportation, few would have the sort of guts, glitz and sheer personality of what had gone before. The new 1974 models heralded the dawn of another era and, for a while, things looked bleak.

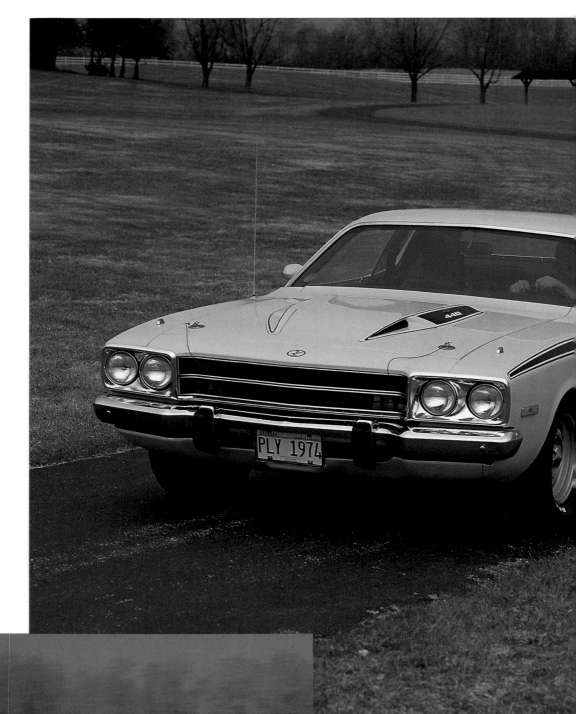

**Above:** Engine-wise, the top Road Runner option for 1974 was the four-barrel-equipped 440 cu.in. V8 that delivered 280 horsepower. The capacity of the engine was lettered on the hood, while bold stripes were applied to the sides and roof pillars. The 440 engine came with an automatic transmission only.

**Left:** The "fuselage" styling of the Satellite body certainly looked right for a muscle car, but by now these looks were more important than the raw power such cars used to deliver.

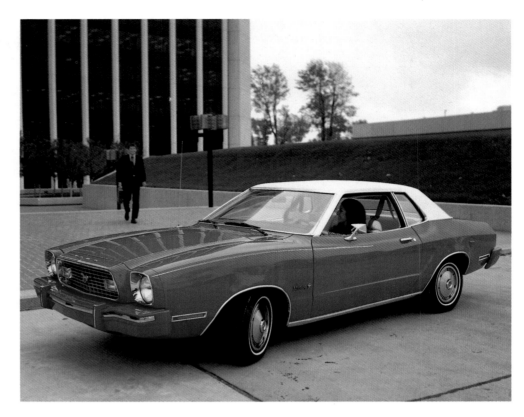

spectacular successes in NASCAR and drag racing helped boost sales. Included in the Dodge Scat Pack and Plymouth Rapid Transit System were the Dodge Super Bee and Charger, and the Plymouth GTX and Road Runner. But, by 1974, strangled by emissions equipment and dogged by high running costs, such cars were no longer selling well.

Typical of these Chrysler products was the Plymouth Road Runner. Based on the "fuse-lage-styled" Satellite body shell, it came with a 170 horsepower small-block 318 cu.in. V8 as standard, which had replaced its previous 400 cu.in. big-block engine in 1973. For the first time on the Road Runner, the engine was fitted with a two-barrel carburetor. The normal transmission was a three-speed manual, although a four-speed and automatic were options. Also optional were 360, 400 and 440 cu.in. engines.

By now, looks were more important than power, and the car sported bold contrasting stripes that curved down from the rear roof pillars and along the waist line to the front edges of the front fenders. Its looks may have promised more than its standard drivetrain could deliver but, nevertheless, it was the last true Road Runner. In 1975, it would be based on the small Fury, and after that merely an options package for the Volare.

A couple of familiar Dodge model names were dropped from the catalog listings during 1974. The Polara series was discontinued but, more significantly, the Challenger name also disappeared – it returned in 1978 on a Japanese import version, showing the direction things were headed.

**Above:** The shape of things to come. Ford's original muscle car, the Mustang, had already been transformed into its new, "more respectable" form. Mustang II was down in size, down on power and down in charisma. Some of the original styling cues were still there – the protruding grille, the side moldings and the running horse emblem – but it was not enough to give the car the raw excitement of the original. Nor were the engines: a 140 cu.in. overhead-cam four and a 171 cu.in. V6. In time, Mustang II would receive a V8 and various trim packages to make it look more aggressive but, even then, it would never match the car that started the race.

The muscle cars which had appeared with the Mustang a decade before were among the casualties. Some had already ceased production, while the rest would not linger for long.

Chrysler, through its Dodge and Plymouth divisions, had been a major contender in the muscle car wars for some years, building a range of machines based on its intermediate models. These were real fire-breathing street-'n'-strip monsters: no-frills quarter-mile machines with powerful engines, four-speed manual transmissions and beefed-up rear ends and suspensions. Engines included the awesome 425 horsepower 426 hemi V8 and the 390 horsepower 44 Six Pack engine, equipped with three two-barrel carburetors. The no-frills approach allowed Chrysler to price them for the younger market, while

# 1975

If there had ever been a competition to select the most unique car of the 1970s, a leading contender for the title would have to be the AMC Pacer. And, as with the Gremlin five years earlier, the American Motors Corporation's "Philosophy of Difference" was to pay handsome dividends initially. The Pacer was the first completely new model from AMC in some years, but the car that eventually made it into production was quite different from the model that was originally planned.

With its vast areas of glass and rounded styling, the Pacer is often referred to as a goldfish bowl and even the factory press release of the time called it "a car that breaks with automotive design tradition" – something of an understatement to say the least. Leaving the Pacer's unusual appearance aside for a moment, it was the engine under that steeply sloping short hood that created the problems for the independent AMC when deciding to bring such a radical car to the marketplace. The intention at the outset of the highly innovative project was that the Pacer should be front-wheel-drive and have a Wankel rotary engine, yet neither of these futuristic ideas made it into the finished car.

Although the Wankel was a very compact and powerful unit for its size, the problem was that the revolutionary engine couldn't achieve the sort of gas mileage figures that buyers were now looking for from smaller cars. Of course, AMC didn't have the research and development resources (or the finances) to build a rotary engine of its own from scratch, so the plan was to buy in engines from General Motors who were proposing to use the Wankel in a number of models. The oil crisis of '73 meant that GM dropped the rotary, which instigated the need for a major re-evaluation at American Motors.

They decided to take a step backward and

**Above:** A massive 'B' pillar was needed to accommodate the Pacer's unique arrangement of having the passenger door 4 inches wider than the driver's. A large rear liftgate provided easy access to nearly 30 cubic feet of carrying space with the rear seat folded down. Slot-style wheels were only available on the Pacer 'X', but an extensive list of optional extras were available and it is estimated that each Pacer sold had more than $1,000 worth of extras added to the advertised price of $3,299.

**Left:** AMC's 2-door Pacer was offered in three versions – a standard model, a sporty 'X' and the luxury D/L shown here. Its compact overall length of 171.5 inches combined with the width of a large car to give the Pacer's proportions the title of "the first wide small car". Under that bodyshell, however, was an old-fashioned straight-six engine and the standard transmission was a three-speed column shift. First year Pacer sales came close to 100,000, but declined thereafter.

shoehorn the reliable old 232 cu.in. straight-six engine into the Pacer, at the same time reverting to a traditional rear-wheel-drive format. While the drivetrain components were readily available from the AMC parts bin, squeezing them into the Pacer required considerable re-engineering and the bulkhead had to be completely revised. The six fitted, barely, with the rear sparkplug virtually inaccessible as it was hidden away under the cowl. Despite the retrograde running gear, some new technology survived, notably the rack and pinion steering and electronic ignition. Overdrive was offered as an optional extra.

However, it's styling that sells cars, and the Pacer's looks were guaranteed to create an enormous amount of interest. Billed as "the first wide small car", the Pacer sat on a 100 inch wheelbase (only 6 inches longer than a Volkswagen Beetle), but at 77 inches wide it was a whopping 16 inches more from side to side than the VW. In other words, the compact-length Pacer gave passengers the same internal space as an intermediate model like the Chevrolet Chevelle. The concept was the brainchild of AMC stylist Richard Teague, who overcame opposition within the company to pursue his vision for the car with

zealous determination.

Apart from the low beltline and obvious expanse of glass used in the design, one totally unique feature of the Pacer is the fact that the passenger door is nearly four inches longer than the driver's door! The idea behind this oddball arrangement was that it made for easier entry and exit, with door hinges that tilted outward as they opened to give even better access. A basic part of the body design was the massive 'B' pillar (described as having the same characteristics as a roll bar), which was used to connect the rear sub-assembly and the forward unit construction section together.

Announced at the Chicago Auto Show in March 1975, the Pacer created something of a sensation. Extensive media coverage had people flocking to the AMC showrooms and 96,769 Pacers were sold – the bubble-shaped car was an outstanding hit. Sadly, although the Pacer provided a much-needed boost to American Motors' sagging sales figures, it wasn't enough to prevent the company from recording a loss of $27.5 million, and things were set to get worse from then.

**Above:** The high-performance limited-edition Chevrolet Cosworth Vega engine featured 16-valves, a DOHC cylinder head, Bendix electronic fuel injection and stainless steel exhaust headers. It developed 120 horsepower from the 122 cu.in. four banger. With close-ratio four-speed manual transmission and heavy duty suspension, the Cosworth Vega was only available in black with gold highlights and matching wheels. Priced at almost double the base model, only 2,061 Cosworth variants were sold in '75. After more disappointing figures the model was dropped the next year.

**Below:** As far as full-sized Fords were concerned, in '75 a facelift produced a Mercedes-style grille on models like the LTD. All new cars were required to run on unleaded gasoline and most now came with catalytic converters. But big was no longer beautiful, and sales of Ford's heavyweights had halved in two years.

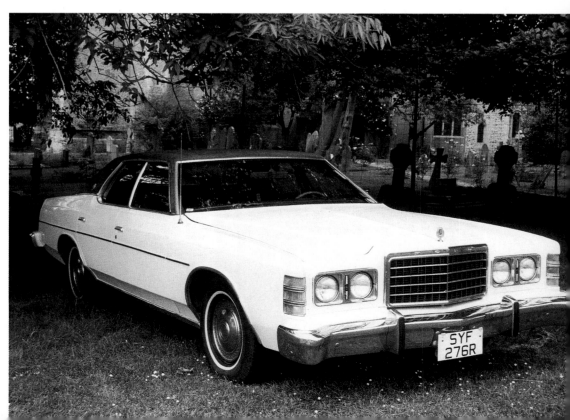

# 1976

This being the bicentennial, marking 200 years of American independence, the fourth of July took on an extra special significance and there were countless celebrations across the country to commemorate the occasion. But, as well as all the fireworks and parades, there were also quite a few departures in 1976: Oil tycoon J. Paul Getty died, as did eccentric billionaire Howard Hughes and film director Busby Berkeley. The death of Chinese leader Mao Tse-tung in September sparked off a power struggle in that vast nation. Meanwhile, in one of the closest elections of the century, Republican Gerald Ford was ousted from the White House when Democratic nominee Jimmy Carter was elected as President.

As far as the auto industry was concerned, there was one type of model that was due to become a thing of the past in '76 – the convertible. The demise of the ragtop had been widely predicted as a consequence of the increasingly vocal demands from consumer pressure groups for improved safety in car design and proposed federal roll-over strength regulations. Indeed, only one major manufacturer, Cadillac, still listed a convertible in their catalog, and the company declared that the 1976 Eldorado would be the last such model to be built.

This generated a huge amount of publicity and speculators clamored to buy the car, convinced it would become an instant "classic" that they would be able to sell on at a big profit. Some people did make money from buying and selling the Eldorado convertible,

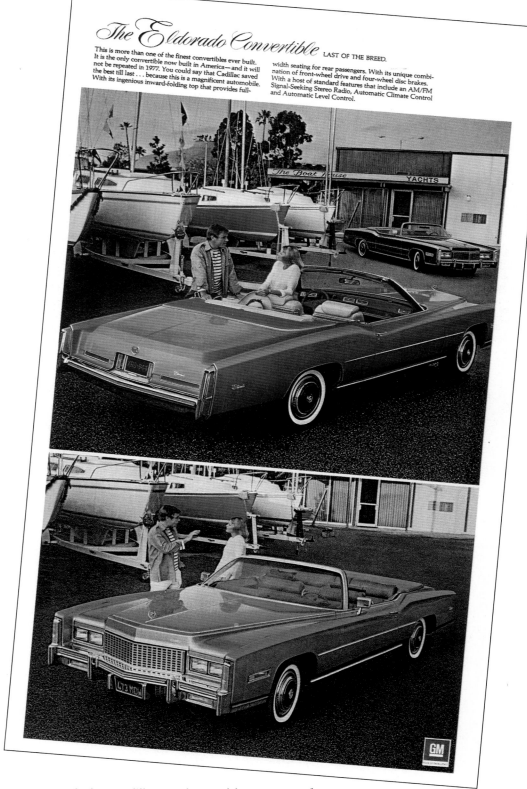

The Eldorado Convertible LAST OF THE BREED.

This is more than one of the finest convertibles ever built. It is the only convertible now built in America— and it will not be repeated in 1977. You could say that Cadillac saved the best till last ... because this is a magnificent automobile. With its ingenious inward-folding top that provides full-width seating for rear passengers. With its unique combination of front-wheel drive and four-wheel disc brakes. With a host of standard features that include an AM/FM Signal-Seeking Stereo Radio, Automatic Climate Control and Automatic Level Control.

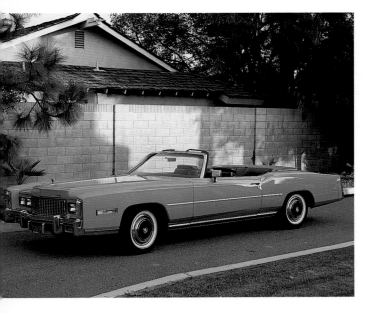

particularly Cadillac, who sold 14,000 of them – over 5,000 more than they produced the previous year.

If the Eldorado ragtop wasn't exactly rare in 1976, it wasn't the last convertible either. A number of specialists soon began offering to chop the roof off an Eldorado coupe and Cadillac themselves would bring the model back in 1984. Today the convertible can be found in just about every dealership. And although the Eldorado still sat on a full-size 126 inch wheelbase, stretched to more than 18 feet 8 inches in length, tipped the scales at well over 5,000 pounds and was powered by a 500 cu.in. V8 (the largest car engine in production), there were signs that the days of the mammoth Cadillac were numbered.

The most obvious indication that things

**Above and left:** Massively over-hyped and massive in almost every other sense, the Eldorado convertible was far from being "the last of the breed" as claimed by Cadillac in their advertising. Thanks to speculators trying to cash in on the model's "instant classic" status, prices zoomed to ridiculous heights before the bubble burst. In the meantime, this huge demand boosted sales by over 50% – immediately destroying the model's rarity value. Cadillac re-introduced a convertible in 1984, which also served to diminish the desirability of the gargantuan '76 ragtop.

**Above:** The dinosaur Cadillacs might not yet have been extinct, but the days of 500 cu.in. engines in cars weighing over 5,000 pounds were definitely numbered. The way ahead was shown by the downsized Seville, which brought European roadholding to the luxury market. Although more expensive than the mammoth models, the Seville sold extremely well and helped Cadillac to a new production record in '76. Padded vinyl roof used to cover up the uneven roof (a modified Chevy Nova panel) until 1977 models.

tomers, with over 44,700 built during '76. It helped to establish a new annual record total for the marque.

Based on the GM corporate 'X' platform and using an Oldsmobile-designed 350 cu.in. V8 equipped with electronic fuel injection, the downsized Seville was a refined package that offered European-style ride and performance combined with the luxury expected in a Cadillac. Acceleration time from zero to 60mph was 11.5 seconds, and it had a top speed of 115mph, but of almost equal importance was the fuel mileage statistic of 15-17mpg. Virtually all '76 Sevilles came with a vinyl-covered padded roof because it was easier to cover up the modified Chevrolet Nova panels on the assembly line rather than spend a lot of time getting the sheet metal smooth enough to be painted.

No doubt many of the bicentennial celebration parades included a new 1976 Eldorado convertible somewhere in the lineup and they will probably continue to appear in lots of future pageants. But the reality is that the only way this Cadillac could be considered as "the last convertible" is if it is positioned at the very rear of the motorcade.

were changing at Cadillac was the arrival of the Seville, introduced mid-year as a '76 model and on sale in the showrooms from May 1975. A thousand pounds lighter, 27 inches shorter and 8 inches narrower than a Sedan deVille, the Seville was designed to take on European luxury cars such as Mercedes. Despite being more expensive than the full-size Cadillacs (it was nearly $1,500 more than an Eldorado convertible) the Seville 4-door sedan found plenty of cus-

**Right:** The Corvette was only available as a coupe in '76 – the convertible had been dropped the previous year due to the threat of safety legislation outlawing ragtops, although the removable roof panels did allow open-top motoring. Thankfully, the ban never happened and convertibles are still on sale. That apart, the 1976 model 'Vette saw only small revisions to the preceding year, but it was a fairly lackluster version of a once great sports car.

# 1977

At first glance, if you were looking for an automotive styling or engineering revolution in '77, the last car you would consider would be the Lincoln Continental Mark V. Indeed, that initial look would probably have convinced you that the new Mark V was bigger – and therefore heavier – than ever before. But appearances can be deceptive and, although it is true that the overall length had increased by a couple of inches, the wheelbase remained unchanged at 120.4 inches; the weight was actually down by around 400 pounds when compared to the Mark IV of a year earlier.

By saving that amount of weight on a full-size family sedan you might expect to see some significant improvements in performance and gas mileage. However, even after putting the gigantic Lincoln luxury 2-door cruiser on a strict diet it still showed an unhealthy appetite for fuel, struggling to better 10 miles per gallon. The reason for this was twofold. Firstly, the Mark V was still a very heavy car, and could easily top 5,000 pounds by the time it was ready to hit the road. Secondly, the standard engine had

**Below:** The Ford LTD II arrived in 1977 as a replacement for the Torino and Elite models, but the A-bodied model was similar in shape and size. Ford promoted the newly-introduced version as "combining LTD's traditional high level of workmanship with Mustang's sporty spirit", but the standard engine was a 130 horsepower 302 cu.in. V8 with a two-barrel carburetor and SelectShift Cruise-O-Matic transmission. The LTD II was also the basis for the downsized Thunderbird, but that didn't seem to deter T-bird buyers.

been downsized to a 400 cu.in. V8 (an enlarged version of the 351 cu.in. Ford Cleveland unit) that produced just 181bhp when fitted with all the emission control equipment required in California. The 460 cu.in. engine, however, was still available as an option.

As far as the styling goes, the changes to the Continental Mark V could best be described as evolutionary rather than revolutionary. Its heritage was immediately identifiable, but designer Don DeLaRossa had cleverly accentuated the angularity of the lines by replacing rounded corners with sharp edges in key places. Other noticeable Mark V exterior features included three louvers introduced behind each front wheel arch, body side moldings dropped down by a few inches and the vertically arranged taillights.

Four model variations that did carry over were those in the special edition Designer Series. Renowned fashion designers Bill Blass, Cartier, Hubert de Givency and Emilio Pucci each gave their names to a model

**Above:** The Lincoln Continental Mark V was new in 1977, although in reality there was little about the model that could be described as being different from its predecessor. At a time when most cars were getting smaller, the Mark V actually grew two inches in length. However, there were some reductions – a marked saving in weight and the base engine was now "only" 400 cu.in., though the behemoth Lincoln remained a heavyweight gas guzzler. Even so, over 80,000 drivers were not to be denied and their choice helped keep a smile on the faces of the dealers.

finished in a distinctive body color and upholstery combination. The Cartier was fairly muted, using dove gray paint with a matching vinyl roof and leather interior, while the Givency came with metallic dark jade paintwork, chamois vinyl roof and dark jade leather. The Bill Blass used midnight blue paint and chamois, and the Pucci was painted in black diamond fire with white vinyl and leather. Other items fitted as standard on the Designer Series models were the gold-finished instrument panel, dual vanity mirrors and turbine-style aluminum wheels.

But if the bulky Mark V seemed to be slightly out of step with what was happening in the world, there were still plenty of people for whom "big was beautiful" and the Lincoln dealers found no less than 80,321 customers willing to pay for this gas guzzler. Less successful, by a long way, was Lincoln's belated 1977 answer to the Cadillac Seville – the Versailles. Based on the Ford Granada/Mercury Monarch platform, the Versailles only lasted until 1980 and never came close to

capturing the compact luxury market in the same way as the Seville.

Yet, even though the enormous Continental Mark V was an undoubted hit in 1977, the most worrying figure for the US auto industry was the 2.1 million imported vehicles that were flooding in to the country. This represented 20% of the sales total, and most of the foreign models were in the compact and subcompact market sectors where fuel-efficiency was more important than flashy special editions. This dominance caused Ford's small car factories to close early for the annual model changeover.

The giants on wheels might have been slow in disappearing from the freeways, but all too many giants of the entertainment world were departing and leaving huge gaps in American society that would prove impossible to fill. The biggest loss of all, and grieved around the globe, was when Elvis Presley died, aged 42, on August 16. Other icons who passed away were Bing Crosby, Charlie Chaplin and Groucho Marx.

# 1978

Facelifts were very much in vogue this year, along with changes of model names. Some manufacturers introduced new names on what were basically revamped versions of '77 models, while others brought back old names from the past. It was all part of an attempt to persuade the buying public that what they were looking at was something totally different from last year's model and, in most cases, it worked pretty well. Otherwise, the status quo remained very much as before. Chevrolet's production fell slightly, while Ford's increased, though not enough to topple Chevy from the number one position in the sales charts.

It was Ford's 75th Anniversary and they marked the event by introducing Diamond Jubilee editions of the Lincoln Mark V and Thunderbird. More pleasing to investors was the announcement of record profits in the first half of the year. The compact Fairmont was a newcomer to replace the ailing Maverick and sold extremely well, equaling the figures of the Mustang's first year. In addition, the Fiesta was shipped in from Europe to compete in the subcompact sector. However, Ford didn't enjoy a trouble-free '78 – there were recalls

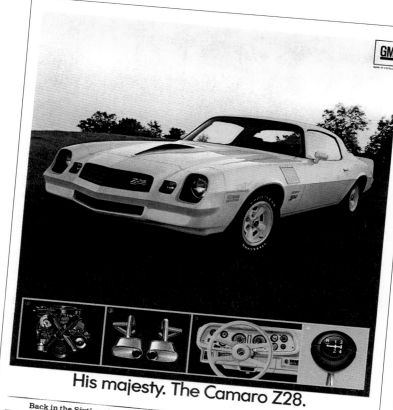

## His majesty. The Camaro Z28.

Back in the Sixties, the Camaro Z28 was a car that could attract an auto buff on just about any street corner in America. It was a King. Now, it's back. And it's still a King.

For 1978, Camaro Z28 bears a sleeker, sharper look, with a new bump-resistant front end and color-coordinated rear bumper styling.

Some of its hardware: ① 350 cu. in. 4-barrel V8. (Camaro is equipped with GM-built engines produced by various divisions. See your dealer for details.) ② Dual exhaust pipes. ③ Special Instrumentation. ④ Close-ratio 4-speed. (Automatic transmission required in California.)

Camaro comes in several other spirited models. Each offers a new option—removable glass roof panels. And each offers you that special Camaro road response.

**Chevrolet**

### SEE WHAT'S NEW TODAY IN A CHEVROLET.

for more than 4 million vehicles (including the infamous problem with exploding gas tanks on the Pinto), which damaged the company's reputation. And in June, Henry Ford II fired company president Lee Iacocca, which

**Left:** The Z28 certainly wasn't a new model in '78, but the final facelift of the second generation Camaro proved to be very successful and sales of hottest version tripled. Apart from a 350 cu.in. V8, the Z28 also came with uprated suspension, a hood scoop, front fender louvers and a rear spoiler. The twin hatch roof with lift-out panels in tinted glass was a new option for the Camaro, and the Z28 also came with a simulated string-wrapped steering wheel.

**Left:** The AMC Concord was little more than a made-over Hornet pushed upmarket and sold as a plush, but economical, compact family car with the slogan "The luxury Americans want – The size America needs". The 2-door sedan was the best-selling Concord model with a base price of $3749. It accounted for almost half of the 121,293 units produced, over 110,000 of which were powered by a six-cylinder engine. Curious styling of a small triangular side window and a thick B-post was presumably an attempt to disguise rather ancient Hornet body origins.

indirectly set in motion the resurgence of Chrysler after Iacocca took over the helm of that troubled organisation in November.

Over at Chevrolet, the second generation Camaro had received its third – and final – facelift, featuring a new grille and taillights with soft, integrated bumpers in the body color. The nose-job worked, and Camaro sales leapt to over 272,000 (up from 218,000 in '77), which was very encouraging, especially as this reworking was only an interim measure pending the arrival of a completely new model in 1982. Part of the Camaro's success was down to its ever-increasing list of optional extras, which included numerous choices of wheels and tires, power-assistance on almost everything and even a variety of radios. But probably the most important option included in '78 was the T-top with removable glass roof panels, at a cost of $625.

The Z28 Camaro had reappeared in '77 (having been dropped in 1974), but the 1978 version obviously caught the imagination of enthusiasts as sales multiplied more than threefold. The revised Z28 featured a hood scoop with a pointed throat highlighted black, functional louvers behind the front wheel arches, a rear spoiler and special graphics. Engine was a 350 cu.in. V8 with a four-barrel carb and dual exhaust that would put out 170 horsepower as sold in California, but 5-10bhp more in other states. Californian Z28s could also only be purchased with an automatic transmission, but a stick-shift was available elsewhere.

AMC were still down at the bottom of the ladder in 12th place but, thanks to their Jeep subsidiary, did better than expected. Of the four AMC model lines, three were virtually unchanged, while the compact Hornet was turned into a more luxurious car called the Concord. It became AMC's best seller of the year but the rest of the range continued to decline and the company began negotiations with French auto-maker Renault with a view to arranging a co-operation deal. This agreement would culminate in Renault becoming a major stockholder in AMC by the end of 1979.

One thing that affected all manufacturers in 1978 was the implementation of the Corporate Average Fuel Economy (CAFE) regulations that specified each company should achieve a set fuel economy figure across its entire model range. The standard set in '78 was 18 miles per gallon, with a target of 27.5 mpg to be reached in ten years time.

# 1979

The year started with President Jimmy Carter announcing "a crisis of confidence" in a half-hour television address to the nation during which he unveiled a six-point plan to combat America's wasteful consumption of oil. His statement was precipitated by the Organisation of Petroleum Exporting Countries (OPEC) increasing the price of a barrel of oil by almost 25% in three months. Carter's conservation program was designed to reduce oil imports and speed up the development of alternative methods of producing energy, with the target of saving 4.5 million barrels of oil a day by the end of the next decade.

Unfortunately, one of the possible alternative sources of energy – nuclear power – suffered a major setback following a disaster at the Three Mile Island facility in Pennsylvania. The accident, caused by a faulty cooling system, released radioactive gases and further reinforced the protests by anti-nuclear campaigners.

In addition to the energy problems, President Carter was also facing difficulties in the financial sector, with soaring inflation and wildly fluctuating interest rates adding to his worries. The consumer price index jumped by 13.3%, the biggest rise for 33 years, and many Wall Street investors lost money as trading leapt to record levels. U.S. Steel closed ten factories, laying off 13,000 workers in the process. The struggling company had been forced to rationalize its operations in the face of fierce competition from overseas and the hefty $1.8 billion expenditure needed to bring plants into line with clean-air regulations.

It wasn't all bad news for Carter, though. He managed to broker a peace deal in the Middle East, bringing the leaders of Egypt and Israel together to sign a treaty at the White House. Carter also signed the SALT II agreement with the USSR to limit strategic missiles.

As far as the automobile industry was concerned, the big story of the year was the decision by Congress to approve a loan of $1.5 billion to rescue the Chrysler Corporation from bankruptcy. Although there were plenty of commentators in Detroit and the media elsewhere who were happy to let Chrysler die, they reckoned without the dedication and determination of the charismatic Lee Iacocca who had taken charge of the company a year earlier. Thanks to his efforts,

**Above:** The third-generation of Ford Mustang arrived in 1979 and the new shape proved to be an immediate hit, boosting model sales by over 80%. Pace cars used for the Indy 500 race used highly modified 302 cu.in. V8 engines, but replicas sold to the public could have either a turbo four-cylinder or a 5-liter V8. Front air dam with integral foglamps, non-functional rear-facing hood scoop and sunroof were standard features on Pace Car models, together with a special paint scheme, but the factory left lettering decals to be affixed by the dealer or the customer.

a deal was thrashed out with the unions for wage cuts and deferred payments to pension funds in order to safeguard the jobs of 150,000 employees, and this agreement helped to secure the government aid.

Iacocca also initiated a morale-boosting campaign using the slogan "We Can Do It!" that not only created confidence throughout Chrysler's workforce – leading to noticeably improved build quality in production – but also gave customers the belief that he would restore the fortunes of the ailing company.

Meanwhile, on the other side of Motor City in Dearborn, Iacocca's old company Ford were launching the third-generation of Mustang. The bare bones of the concept for this version were actually laid down prior to the arrival of the Mustang II in '74, and began as an attempt to come up with a "world car" – in other words, a design that could be built in Ford factories around the world, with only small variations needed to take care of local requirements. As it turned out, the problems associated with the idea proved insurmountable at that time, but some of the original principles set out for a compact, fuel-efficient car, remained.

As they had done previously, Ford gave the task of producing design proposals for the new Mustang to a number of styling studios – three in the USA and Ghia in Italy (owned by Ford and headed by Don DeLa Rossa). Certain fixed parameters were issued to the design teams, including wheelbase, overall length, width, and so on, and using these limits they each had to come up with drawings and models for wind tunnel testing. As a result of this work a number of full-size

**Right:** A rear spoiler was another item fitted to the Pace Car replica. The third generation Mustang was available as what Ford called a 2-door sedan or a 3-door hatchback in '79; a convertible didn't arrive until the '83 model. Almost 2.5 million Mustangs were sold between 1979 and 1992, with only minor changes made to the front and rear of the body.

# THE AMERICAN AUTOMOBILE

mockups were generated for consideration by the Ford hierarchy. The design chosen was that produced by Jack Telnack's group at the company's North American Light Car and Truck Design department. Telnack had earlier spent some time at Ford·Europe and his experience of designing smaller cars was to prove invaluable. From the outset, Telnack's team (which included Fritz Mayhew, David Rees and Gary Haas) looked at ways of making the new Mustang as aerodynamic as possible. This was rather than creating a stylish shape and then modifying it in the wind tunnel to make it more efficient as had been

**Left:** Full-sized Chryslers became a thing of the past, while the Cordoba was promoted as "the contemporary classic". The first use of the 300 nameplate since 1971, the Cordoba 300 package included bucket seats, blacked-out grille, special trim, a 195 horsepower 360 cu.in. V8 and uprated suspension. Adding over $2,000 to the base price of around $6,000, it's no wonder only 3,811 of the Spinnaker White-painted 300 models were sold.

**Left:** A restyled front end came along for the Pontiac Firebird in '79, with two large grilles set low down in the bumper and quad recessed rectangular headlamps positioned above. The Red Bird trim package was an attractive option that included two-tone red paint and custom interior. Pontiac enjoyed one of its best years ever, building nearly a million cars over the 12 months.

**Below:** The Jeep Cherokee got a new grille with rectangular headlamps and a more substantial-looking front bumper, the first changes made to the model since it appeared five years earlier. Apart from these alterations, the boxy wagon remained much as before. After a couple of years of increasing sales, poor economic conditions saw the popularity of big four-wheel-drive vehicles taking a dive and production had to be cut back at the Toledo factory.

done in the past. The result was a drag coefficient of 0.44 for the 3-door fastback and 0.46 for the 2-door notchback – not terribly impressive by modern standards, but a major step forward in 1979.

Like almost any trend-setting design, the success of the Mustang came about from the stylists breaking the rules. The car's slim, wedge-shaped front end was accentuated by the rake of the hood – a feature Telnack's team achieved by ignoring one of the so-called "hard points", the height of the cowl. To get the effect they wanted, the cowl was raised an inch above the dimension for the Fairmont/Zephyr platform that was being used as the basis for the new model. Despite protests from the production engineers, the cost of manufacturing the special items brought about by this change was quickly approved. The integrated spoiler under the front bumper and a small lip on the rear deck-lid were aerodynamic aids that also added to the overall effect.

The new Mustang came with the usual choice of engines, starting with a 2.3-liter four cylinder putting out 88bhp, a turbo version that produced 140bhp, a 109bhp 170 cu.in. V6 and the 302 cu.in V8 that produced 140 horsepower. Later in the model year, problems in obtaining sufficient quantities of the

German-built V6 saw the return of the old 200 cu.in. inline six. Prices started at $4,494 for a 2-door coupe with a four-cylinder engine, with a 3-door hatchback listed at $4,828. You could also get Ghia and Cobra versions.

That the Mustang's new shape proved to be extremely popular is evident by the fact that production went up from around 180,000 in '78 to over 332,000 this year, elevating the model to number 7 in the 1979 sales charts (up from number 22 the previous year). Another acknowledgement of the Mustang's significance came when it was chosen as the Official Pace Car for the Indianapolis 500 – Ford built something like 6,000 replicas.

But possibly the most significant thing about the third-generation Mustang was that it went on to establish itself as one of the most potent drag strip performers of the 1980s. The V8 was briefly discontinued, but quickly made a comeback, and throughout the following decade a whole new industry grew up providing parts for enthusiasts who wanted their Mustang to go quicker. The '79 Mustang might not have created the same sort of sensation as was seen in '64, but if Jimmy Carter was looking for something that could give America confidence in the future, maybe he should have visited his local Ford dealership.

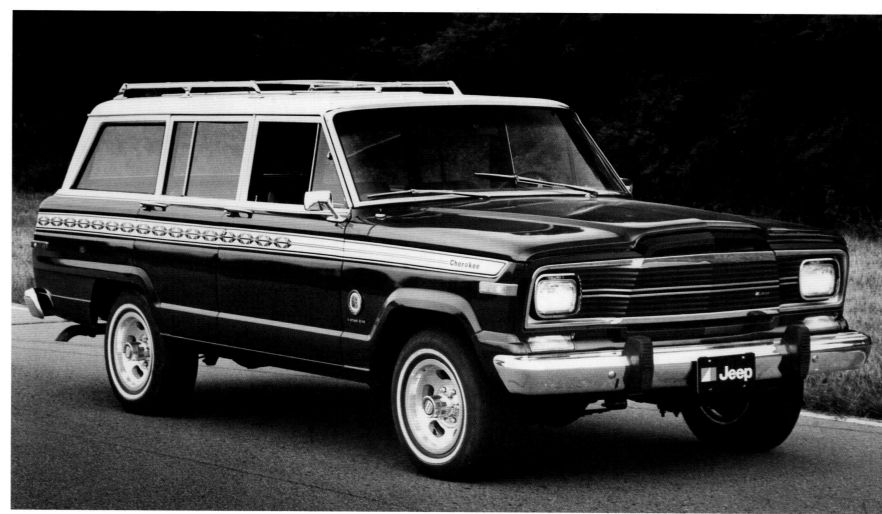

# 1980

If 1979 was a bad year, 1980 was even worse. A mixture of an economy in recession and inflation wreaked havoc across the whole auto industry. Ford were the worst affected, outsold 2 to 1 by Chevrolet and recording a $1.54 billion loss. Henry Ford II resigned as chairman and, for the first time in

**Left:** The front view of Seville is probably the least interesting, but it still retains all the elements of a classic Cadillac design. Sadly, the assertion in the sales catalog that "Through the years, Cadillac has earned for itself an exclusive place... a solitary niche...in the pantheon of the world's truly fine automobiles" was rather let down by the troublesome 350 cu.in. diesel engine fitted as standard.

the company's history, there was no longer a member of the Ford family in charge. Someone else who wouldn't be in charge for much longer was President Jimmy Carter, his popularity undermined by the financial crisis. Republican Ronald Reagan enjoyed a landslide victory in November, making Carter the first elected President to lose an election since Franklin D. Roosevelt defeated Herbert Hoover in 1932 – coincidentally at the beginning of the Great Depression.

The designers and planners working in the

Motor City couldn't help but be influenced by what was going on around them, but the new models they had produced were created well in advance and a couple of automotive gems arrived on the scene in 1980. Wayne Cady's dramatic restyling of the Cadillac Seville was initially not to everyone's taste, but the bustle-back rear deck endowed the car with character and marked it out as a special model that was instantly recognizable as coming from the luxury marque. Unfortunately, under that distinctive Seville bodywork there was one

**Above:** The restyled 1980 Seville was one of the last projects overseen by GM styling chief Bill Mitchell before he retired in 1977. The use of bustle-back design harked back to the razor-edged Rolls-Royces produced by Hooper and Vanden Plas in the 1950s. Although its distinctive appearance was not wholeheartedly welcomed at first, the Seville quickly established itself as a quintessential Cadillac.

particular problem for Cadillac – and it involved the engine.

For the first time ever, a diesel engine was standard in a Cadillac, but the 350 cu.in. V8 fitted into the Seville proved to be a rather troublesome unit. Not only that, it took 19 seconds for the diesel-powered Seville to lumber to 60mph – some 8.5 seconds slower than the '75 model. With the normal 6-liter (368 cu.in.) gasoline engine in place, the front-wheel-drive Seville was in a class of its own, but a number of price increases during the year saw the basic cost of the model escalate by over a thousand dollars and, by the summer, it had reached a whopping $21,000. Reflecting the difficult economic times, Cadillac's overall sales slumped by 30%.

At the other end of the scale, AMC carried out another of their "mix and match" juggling acts and, by combining the body and chassis of the Concord with a four-wheel-drive system from the Jeep, came up with the Eagle. This unique 4x4 car established a hitherto untapped market niche at very little tooling cost but, despite extensive coverage in the media, it failed to sell as well as AMC predicted. In addition, the quirky Pacer had had its day and was dropped to cut costs. Even so, by the end of the year AMC's losses amounted to a staggering $197,525,000.

Production of cars across the industry was hit badly, the total figure of 6.4 million units being some two million less than in 1979, and over 3.2 million down on the record set in '73. Truck manufacturing was similarly devastated – at under 1.6 million, it was little better than half of the '79 figure.

# 1981

In December 1980, Lee Iacocca announced to the press that "1981 belongs to Chrysler, because no other American car company is better equipped to meet the new market requirements of the eighties than the New Chrysler Corporation". His confidence was partly based on the fact that Chrysler was the only auto manufacturer to record an increase in sales during that month compared to the same period in 1979. The rise might have been a very small 2.6% but, put against the 6.2% loss of sales by GM and the even worse

Closer to the October launch date, another catch-phrase was adopted: "America is not going to be pushed around any more". Together with the prominent use of the emotive red, white and blue colors, this new slogan sent out a dual message. The first part emphasized the fact that the K-cars were ultra-modern front-wheel-drive models and pulled the vehicle along, rather than pushing it as in the traditional arrangement that drove the rear wheels. The second was meant to demonstrate Chrysler's commitment to building small cars in America and that the company was not going to hand over this important market sector to foreign imports without a fight.

Today, the K-cars' specification looks like pretty basic stuff. The shape was almost utilitarian, with very squarish styling, and the

**Below:** The Plymouth Reliant K-car arrived in a blaze of publicity. One of the slogans used to promote the new front-wheel-drive model was: "The American way to beat the pump", majoring on the car's fuel economy at a time of rising gas prices. The four cylinder 2.2-liter engine produced an official EPA rating of 25mpg in city driving and, although a compact, the Reliant (and the Dodge Aries sister model) could accommodate up to six passengers. The custom 4-door shown was the middle-priced version of the three models in the Reliant series, with the Special Edition being the most expensive.

12.6% drop for Ford, the gain was significant.

The flagships of the new Chrysler fleet leading this revival were the front-wheel-drive K-cars – the Plymouth Reliant and Dodge Aries. But it wasn't just the arrival of a couple of new models that turned the tide. It was also due to Iacocca's innovative marketing programs that had earlier cleared thousands of old models from stock and then continued by making people aware that things were on the mend at Chrysler. In July '80, a promotional campaign had been launched with the slogan "K-cars are coming" and this was repeated nationwide in newspaper adverts and on radio and television.

**Right:** Chrysler wasn't only selling economy cars in 1981– the luxury Imperial was another new model introduced that year. Frank Sinatra featured in a television commercial and a number of press adverts interviewing Lee Iacocca about the company's products. With its bustle-back styling and vertical grille, the Imperial drew immediate comparisons with the Cadillac Seville, but priced at $18,300 only 7,225 of these limited-edition Chryslers were sold. The Imperial used a fuel-injected 318 cu.in. V8 and had only one optional extra – a powered moonroof priced at £1,044. Everything else was included as standard.

**Left:** One advantage the Chrysler K-car had over compact rivals from General Motors was having a station wagon in the lineup, though the Reliant wagon was only available in the Custom and Special Edition series. The Plymouth Reliant had a small 99.6 inch wheelbase but squared-off styling made it look like a much bigger car. In fact, the Reliant was two feet shorter and half a ton lighter than the Volare model it replaced.

# The Chairman of the Board tells "The Chairman of the Board" why it's time for Imperial.

*Lee Iacocca talks to Frank Sinatra about the future of luxury cars in America.*

On July 18, 1980 Frank Sinatra, the entertainment industry's "Chairman of the Board," joined Lee A. Iacocca, Chairman of the Board of The New Chrysler Corporation, at the first public exhibition of America's newest luxury car, the 1981 Imperial.

This new Imperial is an unusually timely automobile, newer than its competitors and, in significant ways, substantially different from them; it is these differences that make the Imperial the unique automobile it is.

After opening the exhibition and viewing the new Imperial, Sinatra and Iacocca spent some time discussing what America needs in a luxury car today and how this new Imperial fills those needs.

**Sinatra:** When you build a luxury car, where do you start? How do you lay down the specs?
**Iacocca:** You try to build a luxury car that's better than the competition. Say you take your leading potential competitor and you might say, 'I'm going to give a customer 105 percent of this guy's riding comfort. Or 100 percent of his cornering ability.' You can set your sights on what the people are already buying.
**Sinatra:** Is that what you did?
**Iacocca:** Sure. But our standards for this Imperial were based more on what the people need today than on what the competition is giving them. You know, times have changed in the automobile business.
**Sinatra:** You mean the energy crunch.
**Iacocca:** Partly. That's why today you have to try to build a car that's the right kind of car for now and, hopefully, for tomorrow as well. Now, you've owned a lot of cars.
**Sinatra:** You'd better believe it.

**Iacocca:** What do you think today's luxury car should be?
**Sinatra:** I don't know where to start.
**Iacocca:** Start with the way it should look.
**Sinatra:** Well, first of all, I'd want it to look simple. I think things are getting cleaner and simpler looking and that's how it should be.
**Iacocca:** Agreed. That's why we tried to keep the Imperial as uncluttered as possible.
**Sinatra:** The shape is very clean.
**Iacocca:** It's what we call slippery.
**Sinatra:** Slippery?
**Iacocca:** Slips through the air. In the wind tunnel they give it a number they call a drag coefficient. Tells you how aerodynamic the car is. The lower the number, the better.
**Sinatra:** Well, you've come out of the wind tunnel with a very elegant looking automobile.
**Iacocca:** What pleases me more is that the

styling actually helps the car perform the way you need a car to perform these days.
**Sinatra:** Fine, but what about the things I can't see? What about engineering? You guys had a big reputation for engineering.
**Iacocca:** I believe we're still ahead. But engineering a car has changed radically.
**Sinatra:** Come on, Lee, this country can put a man on the moon, but we can't build an automobile right. Where's our technology when it comes to things we use every day?
**Iacocca:** I hear you. But I've been in this business a lot of years and when I look at the new Imperial, I see an electronic marvel.

*"...when I look at the new Imperial, I see an electronic marvel."*

**Sinatra:** An electronic marvel? What does that mean?
**Iacocca:** Okay. You mention the space program. Our electronics division down in Huntsville, Alabama, was a prime contractor on the Redstone missile and the Saturn

2.2-liter overhead camshaft Trans4 engine (rated at 84 horsepower) was the first four cylinder built by Chrysler for nearly half a century. But the Plymouth Reliant was two feet shorter and almost half a ton lighter than the Volare model it replaced. Its EPA figure of 25 mpg for city driving was probably the most important statistic of all. The Reliant also had another advantage over GM's X-body rivals in that there was a station wagon in the lineup, over 50,000 of which were sold in the first year alone. Sales of Reliant coupes and sedans added up to just over 100,000 units; and when you add in the 155,000 Dodge Aries models that were also produced, it highlights the huge impact that the K-cars made on the fortunes of Chrysler.

Ford, on the other hand, were in dire straits. Output fell to around a million units –

the worst annual total for the company since 1958 – and the company was nearly overtaken by Oldsmobile for second place in the sales charts. Losses amounted to $1.06 billion, and about the only bright spot in this very gloomy period was the arrival of the front-wheel-drive Escort compact model. Developed as an "international size" car, the Escort was built in five different countries with small variations to suit local regulations. In the USA it immediately proved to be a winner, easily outselling its ill-fated Pinto predecessor. Escort sales for '81 topped 284,000 units and the smaller-sized Granada model (actually a re-styled Fairmont) also did well. The problem for the company was that the remainder of the range suffered badly – Mustang sales dropped by a third and Thunderbird numbers halved.

# 1982

The recession was finally beginning to bottom out, but there were still some hard times ahead before any noticeable improvements in prosperity would be apparent. In February, President Ronald Reagan announced that the deficit in the forthcoming fiscal year would amount to a staggering $91.5 billion and proposed a program of increased taxation and severe reductions in federal spending. By the end of the year the deficit had risen to over $110 billion, the unemployment rate was 10.8%, industry was working at two-thirds of full capacity, and the number of people classified as being below the poverty line had risen to the highest level since 1967. Interest rates still remained high, yet housing construction and car sales began to show signs of a slight recovery.

One auto company to disappear was De Lorean. Set up in Northern Ireland with substantial UK government grants by the former General Motors executive John De Lorean, the company built a futuristic gull-wing sports car. However, annual production and sales of the model never came close to the 20,000 units forecast. After De Lorean went out of business, many questions were raised about mismanagement of the business. The car was immortalized as Michael J. Fox's time machine in the movie Back to the Future.

The economic recession was being felt around the world and set against this somber background, the arrival of the third-generation Chevrolet Camaro was hardly likely to raise much attention outside the automotive press, but the new model did create a few headlines. Selected as *Motor Trend* magazine's Car

of the Year, the Camaro enjoyed a great first year, selling a very impressive 189,747 units despite only being introduced in February '82. And, for the third time, the Camaro was chosen as the Indianapolis 500 Pace Car, with 6,360 replicas of the Z28 sold to the public.

With an increasing trend towards the use of front-wheel-drive on new models in the '80s it might seem peculiar that the Camaro remained with the traditional front-engine, rear-wheel-drive configuration. A change to front-wheel-drive was considered, but the engineers decided that if the V8 engine was to be retained (and there were plenty of good reasons for keeping the V8) then the only sensible solution was to keep things as they were. That didn't mean that there weren't many changes made to the third-generation. Far from it. The '82 Camaro was almost ten inches shorter than the '81, had a seven-inch shorter wheelbase and was 2.8 inches narrower. A 500 pound weight reduction and fuel economy stipulations saw a four-cylinder engine offered in the Camaro for the first time – the 155 cu.in. Iron Duke from Pontiac.

**Left:** Based on the Chevy Cavalier and Buick Skyhawk J-cars, the Cimarron introduced in 1982 was definitely not one of Cadillac's better ideas. It was intended to compete against the likes of the BMW 320i, Audi 5000 and Saab 900 but, despite the air conditioning and genuine leather seats, the four-cylinder Cimarron didn't appeal to buyers of upmarket imports and was out of step with the tastes of traditional Cadillac owners. While it may not have been a bad car, the Cimarron was definitely the wrong car.

**Left:** Chevrolet announced that they would offer six thousand replicas of the Camaro Z28 1982 Indianapolis 500 Pace Car for sale, with each Chevy dealer given the opportunity to order one of the "Commemorative Edition" models. The replicas were finished in silver and blue, with Indy 500 graphics, sport mirrors and the red highlights on the five-spoke aluminum wheels, but didn't have the roof-mounted lights or chequered flags on the back. "Commemorative Edition" Camaros could be specified with either a carbureted or fuel injected 5.0-liter V8, and manual or automatic transmission, and they were all built at the Van Nuys, California assembly plant in March and April of '82.

Other engines available were a 173 cu.in. V6 of 102 horsepower, and a couple of 305 cu.in. (5.0-liter) V8s. The standard Z28 V8 engine came with a single four-barrel carburetor and put out 145 horses, while the optional fuel injected version was rated at 165hp.

The Camaro was offered in three basic models: the economy Sport Coupe, the luxurious Berlinetta and the high performance Z28. Each was trimmed differently, the Z28 being easily identifiable by having no grille openings above the bumper line and extra air dams on the front and sides. The third-generation Camaro proved to be so successful initially that it stayed pretty much unchanged (apart from juggling with option lists and minor alterations to model specifications) through to 1992. But it was the years to 1987 that were most successful, with 1.1 million Camaros sold in total. Thereafter, only 412,000 were purchased in the final five years. These later years saw the Camaro produced solely at the Van Nuys, California assembly plant following the closure of the Norwood, Ohio factory in '87. In '92 the Van Nuys facility closed and Camaro production transferred to Canada.

**Above:** From time to time, there have been all sorts of styling oddities used by designers, but one of the most superfluous must be the way part of the rear quarter panel was incorporated into the door on the Chrysler LeBaron. Surprisingly, this curious feature was to remain in use for several years on various Chrysler models. In common with many other smaller cars on the market, the downsized '82 LeBaron was powered by a four-cylinder engine.

**Left:** The growing popularity of minitrucks among the younger generation caused a number of examples to be produced. The Dodge Rampage was the first front-wheel-drive pickup to be offered by one of Detroit's "Big Three" and shared the front-end styling of the Dodge Charger. In addition to the base High Line, there was also a Sport version with two-tone paint and graphics.

# 1983

To most people, this year marked the return of the convertible. Of course, to all intents and purposes, the convertible had never gone anywhere at all – although the major auto-makers had dropped the model from their lineups in the '70s, there were always a number of specialist companies who would custom-build a ragtop from almost any make or model if the price was right. Quite a few cars also came with removable roof panels which, if not exactly true convertibles, at least retained the idea of driving with the wind in your hair. When the impending safety legislation that was supposed to outlaw the convertible failed to materialize, a couple of manufacturers almost simultaneously decided they would bring back the ragtop.

Apart from the fact that they both had classic fold-down tops, the two offerings were about as far apart in the automotive spectrum as it is possible to get. The Ford Mustang convertible marked a return to the sporty, front-engine, rear-drive, ultimate fun car ethos of the Sixties, whereas the Chrysler LeBaron Town & Country Convertible was truthfully described in advertisements as "...like no other car on the road today". The front-wheel-drive, "woody"-styled Town & Country actually harked back to a Chrysler model of the late 1940s and was intended as an out-and-out luxury car.

While the Mustang convertible may have been listed as an "official" Ford model, it was actually built by an outside company. After assembly at Dearborn, completed notchback coupes were shipped to Cars & Concepts of Brighton, Michigan, for conversion and installation of interior trim. Sold as either a GLX with a 3.8-liter V6 engine or a GT with the 302 cu.in. (5.0-liter) V8, the ragtop 'Stang also featured a glass backlight, roll-down quarter windows and a power top. Factory price for a GLX convertible began the year at a touch under ten thousand dollars, but jumped to $12,467 after a few months.

The Town & Country wasn't the only LeBaron convertible introduced in '83. There was also a base model and a luxury Mark Cross version, but it was with the "woody" that Chrysler said it was "re-introducing an American classic". Unlike the original, however, the '83 had a fake white ash wooden frame on the body and a 2.2-liter four-cylinder engine under the hood plus Torqueflite auto-

**Above:** "Chrysler brings back the romance of the past with the luxury and technology of the present in the Town & Country Convertible" said the advertisements. The "woody" look was a re-creation of the famous wood-frame exterior used in the late 1940s, but the plush '83 ragtop had a 94 horsepower, 2.2-liter, overhead cam four-cylinder engine under the hood and not a 114 bhp, 250 cu.in L-head six.

**Below:** Movie star Ricardo Montalban was just one of the celebrities used to front Chrysler television commercials and he also featured in newspaper and magazine adverts. The 1983 LeBaron Town & Country Convertible was half the size of the earlier Town & Country classic but twice as fuel efficient. The rebirth of the ragtop brought Chrysler plenty of good publicity and much better sales than forecast, though the "woody" was the least popular of the three versions on offer.

matic transmission. The power convertible top came with zip-down window and weather-seal sides, and there was also a tailored top boot. The LeBaron Town & Country convertible carried a factory price of $15,595 and promised buyers that "No indulgence has been overlooked.'" While that statement was a rather ambitious one, the car was undoubtedly unique to America.

Sales of the two ragtops were directly opposite to the fortunes of the respective companies. When Chrysler re-introduced the convertible they forecast sales of around 3,000 units and hoped to break even, but it was the publicity that would be generated by the ragtop that was the attraction. By the end of the '83 model year, a total of 9,891

**Right:** The new 10th generation Thunderbird had modern aero styling that was, according to the Ford catalog, "Conceived for today with an eye on tomorrow". The wheelbase was reduced by 4 inches (to 104 inches) and the choice of engines was of either a 232 cu.in. (3.8-liter) V6 or the fuel injected 302 cu.in. (5.0-liter) V8. A turbocharged 2-3-liter four also became available during the year. Thanks to the redesign, total T-Bird sales jumped threefold to nearly 122,000.

**Below:** Ford was another marque to bring back the convertible, but the Mustang was converted from a coupe by Cars & Concepts, not built on the assembly line at Dearborn. Available with either a V6 or V8 engine, the price of a Mustang ragtop increased sharply during year and was up by a whopping 25% in a few months. A restyled front end improved the aerodynamics but otherwise the Mustang remained much as before.

LeBaron convertibles had been sold – 5,441 were Mark Cross versions and 1,520 had the Town & Country package installed. Mustang sales for '83 were 23,438, and while Ford hung on to second spot in the sales charts, they slipped to fourth in terms of production numbers behind Oldsmobile and Buick – the first time Ford hadn't been in the top two since 1905. Ford had the best-selling car in the country with the compact Escort and it launched an exciting new Thunderbird, but it was still losing money.

Chrysler, on the other hand, had increased its market share and was making substantial profits – so substantial that Lee Iacocca was able to pay back its government loan in full, seven years early. A proposal for a merger between Chrysler and Ford was made in 1981, but rejected out of hand by the Ford management, who must have had second thoughts about that decision on more than one occasion during this period.

# 1984

As long as examples of the Fiero survive, people will continue to argue whether the Pontiac two-seater was a classic in the making that got prematurely killed off by the accountants or merely an expensive failure that was put on sale before it was fully developed. The truth probably lies somewhere in the middle of these two extremes.

There had, in actual fact, been ideas for a Pontiac sports car bouncing around the division's engineering and styling departments since the early '60s but, apart from a couple of concept cars on the auto show circuit, nothing had come of these proposals. One example of this was back in 1966. As a response to the runaway success of the Ford Mustang, John DeLorean tried to win approval from his GM masters for a two-seater Pontiac for the 1967 model year, but he had to be satisfied with the Firebird — basically a restyled Chevy Camaro with a Pontiac engine.

Although the genesis of the Fiero dates back to around '75, credit for providing the required impetus to get the project moving goes to Bob Stempel, who became Pontiac's general manager in 1978. Stempel's reasoning wasn't based upon producing a mid-engined, high performance sports model but rather a fuel-efficient commuter car to combat the projected escalation of gas prices and likely disappearance of models like the Firebird as a consequence of future government legisla-

tion. This resulted in an immediate conflict as to exactly how the Fiero should turn out.

Another problem was the lack of finance. Stempel had left Pontiac in 1980, to be replaced by William E. Hoglund. Immediately after taking over, Hoglund was informed that there would be very limited funds made available for the Fiero project. The whole auto industry was suffering during the early '80s, with record losses being recorded all round, and these were not the best conditions for

**Above:** The Fiero SE was the top of the range version and came with special WS6 performance handling package and rear deck luggage rack as standard. It also had P215/80R13 tires and a padded Formula steering wheel. Despite costing $1,500 more than the base model, the SE was the top-selling Fiero in '84.

**Left:** On its debut, the Fiero 2M4 (the designation stood for two-seat, mid-engine, four cylinder) seemed to put some real meaning into the Pontiac slogan "We Build Excitement". Unfortunately, lack of development and disappointing performance meant that the excitement soon died out.

trying to get sufficient money allocated to develop a completely new type of car.

Hoglund wasn't to be deterred and set about cutting costs to the bone. The engineering work was subcontracted out to Entech Engineering (under the control of Pontiac's project head Huldi Aldikacti), with a directive to use as many existing components as possible, and pressure was applied to parts suppliers to reduce prices wherever possible. The end result was, predictably, that far too many compromises had to be made and the Fiero suffered badly as a consequence. The underpinnings of the car read like a list cobbled together from the corporate GM parts catalogue: the drivetrain consisted of the four-cylinder engine/transmission unit used in the front-wheel-drive X-body quartet (Chevrolet Citation/Pontiac Phoenix/Oldsmobile Omega/Buick Skylark) and the front suspension was mainly taken from the Chevy Chevette.

Although the designers made space for a V6 engine right from the outset (it was added in '85), the '84 Fiero arrived in the showrooms with a 92 horsepower, 2.5-liter "Iron Duke" four-cylinder mated to either a four-speed manual or three-speed automatic transaxle mounted midships. Although placing the engine in such a position creates the optimum weight distribution – and therefore excellent roadholding – the Fiero's modest power output meant that it was always going to be found wanting when it came to performance.

**Right:** There was no 1983 model (Chevy decided to skip a year) but a completely redesigned Corvette arrived in '84. Lower by 1.1 inch, shorter by 8.8 inches and sitting on a 2 inch shorter wheelbase, the Jerry Palmer-styled coupe was also 2 inches wider than its predecessor and 250 pounds lighter. Powered by a 205 horsepower, 350 cu.in. V8 with Cross-Fire fuel injection and electronic spark control, the aerodynamic new 'Vette would reach 140mph – a significant improvement over the '82 model. Corvette chief engineer Dave McLellan described the car as "absolutely superior to any production vehicle in its part of the market" and though sales figures hit 51,547, they sank to under 40,000 the following year.

# 1992

In some ways, the evolution of the Dodge Viper could be said to have run parallel to the Chevrolet Corvette ZR-1 of 1989, and the on-the-road performance of the two cars is also pretty close. But while GM went looking in England for some technical expertise from Lotus, Chrysler homed in on Italy and Lamborghini for their European connection.

The other major difference is, of course, that while the ZR-1 was a development of an existing production model, the Viper was a totally new vehicle and came from a manufacturer that had never previously been associated with a sports car. And, unlike the Corvette variant, the genesis of the Dodge was a concept car that was built to create publicity on the auto show circuit rather than a serious corporate decision to enter a very specialist market sector.

With a name like Viper there was no doubt where the inspiration for this awesome two-seater came from – the 1960s Shelby Cobra. Another American/British hybrid, the Cobra was the brainchild of Texan racecar driver and constructor Carroll Shelby who married the muscle of Ford V8 engines to the chassis and bodies produced by AC Cars of Thames Ditton in Surrey, near London, England, to create an all-time classic that has been cloned many times over.

As well as providing the inspiration, Carroll Shelby himself was involved at the early beginnings of the Viper idea, but the throbbing heart of this car was its 400 horsepower 8-liter (488 cu.in.) V-10 engine. And the story behind this amazing powerplant goes back to the latter half of 1987, when American Motors Corporation was bought by Chrysler and turned into the Jeep/Eagle division. One result of this amalgamation was the creation of the Jeep & Truck Engineering Department, which was given the task of revamping the Dodge Ram full-size pickup truck range. A prime requirement in this process was the need to provide a larger capacity engine to compete with the big block V8s on offer from Ford and Chevy.

It was apparent that the existing 5.9-liter (360 cu.in.) small-block Chrysler V8 couldn't be stretched any further so the notion of building a V-10 by simply adding two cylinders to the end of the block was discussed.

**Above:** The awesome Dodge Viper RT/10 was a "back-to-basics" exercise bringing the '60s sports car bang up to date. Demand was such that a long waiting list for cars developed after some initial production problems were experienced with the composite body, and this saw Vipers changing hands for double the original $55,000 price. This stunning supercar could accelerate from zero to 60mph in 4.5 seconds and go on to top 165mph.

**Left:** The Viper name and concept harks back to the Shelby Cobra sports car and the design of the badge reflects this heritage. Just like its historic forbear, the Dodge snake was full of venom and lightning fast!

**Below:** The heart-stopping performance of the Viper came from an 8-liter (488 cu.in.) V-10 engine that produced 400bhp at 4,600rpm. Yet thanks to massive torque output of 450 pounds at only 3,600rpm, this car was docile enough to drive in city traffic. By adding a pair of cylinders onto a V8, the all-aluminium Viper engine was developed into its final form by Lamborghini in Italy. And, although the bore and stroke dimensions were the same as the cast iron V-10 used in the Dodge Ram truck, apart from a few small common components the two engines were completely different.

At the behest of Chrysler President Bob Lutz, just such an exercise was carried out and, much to the consternation of those experts who said the V-10 would produce unbearable vibration, the experimental engine performed remarkably well. There was still a great deal of development work needed before the V-10 would be ready for everyday use, but more prototype V-10 engines were tested and one of these was used in the Viper show car that caused such a sensation when it appeared for the first time at the North American International Auto Show in Detroit in January 1989.

This gave rise to the myth that the Viper was powered by nothing more than a truck engine. This was far from the truth. Bernard Robertson (then Vice President of Jeep & Truck Engineering): "As the Viper program evolved, we needed numerous changes to

233

# THE AMERICAN AUTOMOBILE

package the V-10, which led to the low profile cross ram intake with dual throttle bodies, unique cast steel exhaust manifolds and revised oil pan, front end accessory drive system, etc. We also needed a significant weight reduction and were enticed by the 150 pounds or so achievable with aluminum versus cast iron. Because Lamborghini are experts in aluminum and have captive casting facilities, I personally delivered the iron block truck engine blueprints to Mauro Forghieri in March 1989 and arranged for the first five sets of aluminum blocks and heads to come from Italy."

"Lamborghini also proposed some innovative changes to the cooling system and crankshaft balance, which we adopted" he added.

"During the development process, we increased the compression ratio, lightened the pistons, increased the valvetrain critical speed, changed the valve sizes and strengthened the rods and crank, all to achieve 400bhp in Viper configuration. Consequently, the only remaining components shared with the truck engine are some nuts and bolts and minor valvetrain pieces, although the bore, stroke and architecture remain common."

"As you can see, there is a strong family connection between the two versions of the V-10 engine, although each is optimized for its particular application. Both were developed by Jeep & Truck Engineering and both are built at our Mound Road engine plant in Detroit. Lamborghini played a valuable supporting role and their aluminum design and casting expertise probably saved us six months."

But if the V-10 gave the Viper its venom, the curvaceous bodywork undeniably added

**Above:** The Viper is a pure minimalist two-seater, with crude sidescreens instead of wind-up windows and a "build-it-yourself" type of top that was last seen on early '60s British sports cars. But the Viper wasn't intended to be for mundane daily transportation – it's a fun car and one that should be left in the garage when it rains.

**Left:** The Taurus was proof positive of Ford's continuing commitment to building cars for the US market that shared styling and engineering with models produced by the company in Europe. The 1992 Taurus represented the first major redesign since the model's launch in December 1985.

that it would ever be put into volume production. After all, it was nothing more than a "back to basics" front-engined, rear-wheel-drive, two-seat sportster without a top – a no-frills, high-performance fantasy machine from an auto manufacturer that had experienced a torrid time over the previous ten years.

But the Viper struck a chord in the hearts of American drivers like few other show cars before or since. Yes, it was impractical. Yes, its 8-liter engine and 166mph top speed were out of step with 1990s concerns about the environment and safety. But it didn't matter. Every red-blooded person who saw the Viper wanted one. Deposit checks and orders were mailed to Chrysler's head office in Highland Park, dealers were inundated with enquiries whenever the Viper appeared and the media gave it rave reviews. Chrysler had, unwittingly perhaps, tapped into a rich vein of customer demand. Eventually, in May 1990, Lee Iacocca announced that the Viper would go into production in early 1992.

Turning a show car into something that can be used out on the highway isn't a simple task. Yet surprisingly few changes were needed to the original Viper body design in order to make it work. Engineering was more complicated but, even so, the original ethos of the Viper remains. It is not a practical car, there are no side windows and no air conditioning, it is noisy and you get buffeted by the wind at high speed— but,the fact remains it is fun!

When the 1992 Vipers went on sale you could have any color you liked providing you wanted red (black became available in '93 and other colors subsequently followed). But the demand for the $50,000 car was almost insatiable and it still remains popular today.

Looking back, it can be said that the Viper helped enormously in transforming the image of Chrysler. In much the same fashion as the Chevy Bel Air of 1955 altered forever the American public's perception of GM's cheapest brand name, the Viper showed the world that a revitalized Chrysler Corporation was changing into an innovative and imaginative organization that was prepared to take chances. It has certainly paid off, big time.

to the car's immediate appeal. The design concept arose following a series of meetings early in 1988 which, at various times, involved two or more of Carroll Shelby, Bob Lutz, Francois Castaing (Vice President of Vehicle Engineering), Tom Gale (Vice President of Product Design) and renowned Chrysler President Lee Iacocca. Once the idea for a balls-out sports car had been aired, it didn't take Gale longer than a couple of weeks to progress from his "back of an envelope" sketches to a sheaf of styling drawings. With approval granted, the next stage was a full-size clay mockup and from there, the original show car soon followed.

Although all the people involved in the Viper project at Dodge and Chrysler were highly enthusiastic about the car, it is unlikely that many of them believed at the outset

# 1993

The idea of having an exotic car body designed in Europe and then installing an American V8 engine into it isn't a new one. It wasn't new when Cadillac introduced the Allanté in the late summer of '86 as a 1987 model. What was different about the Cadillac ultra-luxury two-seater was the fact that the bodies were handbuilt in Turin, Italy, by Pininfarina and then flown across the Atlantic – 56 at a time – in a Boeing 747 freighter known as the "Airbridge". Some of the body components actually made the eight-hour flight in both directions, because the Allanté was based on an Eldorado underbody and these were shipped out to Italy (along with various other parts) for modification.

After Pininfarina's craftsmen shortened the Eldorado platform slightly and assembled the Allanté body onto it, the finished unit was fully painted and trimmed before being sent to Detroit for completion. In a relatively small corner of the GM Hamtramck assembly plant the front-wheel-drive powertrain and suspension were added to produce an unusual combination of Italian style and US muscle. Unfortunately, although the understated (for a

**Above:** Although the price of the Allanté had risen to over $60,000 by 1993, its Northstar V8 and other improvements over the years meant that Cadillac's two-seater was now capable of beating Jaguar and Mercedes models in the same class. Regrettably, just as they seemed to have got it right, Cadillac decided to axe the Allanté. The problem that proved impossible to overcome was its image of being an under-performing luxury cruiser.

**Left:** Cab-forward styling, a wider stance and new engines were introduced on the revised '93 Ford Probe. The body and interior were designed by Ford's studio team headed by Jack Telnack, while Mazda supplied the engineering input.

rior being another step in the right direction. An antilock braking system was introduced in 1990 but, positive though these changes were, the Allanté couldn't seem to shake off its image as being a luxury cruiser rather than an exclusive, high-performance machine. Sales hovered around the 3,000 mark for most years, but fell disastrously to 624 in '92.

The 1993 Allanté was by far the best yet, thanks to the arrival of the fabulous Cadillac Northstar V8. This 4.6-liter all-aluminum engine, with double-overhead camshafts for each cylinder bank and 32 valves, pumped out a mighty 290bhp, turning the Allanté into the quickest and fastest Cadillac ever tested by *Road & Track*. Zero to 60mph was achieved in 6.7 seconds, while the top speed had jumped to 145mph. In recognition of the Allanté's elevation to performance car status, the Cadillac was chosen as the Pace Car for the Indianapolis 500 which it was said to have undertaken the role in completely standard form (apart from additional safety equipment, like the roll bar). But it still wasn't enough. Demand remained depressingly low and the '93 model was decreed to be the last after approximately 3,500 were built – it was a sad ending.

1993 was also celebrated as the centenary of the gasoline-powered American automobile. It was exactly one hundred years ago – on September 21 1983 – that Frank Duryea took his buggy for its first test drive on public roads in Springfield, Massachusetts. Steam-powered contraptions had been around for much longer of course, but the Duryea is usually regarded as the forefather of the modern car.

**Inset:** Cadillac's first all-new engine for a decade, the 4.6-liter Northstar V8 is one of the truly great automotive powerplants. Featuring dual overhead camshafts on each cylinder head and 32 valves, with a compression ratio of 10.3:1, the Northstar produced 290bhp at 5,600rpm and 290 pounds per sq. foot of torque at 4,400rpm. Redlined at 6,500rpm, the computer-controlled sequential port fuel injection would automatically cut off fuel delivery at 6,700rpm.

**Right:** November 10, 1993, and the first 1995 model year Dodge and Plymouth Neon small cars roll off the assembly line at Chrysler's Belvedere, Illinois, assembly plant. Over 1,000 guests witnessed the occasion that represented a $1.3 billion investment.

Cadillac) looks were generally well received, the performance of the Allanté never quite lived up to potential customers' expectations.

The interior, with its hugely intrusive rectangular central console set into the dash was also criticized, as was the amount of plastic used on a $50,000 automobile. And the disappointing 4.1-litre V8 only produced 170bhp, which gave the '87 Allanté a 0-60mph time of 9.5 seconds and a top speed of around 120mph. While those figures aren't too bad, a *Road & Track* comparison test with a Mercedes-Benz 560SL showed the German sportster to be two seconds quicker to 60mph and more than 15mph faster.

Allanté sales in the first year amounted to only 3,363 cars, and the figure dropped to 2,569 in '88. A bigger 200 horsepower engine was fitted for '89 and this, together with the uprated suspension, helped the performance aspect with various improvements to the inte-

# 1994

After 15 years and 2.5 million cars, Ford decided to introduce a brand-new Mustang and dealers nationwide were inundated with people wanting to see it on the official launch date of December 9 1993. Although the styling changes were immediately apparent, the designers had cleverly combined the modern aero look with the traditional "running horse" identification features in a great package. However, just as important as the bodywork were the changes that had been engineered in the running gear to update the Mustang's performance.

Based on a much revised version of the well-proven "Fox" platform that had served the previous decade and a half of Mustangs so well, the Fox-4 featured a slightly longer wheelbase (by three-quarters of an inch) and a wider track (increased by 3.7 inches on the standard model and 5.6 inches on the GT), together with improved steering and suspension geometry. The aim was to iron out the shortcomings of the earlier model – primarily in the high-speed handling and tire wear — and 85% of the '94 Mustang platform was either modified or new. The addition of a rear sway bar as standard also helped to eliminate the "tail happy" tendency experienced with the third-generation 'Stang, and the overall effect was to create superior handling as well as improved ride quiality.

The 79 Mustang had quickly established a reputation for itself as an affordable high

**Right:** Triple lens taillights were also styling cues taken from original Mustang design, but arranged horizontally. The GT had a rear spoiler and foglamps, plus a 215bhp 5.0-liter V8. Four-wheel disc brakes were fitted on all Mustangs, with the option of ABS in the '94 catalog.

**Below:** The Mustang got its first major redesign since 1979, bringing back traditional styling elements like the running horse grille badge. The GT in the foreground is fitted with optional 17 in. alloy wheels. The full heritage of Ford's pony car is shown here, including 1965 models. The 1994 Mustang would never match the first year sales of 30 years earlier, but the new version was well received.

**Above:** While the Mustang's exterior was completely revamped, the Fox-4 platform it was based on dated back some years. Engineering alterations were made to the steering and suspension for '94 to improve road holding and ride. The base coupe model illustrated had a 3.8-liter V6 engine.

**Above, top right:** The Aurora was the new flagship model for Oldsmobile and lined up against luxury imports like Lexus and Infiniti. Using a 4.0-liter, 250bhp derivative of the Cadillac Northstar V8, the Aurora was part of an effort to reverse troubled fortunes at the Oldsmobile division. Although the Aurora won much approval and sold well, Oldsmobile continued to lose money.

**Right:** Dodge set the fullsize pickup market alight when it introduced the powerful Ram truck. The bold styling would set the trend for every manufacturer, and, with its 300 horsepower, 8-liter V-10 engine, Dodge claimed the Ram would out-run, out-haul and out-pull any competitive pickup. First year sales of 206,000 – an increase of 163% and the best 12-month figure for a full-size pickup in the company's history – proved the point.

performance car and throughout its life was regarded as excellent value for money. Ford weren't about to change this philosophy of providing "the best bang for a buck", but they did make some alterations to its range of engines. It may be hard to believe that any enthusiast regretted the passing of the 2.3-liter four banger, especially as it was replaced with the 145 horse, 3.8-liter V6 as used in the Thunderbird Super Coupe. However, the news that production of the 5.0-liter HO V8 was to cease because of rationalization at the Cleveland engine building plant was disappointing.

In its place came the Thunderbird version of the V8 (designated the MN-12) with a new low-profile fuel injection system that produced a maximum of 215 horsepower at 4,200rpm. So equipped, a Mustang GT could gallop from zero to 60mph in 6.7 seconds and reach 140mph in the stretch. For those more interested in quarter horses, on the drag strip a '94 Mustang could traverse the 440 yards in 14.8 seconds and reach 93mph at the finishing line. Once again, the numbers were impressive and once again the Mustang was chosen as the Pace Car for the Indy 500 – it was 1979 all over again.

The actual car used to lead the pack around the famous Indianapolis oval was a Cobra convertible, harking back to the ragtop Mustang used for the 1964 race. A thousand Cobra Pace Car Replica convertibles were

built by Ford, as well as 5,000 Cobra coupes, but the Indy 500 decals only came on the soft top models.

The 2-door coupe and convertible models were available from the outset (the 3-door fastback now eliminated from the range), but later in the year a convertible/hardtop version also appeared. Similar in concept to the detachable hardtop offered on the original 1955 Thunderbird, the Mustang version weighed in at only 84 pounds and was rollover certified. The ragtop also came with a dome light and rear window defogger, as well as its own storage dolly.

Car and truck sales increased across the industry in '94, with a total of 15 million vehicles streaming off the assembly lines. Over 137,000 of these were new Mustangs. But the automotive event that grabbed the most media attention of the year was the high-speed police pursuit of former football star O.J. Simpson along the highways of California that was shown live on TV.

# 1996

Although Chrysler had been the leading player in the minivan market ever since it introduced the front-wheel-drive Plymouth Voyager and Dodge Caravan in 1984, the opposition was getting stronger year by year as other manufacturers brought out their own versions of the multipurpose vehicle. In order to maintain their dominant position as the

the Chrysler corporate identity.

But as well as the modern styling, there were a couple of innovative touches announced on the new models. The first surprise was the option of a left-side sliding door, making it possible to have sliding doors on both sides. Then there were the patented "Easy Out" roller seats and first-for-minivan features such as dual zone climate control, memory seats and mirrors. An all-new 150 horsepower, 2.4-liter, 16 valve, dual overhead camshaft four cylinder engine was one of the powertrains available, the oth-ers being a 3.0-liter SOHC V6, a 3.3-liter V6 and a 3.8-liter V6. A 2.5-liter turbo

**Above:** A new badge was chosen by Chrysler in '96, the design based on the original "gold seal" emblem used by founder Walter P. Chrysler in 1924. The famous Pentastar logo was retained to represent the Chrysler Corporation as a whole, but all Chrysler-branded cars would henceforth carry the new badge.

**Left:** Plymouth's Grand Voyager was one of a family of new minivans introduced by Chrysler as '96 models. It sat on a 119.3 inch wheelbase (six inches longer than the normal Voyager/Caravan) and could carry seven passengers plus their luggage. Modern aerodynamic styling and an optional left-side sliding door were part of Chrysler's initiative to keep the number one slot in this valuable market sector. All-wheel-drive was also available on the long wheelbase versions, though this didn't arrive until later in the year.

number one seller in this lucrative sector, the Chrysler team realised that they had to come up with something new for '96. The answer was revealed at the 1995 North American International Auto Show held in Detroit.

In addition to the Dodge Caravan and Grand Caravan, Plymouth Voyager and Grand Voyager, and Chrysler Town & Country luxury minivan models on display, there were also the Chrysler Voyager and Grand Voyager versions to be sold overseas. But the star of the presentation hosted by Chrysler president Bob Lutz and chairman Robert Eaton was a bright red Dodge Caravan that was connected to a hidden mechanical arm to make it jump into the air. With the aid of a Kermit the frog look-a-like and some humorous poetry, the point was made that, with this new model, Chrysler were leapfrogging ahead of the competition once again. The stylish, more curvaceous lines of the cab-forward design marked a definite advancement of the minivan concept, while at the same time clearly retaining

diesel four cylinder would be offered in those vehicles sold outside the USA. Transmission options were a three-speed manual or a four-speed automatic (only on V6 models).

Another surprise at the Detroit show was the 1996 Ford Taurus and Mercury Sable models, the first complete redesign of the pair

**Below:** Chrysler president Bob Lutz (left) with chairman Robert Eaton and the leapfrogging Dodge Caravan that made its debut at the '95 Detroit show.

since their introduction ten years previously. Although the sleeker Taurus seemed smaller than before, it was actually larger, with two-inches longer in the wheelbase and 5.4 inches longer overall. The width had increased by 2.4 inches and a new 3.0-liter, 24 valve, "Cleveland" V6 engine rated at 185 horsepower was offered, as well as an improved version of the base 3.0-liter V6. Both Taurus and Sable followed the trend of the cab-forward styling school, but subtle alterations to the front and rear were used to try and give the Mercury a different appearance to its stablemate from Ford. Later in '96, a further example of the growing globalization of the industry became evident when Ford announced that it had bought a controling interest in Japanese auto-maker Mazda.

While all manufacturers were busy looking ahead and trying to come up with an edge over their rivals, there were still a few who were prepared to cater to customers with more traditional demands. It's true that Buick produced their fair share of futuristic concept cars and radical new models, but in 1996 you could still buy an old-fashioned, full-size Roadmaster Estate Wagon – and it even had the fake wooden panels stuck on the sides! But this was to be the last year for the rear-wheel-drive Roadmaster sedan and wagon and the models were given the Collector's Edition designation.

**Above:** The first major redesign since 1986 saw the Ford Taurus adopt a prominent oval theme in its styling, which wasn't universally approved. That didn't stop the car from selling very well. To begin with there were only two trim levels offered – GL and LX – but a base G and the high-performance SHO model were added midway through the year. The station wagon also made a comeback as part of the Taurus line.

**Left:** It was the end of the line for the Buick Roadmaster Estate Wagon, and it carried the Collector's Edition designation for its final year. A 260 horsepower, 5.7-liter V8 was standard, combined with four-speed automatic transmission, but a new generation of multipurpose vehicles was supplanting these full-size, rear-wheel-drive wagons. Once production of these models was phased out, the Arlington, Texas, assembly plant where they were built was converted to truck manufacturing.

# Acknowledgements

The publishers would like to thank the following for their kind loan or supply of photographs for this book:

**Courtesy of Ford Motor Company**
page 8/9 top, 29 top, 38, 42 bottom, 51 bottom, 64/5 top, 88/9 bottom, 96/7 bottom, 114/5 bottom, 120 bottom, 135, 144/5 top, 156, 157 bottom, 160 top, 172/3 top, 175, 180 top, 182/3 top left & bottom left, 183 bottom, 187, 189 right

**General Motors Corp., used with permission**
page 9 bottom, 25 bottom right, 34/5 bottom, 58 bottom, 72, 73 top, 82/3 bottom, 87 top, 124/5 bottom, 131 bottom right, 133 bottom, 134, 152 bottom, 153, 162/3 top, 173 bottom, 178/9 top

**Courtesy Oldsmobile History Center**
page 15, 43 bottom, 70, 71 bottom, 79 top, 109, 120/1 top left, 137 top, 140/1 top, 157 top, 160 bottom, 172 bottom

**Free Library of Philadelphia**
page 1, 8 bottom, 12, 16/7 bottom, 18 top, 18/9 center, 20 center, 20/1 top & bottom, 26 bottom, 30, 31, 32 bottom, 36/7 bottom, 42/3 top left, 48/9 bottom, 52, 53, 55 bottom, 85 top, 63 bottom, 66 bottom, 78, 86, 98 top, 152 top, 183 top, back of jacket (bottom)

**Studebaker National Museum**
page 80/1 bottom, 81 top

**IMS Photos, Indianapolis Motor Speedway**
page 13 bottom, 14 bottom, 23 top, 56, 99, 112/3 top, 141 bottom, 158 bottom

**Daimler-Chrysler Historical Collection**
page 146, 154/5 top & center, 196 bottom, 200 top, 207 top, 208 top, 244

**National Motor Museum, Beaulieu**
page 13 top, 14 top, 17 top, 19 right, 21 top right, 22/3 bottom, 25 top, 27 bottom, 32/3 top, 34 top, 35 right, 36/7 top, 39 top, 40/1 bottom, 43 top right, 45 right, 46 bottom, 46/7 top, 50 bottom, 54 bottom, 57, 60/1 left, 62, 65 bottom, 66/7 top, 74, 90 top, 98 bottom, 100 bottom, 116, 131 top, 138/9 bottom, 140 bottom, 144 bottom, 145 bottom, 161, 164 top, 166/7 bottom, 168/9 bottom, 170/1 bottom

**Tony Beadle Collection**
page 25 left, 26/7 top, 35 top right, 75 bottom, 76/7 bottom, 79 bottom, 100/1 top, 110, 111, 113 bottom, 123 bottom, 148 bottom, 149, 150, 151, 163 bottom, 171 top, front of jacket, 195 bottom, 206/207 top, 212, 213 top, 214 bottom, 217 top, 219 bottom, 220 top, 222/223, 223 bottom, 224both, 225both, 226/227, 227 top, 228/229, 229 both, 231 bottom, 235 top, 236/237 top, 236 bottom, 237 both, 238, 239 top left and center, 241 both, 242 top and center, 243 top, 244, 245 all, 246/247 all, 248 both, 250/251 all, 252/253 all

**The Advertising Archive**
page 28 top, 33 bottom, 48 top, 63 top, 75 top, 80 top, 96 top

**Nicky Wright/National Motor Museum, Beaulieu**
page 37 top right, 47 bottom, 82 top, 87 bottom, 121 bottom, 124 top, 137 bottom, 148 top, 158/9 top, 177, 179 bottom, Page 193 bottom, 194 bottom, 200 bottom, 210 bottom, 210/215 top, 216 top, 219 top, 220/221 bottom, 230, 234 bottom

**Nicky Wright/Chrysalis Picture Library**
Page 192 bottom, 202 both, 211 bottom

**Nicky Wright, Marshall, Michigan, USA**
page 4/5, 10, 11, 22 top, 41 top right, 44, 64 bottom, 83 top, 84/5 top, 114/5 top, 136 top, 143 bottom, 176, 181 right, 184, 185, 188 bottom, 188/9 center, 191 top, 198/199, 199 bottom, 208/209, 215 bottom, 231 top, 232/233 top & bottom, 234 top, 239 top right, 240/241 top, 240 bottom, 242 bottom, 243 bottom, back of jacket, endpapers

**Mike Key**
page 68, 69, 73 bottom, 94, 102, 103, 104 top, 117 bottom, 118, 119, 127 bottom, 128, 129, 147, 169 top, 186

**Dan Lyons**
page 54/5 top, 92, 93, 101 bottom, 105, 112 bottom, 117 top, 142/3 top, 164 bottom, 165, 168 top

**Andrew Morland**
page 28/9 bottom, 40/1 top left, 50/1 top, 59, 61 right, 122 bottom, 122/3 top, Page 221 top

**William D. Siuru**
page 24, 67 bottom, 71 top, 77 top, 84 bottom, 85 bottom, 90 bottom, 91, 121 top right,, 126/7 top, 130, 138/9 top, 154 bottom, 180 bottom

**Jim Maxwell**
page 2/3, 6/7, 159 bottom, 162 bottom

**Anders Odeholm, The Media Factory AB**
page 108, 167 top

**Colin Burnham**
page 95, 132/3 top, 136 bottom

**Julian Balme**
page 106, 107

**Rod Blackaller**
page 174, Page 190/191 top, 190 bottom, 197 top, 201, 203 bottom, 213 bottom

**Vintage Ad Gallery**
Page 192 top, 196 top, 205, 207 bottom, 208 bottom

**Neill Bruce Motoring Photolibrary**
Page 194/195 top, 206 bottom

**Pete Roberts Collection/ Neill Bruce Motoring Photolibrary**
Page 197 bottom, 204/205 top, 204 bottom, 209 top, 216 bottom

**Quadrant Picture Library**
Page 203 top, 210/211 top, 217 bottom, 218 bottom

**Peter Robain**
Page 239 bottom

# Discovering London for Yourself

This book has tended to emphasize the enduring traditions of London and its uncanny ability to assimilate the twentieth century. The narrow lanes have surrendered to complex one-way schemes as the City fathers attempted to solve the conundrum of how to pour a quart of traffic into a pint pot of roadspace. The skyline has been colonized by a plague of tower blocks overshadowing Wren's more elegant contribution.

Yet unlovely as all this undressed pre-cast concrete may appear it too is part of what London is. One could even ask which is the more incongruous: towers and office complexes that maintain the city's pre-eminent position in world finance or soldiers in scarlet uniforms of the last century protecting Buckingham Palace with unloaded rifles? The answer, I believe, is not a straightforward one. That the Palace can be guarded by men in comic opera uniforms instead of men in flak jackets hiding behind sand-bags is possibly the most positive statement anyone can make about London today.

Ultimately these traditions do not exist purely for tourists, important though they are to the country's economy, they continue because we Londoners like them. Horses and shining armour, state coaches and powdered wigs, absurd as they may appear, infuse a little sanity and instant theatre into everyday life.

Although Britain and London in particular has acquired a reputation as the most accomplished organizer of pageantry and tradition anywhere in the world, yet not all our traditions are so formalized.

For example, most overseas visitors in search of some relaxed English atmosphere inevitably find their way to one of the great institutions of our country, the pub. Pubs like the George at Southwark, the Anchor, Bankside, the Prospect of Whitby and the Cheshire Cheese are well known to visitors and Londoners alike because of their architecture and their historic associations. But every area has its 'local' and whether it's a centuries-old inn, a Victorian palace rich in velvet and etched glass or a brand new house it invariably takes on the character of its regulars and its landlord or 'guvnor'.

However pubs are not only interesting buildings they are businesses and their product is drink – in the main, beer: light ale, brown ale, mild, bitter, special, stout, export pale, lager the list is endless as the tastes are varied. Along with the beer a wide range of spirits and in some cases over twenty different scotch whiskies can be had. (I even know of one publican who serves a range of thirty-eight different scotch whiskies.) Over the years many pubs have introduced pub grub which can range from simple rolls and sandwiches to four- and five-course meals.

A good place to go pub crawling and see an old area of London is Islington. The Kings Head pub near Highbury and Islington tube puts on plays and food and other pubs in the area are good for music. Nearby is Camden Passage with restaurants, antique shops and militaria shops. So hop on a bus or hail a cab and ask for the 'Angel'. From the Angel it's only a short hop over to Hampstead where a more 'refined' type of drinker can be found. Refinement doesn't stop them getting drunk over there but only on real ale or a tempting little teaser from Haut Medoc. Their reasons for getting drunk are more likely to be artistic tension or the trauma of a second divorce rather than where next weeks rent's coming from, and as they invariably talk loudly it's a great entertainment to eavesdrop! Hampstead also contains some good restaurants, bistros and wine bars squeezed between antique shops and bookshops and of course Keats house in Keats Grove.

In spite of some of its inhabitants Hampstead is a fun place to visit, a walk across the Heath on an autumnal morning, a pint of Young's Special in the Flask with a Ploughman's Lunch – strong Cheddar, crusty bread, hold the foliage – is one of the enduring pleasures I enjoyed when I was a teenager and, though the price has changed, it's still great value.

In mentioning Hampstead and Islington I've written about areas undergoing change, that is going up in the world, though Hampstead has always been an 'acceptable' address. However, other areas that at first sight may be termed depressed still have a strong community spirit. The East End is a term that covers an area that stretches from Aldgate Pump eastwards taking in the docklands and Mile End and Stepney. Here the local really is the local – no decorative drinkers here. Though the district has suffered its fair share of tower blocks and waste areas – a hangover from the blitz – it is still the place to visit if you're looking for that nebulous item the 'cockney'.

Like pubs, another facet of London life is the auction rooms, Sotheby's and Christie's are rightly world famous, but London has several auction rooms where bric-a-brac, object d'art and collectable ephemera are sold, you don't have to be a representative of the Guggenheim to enjoy a day at the sales. Philips, Bonhams and Sothebys run auctions most days of the week in South Kensington and the West End.

For those who want to go further, to pursue a particular interest or discover more for themselves, London will repay as much time as anyone has to spare. The best way, of course, to discover any city is to buy a decent map and walk. It is also well worth doing any of the London walks or tours organized by the London Tourist Board and registered guides. The City Corporation has a tourist information service close by St Paul's Cathedral which is very useful to casual visitors and has on sale a number of books and pamphlets. Also the London Tourist Board in Grosvenor Gardens, SW1 provide tourist and sightseeing information as well as tickets for visitors.

If you are planning on finding out more about London for yourself you could also purchase a decent guide book. I would recommend *The Penguin Guide to London* by F. R. Banks to take around with you. It has the advantage of being pocket sized and packed with information. If you want a book for the home then Kent's Encyclopedia is a good reference work. Along with these general reviews of the city there are specific histories of guilds and churches. Also, all of London's tourist attractions publish booklets though not always of the quality of that produced by Westminster Abbey.

So armed with map, guide book and a keen sense of curiosity the city awaits. The rule to follow is that there is no rule, go where your nose leads you and discover for yourself. London is a city for all seasons and all people.

## Dates to Remember

**AD43** Roman occupation of Britain. Accepted date for the founding of Roman London.

**61** London, by now a busy port, is burnt to the ground during the Revolt of the Iceni led by Boadicea.

**120** Emperor Hadrian comes to Britain. Defensive wall started round the rebuilt city.

**410** End of the Roman Occupation.

**604-7** Building of first St Paul's Cathedral.

**616** Legendary consecration of first Abbey at Westminster.

**883** King Alfred recovers London from Viking invaders.

**1065** Consecration of Edward the Confessor's Westminster Abbey.

**1066** Norman invasion. Harold defeated and William The Conqueror crowned at Westminster Abbey. Gives charter to the City confirming rights as they were in 'good King Edward's day'.

**1078** Building of the White Tower.

**1097-9** Building of Westminster Hall under William II (Rufus).

**1135** London obtains a charter of liberties from Henry I.

**1190** William Fitzstephen dies. His biography of Thomas Becket contains a description of London which is the chief authority for our knowledge of the social life of this city in the twelfth century.

**1215** King John signs Magna Carta at Runnymede and grants a charter confirming the City's right to elect its own Mayor.

**1245** Present Westminster Abbey begun.

**1292** Lincolns Inn, first of the Inns of Court, founded.

**1295** 2nd Westminster assembly summoned by Edward I (1239-1307) in Westminster Abbey chapter house. Later parliaments took their form from this assembly.

**1348-9** First outbreak of the Black Death in London.

**1381** The Peasants revolt. Rebel leader Wat Tyler killed at Smithfield.

**1398** Dick Whittington elected mayor for the first time. He was mayor again in 1406-7 and 1419-20.

**1476** William Caxton sets up his printing press.

**1586** Shakespeare comes to Blackfriars.

**1598** Publication of *A Survey of London*, the first detailed history of the City, by John Stow (1525-1605) the Elizabethan historian and antiquarian.

**1605** 5th November – The 'Gunpowder Plot': conspiracy to blow up Parliament and King (James I).

**1631-5** Inigo Jones lays out London's first residential square (for the fourth Earl of Bedford) in Covent Garden and designs St Paul's Church (1633) – first renaissance church in London – on the west side of the square.

**1642-46** The Civil War. Charles I executed in 1649.

**1649-60** Period of Commonwealth rule under Oliver Cromwell. Puritan ban on all entertainment and festivities.

**1652** London's first coffee house opens.

**1660** The Restoration of the monarchy. Theatres re-open. First year of Pepys' diary. Margaret Hughes plays Desdemona. First public performance by a woman on the stage.

**1665-6** The 'Great Plague' (the worst outbreak of the plague in which thousands of Londoners died) and the 'Great Fire' (1666) which started before the plague had entirely died out. The Fire consumed 89 churches and 13,200 houses.

**1669** Last entry in Pepys' diary (begun 1 Jan 1660).

**1675-1710** Building of new St Paul's Cathedral, designed and supervised by Sir Christopher Wren.

**1688** William of Orange (William III) enters London.

**1694** Bank of England opens.

**1702-3** Court moves to St James's. Buckingham House built – later renamed Buckingham Palace when it became a Royal Residence (it was purchased for George III in 1762) for Queen Victoria.

**1720** South Sea bubble: financial disaster in the City.

**1745** Hogarth auctions his *A Harlot's Progress* (1731) and *A Rake's Progress* (1735).

**1749** Performance of music for the royal fireworks for George II's peace celebrations at Green Park costing £90,000.

**1763** May. Boswell's first meeting with Dr Johnson.

**1768** The Royal Academy established.

**1780** June. The Gordon Riots in which 458 Londoners were killed or wounded and over 100 buildings destroyed or damaged.

**1801** First population census 958,865 people.

**1814** Gas street lighting established in London.

**1817** Waterloo Bridge built.

**1828** Zoological Gardens established.

**1829** Sir Robert Peel founds the Metropolitan Police.

**1837** Euston Station opened.
Queen Victoria comes to the throne.

**1840** Penny post introduced throughout England.

**1850** First slum clearances.

**1851** Prince Albert's Great Exhibition: attended by 6 million people.

**1855** First London letterbox, Fleet Street. It had 10 clearances a day.

**1860** Sir Charles Barrie and August Pugin complete the building of the new Palace of Westminster.

**1862** Mayhew's *London Labour and the London Poor* published.

**1863** First underground railway (the Metropolitan Railway) between the City and Paddington opens.

**1879** London's first telephone exchange opens in Coleman Street in the City.

**1886-94** Tower Bridge built.

**1914-18** World War I. 25 air raids on London.

**1923** BBC sets up its first headquarters, on Savoy Hill.

**1934-45** World War II. September 1940, Germans bomb London and the blitz begins.

**1951** The Festival of Britain on the South Bank.

**1953** Queen Elizabeth II crowned at Westminster Abbey on 2 June.

**1963** Barbican development – a scheme to attract residents to the City – begins.

**1964** Post Office Tower built.

**1976** The National Theatre opens.

**1981** 29 July. The Prince of Wales and Lady Diana Spencer are married at St Paul's Cathedral.

**1982** March. The new Barbican arts centre opens.

# Index

**Photographic Acknowledgements**

John Bethell, St Albans 15, 27 bottom, 28-9, 30-1, 33, 39 top, 53 bottom, 54-5, 64, 81 top, 86, 86-7, 88-9, 89 top, 89 bottom, 92 top, 96 bottom, 101 top, 108 top, 108 bottom, 112 bottom, 113 top, 113 bottom, 114-5, 116, 121 bottom; British Museum, London 81 bottom right; British Tourist Authority, London 13, 14, 16 bottom, 22, 23, 27 top, 43 top, 43 centre, 47, 53 top, 56 top, 58-9, 59, 62 top, 65 top, 71, 72 top, 85 top, 85 bottom, 112 top, 117; Colour Library International, London front and back endpapers, 4-5, 6-7, 19, 20-1, 24-5, 26-7, 37, 38-9, 39 bottom, 40-1, 50-1, 52-3, 56 bottom, 57, 61, 62 bottom, 66-7, 74, 75 bottom, 76 top, 77 bottom, 79, 80, 82-3, 84-5, 87, 91, 92-3, 94-5, 96 top, 97, 99, 102-3, 104, 106-7, 109, 111, 118-9, 120, 122; Daily Telegraph Colour Library, London – G P Eisen 101 bottom, Tim Mercer 17; André Goulancourt, Ashford, Middlesex 46; Hamlyn Group Picture Library 43 bottom, 121 top; Robert Harding Picture Library, London 48 top, 103; A F Kersting, London 42, 44-5; Keystone Press Agency, London 76 bottom; Andrew Lawson, Charlbury 16 top, 29 top, 29 bottom, 34 top, 35 top, 35 bottom, 58 top, 68 top, 69 top right, 72 bottom, 75 top left, 75 top right, 92 bottom, 100-1, 105 top; Ian Muggeridge, Reigate 48 bottom; Mike Peters, Twickenham 34 bottom; Science Museum, London 81 bottom left; Stock Exchange, London 32 top; Homer Sykes, London 68 bottom, 69 bottom; Whitbread & Co, London 32 bottom; ZEFA (UK) – Colin Maher 49, Marché 58 bottom, J Pfaff 105 bottom, P Phillips 72-3, Clive Sawyer 8, 62-3, 69 top left; Zoological Society of London 65 bottom.

The photograph on page 77 top is Crown copyright and is reproduced with the permission of The Controller of Her Majesty's Stationery Office.